Fairbairn's Journey into the Interior

This is a uniquely authoritative and intimate psychobiography. Most psychobiographies are inevitably speculative about the inner lives of their subjects. *Fairbairn's Journey into the Interior* is an intimate account of one psychoanalyst by another who was pupil, colleague and friend for over thirty-five years. Ronald Fairbairn (1889–1965) was – with Melanie Klein and Donald Winnicott – one of the founders of the 'object-relations' approach to psychoanalysis, which bases personality development on the experience of the infant in its early relationships within the family, rather than on great instinctual forces, the classical Freudian view.

Fairbairn worked in relative isolation in Scotland, but his clinical and theoretical contributions were so original that he was made a Member of the British Psycho-Analytical Society without having undergone the normal training.

John Sutherland has drawn on his own knowledge of Fairbairn and on important private documents to bring about a close integration between Fairbairn's life and ideas, on the one hand, and his fraught inner world and symptoms, on the other. It is a moving account, one which sheds important light on the history of psychoanalysis and on the wellsprings of creativity in relation to severe inner turmoil. Sutherland's exposition of the interrelations between Fairbairn's and Melanie Klein's ideas are particularly fine. The book will be of great interest to all those who value psychoanalytic thought.

Dr John D. Sutherland taught Psychology at Edinburgh University, joined the 'Tavistock Group' in the Army during World War Two, and the Tavistock Clinic after the War, where he was Medical Director from 1947 until 1968. He was awarded the CBE and retired to Scotland, where he helped to set up the Scottish Institute of Human Relations. He is a Member of the British Psycho-Analytical Society and has been Editor of the *British Journal of Medical Psychology*, the *International Journal of Psycho-Analysis* and the International Library of Psycho-Analysis.

Fairbairn's Journey into the Interior

J.D. SUTHERLAND

'an association in which the free development of each
is the condition for the free development of all'

Free Association Books / London / 1989

First published in Great Britain 1989 by
Free Association Books
26 Freegrove Road
London N7 9RQ

British Library Cataloguing in Publication Data
Sutherland, John D.
   Fairbairn's journey into the interior.
   1. Psychoanalysis. Fairbairn, Ronald
   I. Title
150.19'5'0924
   ISBN 1 85343 058 7
   ISBN 1 85343 059 5 pbk

Typeset by Selectmove Ltd
Printed and bound in Great Britain by
Short Run Press Ltd, Exeter

Manufactured in the United States of America. Psychotherapy Book Club offers books and
cassettes. For information and catalog write to Psychotherapy Book Club, 230 Livingston Street,
Northvale, NJ 07647.

CONTENTS

INTRODUCTION

Fairbairn's views on the basic aetiological factors underlying the psychological disorders are now recognized as constituting a development from Freud's metapsychology that was needed. Revisions of psychoanalytic theory and practice have frequently faded from the scene when they have been deemed to be abandoning some of its core principles, especially those related to the depth and persistent power of unconscious conflicts in the person. Such views have been discredited as 'deviations'. Fairbairn's assimilation of the full nature of these unconscious forces, as Freud had exposed them, made it clear that his contribution was not in that category. Adhering to the strict psychoanalytic method, Fairbairn found that the characteristic problems presented by schizoid patients, far from making these individuals unsuitable for psychoanalysis, as had been hitherto held, had quite the opposite nature. Their difficulties, essentially stemming from distortions in the capacity to make personal relationships, needed explanatory concepts other than those founded on the vicissitudes of instinctive energies as conceived in the models of nineteenth-century science.

As usual with challenges to a well-established scientific paradigm, Fairbairn's new line of thought was somewhat patronizingly ignored for a number of years. Today, however, it is seen as a remarkable early manifestation of a swelling tide: the expanding studies in child development, and in psychology, the new psychoanalytic data from the inner worlds of very young children pioneered by Melanie Klein, and from the treatment of the more serious disorders in adults, have all been pointing to radically different theoretical premises.

The growing mass of data on the development of the personality increasingly suggested that the person's effective capacity in managing the business of living is governed by the extent to which he (or she) can maintain satisfying relationships with himself (or herself) and others. The psychic structures mediating this capacity could not be derived solely from the satisfaction of instincts. They were founded in 'good enough' experiences with others, of being treated as a person from the earliest phases. Correspondingly, deformations in these structures were the major source of the wide range of psychological disorders. The central theoretical issues for psychoanalysis were therefore moved by Fairbairn to those around the organization of the experiences of relationships, or, in his phrase, to an 'object-relations theory of the personality'.

This notion of taking the critical locus for the structuring of the personality to be the central self-system resonated sympathetically with Ernest Jones. Always a rigorous critic, and well known on the London scene for his sharp treatment of what he considered to be intellectual woolliness, Jones had at the same time an open-mindedness which allowed him to sense the potential importance of new ideas, when many of his colleagues reacted either negatively or indifferently. (It was Jones who saw the great relevance of Melanie Klein's work, and so welcomed her immigration to London.) Although Fairbairn had, throughout the 1930s, attended a few meetings of the British Psycho-Analytical Society each year, he had never been able to maintain frequent contacts with the London group, because of his geographical isolation; later, the outbreak of war made contact impossible. He had published a paper in 1931 in which he took Jones and psychoanalysts in general to task for getting into conceptual confusions which could be avoided by paying more attention to the writings of some of the general psychologists. Jones was clearly appreciative and shortly afterwards Fairbairn was elected to associate membership of the Society – quite a tribute to one who had not had the usual psychoanalytic training.

This favourable attitude prompted Fairbairn, twenty years later, to ask Jones to write a preface to the volume in which his papers were first to be presented in one collection. Jones described Fairbairn's train of thought as of 'great interest and indisputable originality', and, with exceptional prescience, expressed 'the firm opinion that it will surely prove extremely stimulating to thought'. He then wrote what has always seemed to me to be a paragraph of brilliantly terse appraisal:

If it were possible to condense Fairbairn's new ideas into one sentence, it might run somewhat as follows. Instead of starting, as Freud did, from stimulation of the nervous system proceeding from excitation of various erotogenous zones and internal tension arising from gonadic activity, Fairbairn starts at the centre of the personality, the ego, and depicts its strivings and difficulties in its endeavour to reach an object where it may find support. Fairbairn has elaborated this theme . . . and he has worked out its implications both biologically in regard to the problems of instinct and psychologically in the baffling interchange of external and internal objects. All this constitutes a fresh approach in psychoanalysis which should lead to much fruitful discussion. (in PSOP,* p.v)

Coming from the most senior analyst of this period, the last survivor of Freud's group of trusted colleagues ('the Committee') and currently immersed in the preparation of his great biography of Freud, there could hardly have been more respect paid to the views of any analyst, especially when they contained such a radical challenge. Nevertheless, judging from the way the book was received by the greater part of the psychoanalytic establishment, it seems as if this passage was scarcely noticed.

Fairbairn's originality is all the more striking when it is recalled that, as Jones also commented, his ideas developed from his daily working experience in his isolated situation as a psychoanalyst in Edinburgh hundreds of miles from his nearest colleagues, whom he seldom meets. Furthermore, his main ideas were conceived before the availability in English of H. Hartmann's ego psychology, and of all the advances in our knowledge of child development and general biology that have in recent decades stimulated so many lines of thought in psychoanalysis. His work therefore arouses interest both for itself and in the factors that helped to create his highly innovative thought. We cannot but imagine that special processes were developing in Fairbairn's inner world under the impact of his experience with patients, and from his life in general. As more psychoanalysts and others learned of his work, the question was asked more often: what were the personal resources that stimulated his new ways of looking at the clinical phenomena, and which sustained an intense creative commitment over the years with patients who had tended to be regarded previously as not very suitable for analysis?

My account of the background of the development of Fairbairn's personality, with reference to his contribution to psychoanalysis, started in response to a request from H. Guntrip to write a biographical chapter for a new book devoted to a further appraisal of Fairbairn's work. Sadly, this book had not been taken beyond the early stages when Guntrip died. His reaction to my first draft, however, was one of encouragement because the emergence of some of Fairbairn's ideas clearly stemmed from the dynamics of his own inner world. At this point I had done little more than describe the stressful situations occurring at various times in his life. While these illumined broad features, I felt the links between Fairbairn's inner and outer worlds could be made much more specific by reference to his self-analytic notes, which

* Fairbairn's *Psychoanalytic Studies of the Personality*, 1952, London: Tavistock, is referred to throughout as PSOP.

had only recently become available to me. I therefore discarded my original chapter and began all over again.

The following account is not as detailed as many of those who value Fairbairn's contribution to psychoanalysis might wish. However, as almost the only survivor of those who knew him well throughout his working life, it seemed important to get some of my knowledge of his personality recorded. It will be transparent that this personal statement is by one in whose life Fairbairn played a unique part – a part that placed me for ever in his debt, and a debt which I feel proudly privileged to have incurred. I hope, nevertheless, that my account is not thereby too distorted.

In writing this book, the limited scope of my aims has been to give a narrative of one person's efforts to use psychoanalytic understanding in order to illumine the development of the person. From this account I hope to answer in some measure the questions so often asked: what took Fairbairn into psychoanalysis as a career, and what sustained him in it? The origins of creativity are notoriously elusive, but I hope that some of the factors contributing to his originality emerge from what I have to describe about his journey into the deep interior areas of the mind.

I do not attempt any comprehensive critique of Fairbairn's work. The specific views put forward in his papers have been amply discussed by Guntrip (1961), and in recent appraisals by various psychoanalysts (e.g. Greenberg and Mitchell, 1983; Kernberg, 1980; Rinsley, 1979). I do, however, make some comments in the final chapter on how I see his significance for the development of psychoanalytic theory. In brief, I consider that he marks a watershed in its theoretical development because of the changes he suggested in its basic assumptions. He saw these clearly as essentials for the future, and he expounded them fearlessly. His was no iconoclastic urge to attack Freud, and I hope I shall show that this can no longer be used as a pretext for avoiding the careful study of Fairbairn's ideas: the picture I give is of a disciplined, critical mind in a gentleman scholar whose aim was to advance our knowledge of man as a person. To my mind, there has been in the psychoanalytic movement an excessive persistence of what can rightly be termed an idolatrous worship of Freud and his work. The profoundest appreciation of any thinker's ideas is surely to explore where they lead. Fairbairn never thought of himself in any other way than as a diligent student groping forward with his assimilation of the unique contributions Freud had made. Freud's thought remained a constant inspiration to him as well as being the *fons et origo* of his whole psychoanalytic self.

The sources I have drawn upon are: (a) my personal relationship with him during thirty-six years; (b) impressions and recollections of his family and others who knew him well; (c) some diary notes he kept in boyhood and during his student years; and (d) some notes of a self-analytic nature that he left amongst his papers.

My personal relationship began in 1928 when I became a junior assistant on the staff of the Psychology Department in the University of Edinburgh. For the first few years there were only three members on the staff apart from myself: the Professor; a senior lecturer; and Fairbairn, who was part-time. I shared with him the supervision of students doing 'experiments' several times a week for the next few years. There were ample opportunities for informal talk and, while I was rather awed by a kind of aristocratic superiority about him, he proved to be extremely friendly and interested in discussing all kinds of issues in a very open-minded way. By the end of this period, as a result of all my contacts with him, especially in the Child Guidance Clinic conducted in the Department, I became drawn to the kind of work he did, and I decided to become a psychoanalyst. To this end, he encouraged me to take a medical training, which I completed while remaining on the Department staff. In these years I observed the hostility shown towards him because of his psychoanalytic interests, an animosity that became increasingly active within the immediate University circles.

When he left the Department I began a personal analysis with him which I continued for the next five years. Again, I was greatly helped in this endeavour by the very low fee he agreed upon. Naturally, I did not see so much of him in that period, although in the very small network in Scotland I inevitably had some contacts with him in local professional groups. These were continued when I left Edinburgh to gain general psychiatric experience in Glasgow from 1938 to 1940. I then moved to a hospital for the expected psychiatric war casualties, and there Fairbairn again became a colleague when he joined the staff for eighteen months.

The hospital closed at the end of 1941 whereupon I went into the Army. I was stationed in Edinburgh for the next eight months so that I was still in fairly close touch with Fairbairn. The unit I joined was a new one established to pioneer improved methods of selecting candidates for officer training. My colleagues there included the psychoanalysts Wilfred Bion, John Bowlby and Eric Wittkower, and, once a procedure had evolved, a considerable number of psychoanalysts and psychotherapists visited the unit prior to the setting up of other units throughout the country. I was thus able to introduce many of them to Fairbairn and his ideas.

I was in London for the next twenty-six years and would meet with Fairbairn several times each year, either when he visited there or when I went to Edinburgh. I also had a good deal of contact with him over the publication of several of his articles while I was editor of the *British Journal of Medical Psychology*. Although separated geographically, I always felt I was in fairly close touch with what he was thinking, and with his personal and family life in general. These contacts were increased when Guntrip began to publish his papers on Fairbairn's views. I then became involved in a triangle which, I think, was much enjoyed by all of us.

For personal recollections, I am grateful to Mrs Ellinor Birtles, Fairbairn's daughter, his older son, Mr Cosmo Fairbairn, and his younger son, Sir Nicholas Fairbairn. For the opportunity to read the diary, the personal notes, and for many talks about him, I am greatly indebted to Mrs Marian Fairbairn, his widow.

Because of their intimate character, some of Fairbairn's self-analytic notes raised acutely for me the question of the propriety of using them for publication. Many prominent individuals have held strong views on the irrelevance to their achievements of their private worlds, and have often taken pains not to leave material about the latter. When their work has little apparent connection with their inner conflicts, this question can be side-stepped. It is not possible to do that when their contributions are necessarily centred on the most subjective areas of their person.

Fairbairn had often commented to me on the intimate interplay of theoretical preferences and personality features, not only in psychoanalytic, but in all scientific theorizing. My reservations about using his notes were ended by two main considerations. First was the fact that many of the notes were written in the years around his most creative thought, and the way in which they were set down clearly indicated that he was trying to get further understanding of himself. He had been steeped during the early years of his psychoanalytic work in the conflicts of deeply schizoid personalities, and this experience had confronted him with disturbing forces. By itself that challenge would have been met successfully. There were, however, other stresses that, in the early 1930s, added to the clinical challenges and precipitated a disturbing symptom that preoccupied him for the rest of his life. The first of these unfortunate situations was particularly painful as it arose from a growing hostility in his wife to his work and the way it isolated him. The second was of the same nature, but emanated from his seniors in the University departments to which he was attached. The work which he valued so highly and to which he was deeply dedicated was thus attacked on all sides in his immediate world. There was support from outside Edinburgh but, unfortunately, no analytic help was available locally for the deeper disturbances that were released. The self-analytic notes struck me as a serious and persistent attempt to grapple with conflicts underlying his symptom and from which he could not gain relief.

The second influence on my decision was the fact that Fairbairn had not only written his notes carefully, but had preserved them for the rest of his life, that is, for over twenty years. They are not very extensive, about ten thousand words, and are largely devoted to early memories and some later dreams and phantasies. They give a strong impression of being intended as part of an eventual contribution to psychoanalytic understanding: the advancement of psychoanalytic knowledge was indeed a central endeavour of Fairbairn's self.

The existence of domestic stress and of the symptom was freely talked about in later years by his family, so to omit reference to them would have been to present a very incomplete account of Fairbairn's inner and outer worlds; and having revealed their presence, I decided that to print the self-analytic notes was the right course. I also increasingly gained a conviction that he had left them to be of help in understanding himself and his work; and I still believe this is not a complete rationalization on my part. Moreover, the likely recipients of the notes would be his close friends, either Guntrip or myself. They illuminate processes of great general psychoanalytic interest which, to me, constitute a tribute to the dedication of this isolated research worker. The creative use of them is to honour Fairbairn's lifelong work.

Analysing some of the inner forces that forge innovative thought is in no way to detract from its value as a contribution to knowledge. Specific constellations of factors in one individual, however much we may feel they would distort his perceptions and conceptualizations, facilitate a particular insight that leaves us in his debt for that illumination. Our judgements of the product have then to be made from our own experience – and judgement has already been made on Fairbairn's work by many analysts long before what may here be said about some of its unconscious determinants.

In the first chapters of this book, I describe the course of Fairbairn's life as seen from the everyday, external point of view. My aim here is to highlight the most relevant aspects of the environmental interactions that shaped the choice of his profession, and thereafter his progress in it. Naturally, this account can provide little more than a scaffolding of events behind which is the architecture of Fairbairn's self, with the inner powerhouse in which his understanding of his patients was fashioned.

In ensuing chapters, I have tried to give a picture of the interaction between Fairbairn's inner and outer worlds in relation to the papers he wrote. This takes us up to the outbreak of war in 1939, with its inevitably disturbing impact on the whole circumstances of his life. It was in 1940 that the ferment of his creative ideas became most active and, as I shall suggest, this activity was the stimulus to the writing of his self-analytic notes. Having decided to use the notes, I had to settle at what point I should bring their contents into my narrative: whether to use them early, to give a fuller description of his childhood experiences, or later, when they occurred in his own development.

I chose the latter course because they had originated under the tensions of that particular phase in his life. It seemed that in this way their dynamic origin would be more vividly conveyed.

In the final chapter, I make some comments on what I consider to be Fairbairn's essential significance for psychoanalytic theory. His specific formulations on the basic endopsychic structuring may well require amendment as knowledge grows. His theoretical premises, however, will stimulate such development as part of the next phase for psychoanalysis.

Like many an author on the completion of his book, I have an enormous sense of gratitude to a large number of people. To Fairbairn's widow, Mrs Marian Fairbairn, I repeat my special acknowledgement of her assistance. The other members of his family also could not have been more helpful. For the innumerable changes that kept being made throughout, I have again been most fortunate in the way Mrs Davina Stewart of the Scottish Institute of Human Relations has kept up her cheerful patience. I also wish to thank Robert Young, the Managing Director of Free Association Books, and his staff for their generous tolerance and encouragement. The sad aspect of some of Fairbairn's experiences added to my appreciation of the caring forbearance of my wife.

To Eric Trist, my former colleague at the 'Tavistock' Clinic–Institute, I owe a very special debt. From the time I began to work as a psychoanalyst, his generous friendship has kept my focus on the inner worlds of persons open to the contributions of social scientists who are concerned about what happens to people in their outer realities, and so to consider always the person within his social matrix at every stage of his life.

I Making a choice of career

FAMILY BACKGROUND AND SCHOOLING

THE FAMILY ATMOSPHERE into which William Ronald Dodds Fairbairn was born in 1889 in Edinburgh was pervaded by the contradictions of devoted loving care combined with oppressive strictness. There was a liberal quality, however, in the provisions made by his parents for the development of his talents, and in the degree to which he shared in their social life. They had a large circle of relatives and friends all over the country with whom regular visits were maintained, and in which Ronald was encouraged to be an active participant.

The restrictive aspects of his upbringing were the result of various factors. Ronald was to remain an only child within the cramping milieu of parents dominated by a culture which demanded a high degree of conformity to its moral and formal standards. Most prominent, perhaps, was the fact that his exacting mother maintained an over-intensive supervision of all his activities throughout his early years.

Thomas Fairbairn, his father, was a valuer and surveyor able to provide the comfortable setting of the successful middle-class professional of the late Victorian age. His background had been the stern school of Scottish Calvinism, with its heavy stress on moral values inculcated by the powerful influence of the Church and its strong pressures towards regular attendance at its weekly services. Great emphasis was laid on hard work and achievement – especially praiseworthy when gained without pampering or indulgence.

The social stratification and self-conscious differentiation between classes which was so prominent in Victorian Britain was also a conspicuous feature of Edinburgh society. As the capital of Scotland, its population had been for centuries dominated by the hierarchies of the aristocratic and landed families whose importance rested both on their economic power and on the fact that they had provided the occupants of many of the chief political and legal offices. The University had a high reputation with a social influence in a not very large city that was considerable. Scholarly traditions were enlivened by the great figures of the not-too-distant past. Fairbairn's father's generation were the grandchildren of those brought up in the period of the *Edinburgh Review*, when the city was a literary centre of European renown, with writers like Francis Jeffrey, Sydney Smith and Sir Walter Scott, who, in turn, had grown up in the intellectually brilliant Scottish Enlightenment, focused around the philosophers David Hume and Adam Smith.

Traditions of learning, and especially family ones, were very important in the national culture so that within the professional classes there were many who were artistically cultivated and intellectually sophisticated as well as being politically and economically influential. A common aspiration was to be the 'gentleman' – the man who combined high moral principles, elegance and the intellectual and artistic culture of the upper classes, with a genuine humanistic concern for, and an informed involvement in, the general improvement of mankind. Nevertheless, and despite the Enlightenment, it was a culture in which the oedipal super-ego was virtually deified to uphold the prohibitions of the Church, especially against immoral sexuality, and to preserve the authority of parents along with their class privileges. It was inconceivable in that society that there might have been some reference within the Ten Commandments to the duty of parents to understand and respect the autonomous nature of their children. The repressed, of course, had its re-entries, notably in the adulation of the national poet, Robert Burns, whose life and poetry celebrated the earthy vitality of human nature, as well as scorning the hypocritical trends within the excessively moralistic precepts of the Church.

With the drive to achieve – which, for the young professional man meant getting enough income to afford the comforts of success, such as an appropriate house in a desirable neighbourhood – it was common for the husband to marry relatively late. Fairbairn senior was in his middle thirties when he married an Englishwoman about his own age, Cecilia Leefe. She came from Yorkshire yeoman stock who had farmed their lands since Norman times. That her staunchly Presbyterian husband should choose an English Episcopalian to be his wife, perhaps represented a latent need on his part to mitigate the harshness of the Calvinistic tradition. There was, however, little yielding in this respect, because Cecilia Leefe was strict to the point of being a martinet in bringing her son up to conform to the formalities of their class, religious and otherwise. Fairbairn senior, however, was a friendly man, to those who knew him, fond of entertaining and interested in his society as he saw it. His wife was known amongst their friends as one who maintained a well-ordered establishment with a marked sense of what was 'proper'.

Ronald was born in a substantial villa that his parents had acquired in Morningside, a suburb then extending to the southern fringes of Edinburgh. The house stood near the edge of this developing area, with houses of similar social status around. A suburban railway line ran by the foot of the garden, and the opportunity to watch the passing trains at close quarters gave the little boy an interest which he maintained for many years. (He had a good collection of railway tickets which he sold in his later life for a sum that surprised him.) On the other side of the house the landscape stretched towards the Pentland hills, immortalized by Robert Louis Stevenson.

The household had the usual complement of domestic staff of the period – maids plus a nurse for the child. Within this highly formalized and controlling background, the young Ronald received a great deal of attentive care and, as mentioned, he was very much a part of his parents' social life. His father, in the customary way of his times, did not spend much time with his son in his early years, though he showed the normal paternal concern in taking him to places of interest, then later played games with him, especially golf – one of the main national pastimes in Scotland. As an only child, however, Ronald was enveloped in the paramount values of 'good behaviour', morally and socially; and for the upholding of these, his companions were carefully scrutinized.

To compensate for the restrictive aspects of Ronald's parents, there was the freer relationship with his nanny. It was thus inevitable that the little boy was thrown rather much into his inner world. He had an active fantasy life with systematized creations such as a country of which he evolved the features in great detail. The positive aspects of his family experience, as well as establishing a rich inner world, enabled the boy to enjoy the company of others and especially those of similar mould. He often referred in later life to the great joy of spending holidays in Yorkshire and in London where he always felt warmly welcomed by his uncles, aunts and cousins. He noted, too, his gratitude at having so many friendly homes for these frequent holidays, three and four times a year, which he felt compensated for the absence of brothers and sisters. That these relationships with many of his relatives were deeply valued (he thought of them as second homes) was shown by the way he maintained them like an extended family in later life.

His parents' restrictions inevitably had their effects. An omnipresent mother, ever watchful lest inappropriate influences or activities should be adopted, produced a rather unassertive young man with a strong lifelong attachment to her. This tie was made the more intense by his mother's frequent illnesses, which caused, at times, a good deal of anxiety in the home about her welfare. Her Victorian taboo on sex was so strong that sexual curiosity became an anxiously preoccupying concern for the boy. While little is known of more specific features in his father's personality, one symptom he had suggests there may well have been a good deal of neurotic difficulty. This consisted in an inability to urinate in the presence of others so that, even at home, there had to be no one near the toilet door when he went to urinate. Ronald was thus made regularly aware of his father's mysterious affliction.

In response to the parental ideals so consistently held up to him, the young Ronald developed into the dedicated, concerned 'gentleman' from an early age. He was sent to Merchiston Castle*, a private school for boys up to the age of about eighteen, which, though normally residential, included a few non-resident 'day boys'. The school was near the Fairbairn home and Ronald remained a day boy throughout his school years. All pupils came from families who could afford private education and so all were of similar background. Here he was well grounded in the humanities. While he felt ill at ease with the 'hearty' athletic extroverts, a stereotype many of these schools tended to emphasize, he did not refer openly to his schooldays as an unhappy period. He told his children later, however, that he had hated school. Football he disliked but cricket and golf appealed to him. He was also in the school Officer Training Corps, an institution that was then a feature of most private schools for boys in the United Kingdom, whereby an introduction was provided for the common careers in the armed services or in colonial administration.

FURTHER EDUCATION AND MILITARY SERVICE.

On leaving school, Ronald was a fairly typical youth of his social class, albeit notably identified with intellectual preferences. His participation in conventional social activities and his enjoyment of friends were much influenced by his interest in 'serious matters' such as religious, moral and social questions; yet he was not regarded as unduly priggish or aloof with others. He always had a keen sense of fun and enjoyment, and he was, from early years, a good listener – a quality that enabled him to make many friendships, not a few of which he kept up until his death. Artistically, he was highly responsive to the visual arts, an interest of his father's. He liked classical music, although, perhaps because neither parent played an instrument, he refused to learn the piano at school.

There had been thoughts of a career in law until his early interest in moral and psychological issues progressed to the point where philosophy became the choice for his first studies at Edinburgh University. (The Philosophy Department at that time provided the academic teaching in psychology.)

---

* This school was located at that time in and around the ancestral home of the Napiers of Merchiston, a family prominent throughout several centuries in Scottish history. One of them, who had a considerable reputation in Europe as a philosopher and mathematician, published in 1614 his invention of logarithms.

Enrolling as a student in 1907, when he was eighteen years of age, Ronald graduated four years later with honours in philosophy.

By this time he had decided to become a clergyman, a vocation not unusual for a young man from his background. Throughout boyhood and adolescence he had attended church with his parents every Sunday for both morning and evening services. This custom did not strike him as tedious, for he would listen with increasingly critical appraisal to the arguments, unless the sermons were unduly long (over an hour, say). The Presbyterian services, however, gradually came to seem harsh and drab for him compared with the Episcopalian ones which he often attended on holiday with relatives and family friends, who included some Anglican clergy.

As well as such prolonged contacts with the formal expressions of Christianity, Ronald joined in much 'practical Christianity' by helping with various clubs and organizations for the deprived sections of the community. That his marked altruistic and religious feelings were merged with his whole upbringing is clear from his general conservatism. His impulses to improve the lot of the deprived or the suffering, to make life more tolerable and to provide opportunities for all, were unquestionably strong and sincere. They were, however, to be expressed within the established structure of society, to which his attachment was unusually strong. He was devoted to the monarchy with its deep parental significance in the symbolic family of the nation. The contemporary Fabians with their socialist belief that society's traditionally hierarchical structure, its economic organization and its institutions had to be abandoned, were abhorrent to him. To have accepted notions of that kind was not an option for one so enmeshed with his powerful conservative mother and his successful father. For Fairbairn, a benevolent, concerned élitism was the only effective way to foster what was best for society. He had an idealized idea of the traditional social orders and values, and in addition had a deeply rooted conviction that social change had to proceed by evolution; for, together with the influence of his parents, his classical studies buttressed his view of the inescapable tyranny that followed revolutionary change.

His conception of the religious life and his decision to adopt it are described with a rather youthful fervour in his diary on his twenty-first birthday. In early years this diary is mainly a catalogue of holidays and other events, with considerable gaps. For the period around his twenty-first birthday, the entries are much more expansive (there is very little subsequently). I quote the entry on his birthday in full (see below) as it brings out so much of his inner self at this time. While it reflects the strength of his religious feelings, these were probably to the fore at this point because a few days earlier he had attended a Bible conference at which there were several students. He refers to them and to some of their social activities, serious and frivolous, from which he is clearly 'one of the boys' in this group. Surprisingly enough in view of many of his later comments about his lack of masculine assertiveness, he describes an incident while playing golf when he and his partners were involved in fisticuffs with some aggressive players on the golf-course. In short, his religious interests were certainly not pursued in solitude, nor in a notably passive self.

Diary entry for 11th August, 1910:

August 11th, which is notable as the 21st birthday of that humble servant of King George V, Ronald Dodds Fairbairn. Not only a humble servant of King George, I hope, however, but also of Jesus Christ; for, at a time such as this, it is well to be serious for a moment, and to pause at this great turning-point of life to take a breath of heavenly air, before plunging into the work and stress of manhood. It is hard to combine in the right mixture the jollity and the seriousness which are both essential for a presentable life. It is of ultimate importance to be solid at the bottom, but continuous solidity acquires a 't' and becomes 'stolidity'. Now, of all things, stolidity is the most depressing, and, therefore, to be consummately avoided. This is where so many Christians cut themselves off from life. They are serious, and rightly so, but never jolly. There is a call to look on the happy side of life and things, no less divine than that which bids us remember that life is a Great Reality. Excessive seriousness is to [be] avoided for several reasons. We must remember that cheerfulness and cheery demeanour bring happiness into others' lives. The 'damp cloth' gentleman is deservedly the *bête noire* of all society. And not only does a happy heart lighten the burden of our toiling fellow man; it exalts ourselves. For those whose pursuit in life is of a serious nature, nothing is a greater Godsend than the possession of a light and cheerful heart, to smooth away the stony path, and prevent fossilization. It has now been demonstrated beyond possible doubt, that, from a purely physiological point of view, happiness has an uplifting influence upon the vital forces, and conduces to health and usefulness. The ideal man, in my opinion, is one who, while realizing the seriousness and responsibility of life, yet sees life's whimsicalities and joys as well. But, how few of such there are! Would to God, there were more in the Christian Ministry! The serious side must never be neglected, but what I shall call full-bloodedness must be remembered too. It is neglect of this, for one thing, that alienates modern youth from the Church. We are continually being told how young men and young women wander from the Churches' portals in search of pleasure. It is a sad thought. But what is the cause? Is it the frivolity and foolishness of modern youth as we are so often told amid groanings and tears from the pulpit? Is the youth of the 20th century really so much more depraved than that of centuries gone by?

Surely we ought to look elsewhere, before declaring that to be the only cause. It is easy to blame young men and women for not being attracted by religion; but it is wiser to inquire if religion is being presented to them in a way calculated to attract. Is the religion of the average Church of today of a nature to capture and mould the full-blown life of the healthy-minded young man and woman? Or does it only provide for one type of mind? Is it only suited for half of the individual's life? True Christianity ought to satisfy every legitimate instinct and aspiration. It ought to be a working and workable philosophy of life for man and boy, matron and maiden; it ought to be adaptable to the condition of schoolroom and football field, of office and golf-course, of factory and home. God give me strength to do my share, however little, to effect that unspeakably desirable consummation. I have decided to devote my life to the cause of religion; but may it be a manly, healthy, whole-hearted strong religion, appealing to enthusiasm of youth, as well as to the quiescence of old age – in other words may it be a Christlike religion.

Leaving aside its old-fashioned tone, we are struck by the naïve earnestness, as though this is a young adolescent with a strong sense of a dutiful destiny expressed like a sermon. He is determined to put right the Christianity with which his parents have emasculated him. His mission will not alter his submissive loyalty to God and King, although he indicates clearly his intention to own his masculinity.

What struck me most forcibly on reading his declaration, was the extent to which his self had been transformed by the time I first knew him about twenty years later. The delays in his development had been overcome most successfully, presumably from the experiences of getting away from home, to his years in the Army, his personal analysis with Connell who was a very full-blooded Christian, and then his marriage and work, all of which will be referred to presently.

There is no mention anywhere in his diary notes of his being attracted to any young woman. Neither is there anything expressed of a physical interest in boys or men.

Having chosen the Church as his future field of work, there seem to have been doubts in his mind about it, or at least about his readiness for it, for prior to the divinity course he pursued Hellenic studies in short periods at the Universities of Kiel, Strasbourg and Manchester. These further broad studies in the humanities were possibly felt as likely to give him some insight into the aspects of man that he noted later as missing from the academic teaching in psychology, namely, conscience, guilt, sin and sexuality. That he was searching for some guidance on the management of inner conflicts is more clearly suggested by the fact that in this period he was reading about hypnotism and suggestion. Such trends did not divert him from his decision, however, for he went on to take the intermediate degree in divinity at London University; and in the autumn of 1914, now aged twenty-five, he was back at Edinburgh University in the regular theological course of the Presbyterian Church.

The outbreak of war in 1914 did not pose a conflict for the theological student rooted in the staunch Victorian patriotism fostered by the Churches and which his parents embodied. It was his mother who was very much against his joining the Army as a combatant – perhaps an indication of her need to hold on to him. In the spring of 1915, he settled the issue by joining the engineering unit of the University Officer Training Corps. Two months later he was rejected medically when he went to be commissioned as an officer in the Army. The varicocele, which had led to his rejection, was removed by operation and in November he joined the Royal Garrison Artillery as a second lieutenant, being stationed locally for the next eighteen months. Amongst his social engagements during this period was a visit with an Army doctor to a hospital in Edinburgh for 'Nerve-Shocked Officers' to meet Captain Rivers, that is, Dr W. H. R. Rivers of Cambridge, a well-known anthropologist and pioneer of medical psychology – another indication that he was attracted by the 'new psychology'. The manifestations of conversion hysteria that he saw on this visit greatly impressed him.

The autumn of 1917, by which time Fairbairn was now promoted to the rank of lieutenant, saw his battery move off to the Middle East. Within a few months, he was in the midst of Allenby's successful campaign against the Turks in Palestine that ended in the triumphant entry into Jerusalem in December. A spell of illness later in the following year necessitated hospitalization in Cairo. In October 1918 he was back on leave in his parents' home, with demobilization following on Christmas Eve, his total period of combatant service having been three and a half years. He never spoke much about his war experience and his family received no impression of it as a traumatic one. Indeed, he seemed to have enjoyed the close relationship with others. It had, of course, a special significance for one whose Christian ideals were not only tested by the brutalities of war, but on the sites of Christ's life and work. The fact that he had participated in the liberation of Jerusalem pleased him and, as a memento of that campaign, he kept a model of the kind of guns he had been using in it.

It was in Palestine that his interest in medical psychology took definitive shape. His first choice of the Church as a career had not satisfied his need to understand and help with human conflicts. Moreover, he had developed an increasing aversion to the prospect of preaching sermons, an attitude which, in the light of later notes, possibly derived from a degree of associated phobic anxiety. It needed only the few contacts his reading had provided with the new psychology to set the direction of his future. He moved fast so that by early January 1919 he had embarked on a condensed four-year training in medicine with a view to becoming a psychotherapist.

In the second year of his course he was reading books by Freud and Jung and in the middle of 1921 he began a personal analysis with E. H. Connell. Connell was a wealthy Australian who had sold his business to train in medicine and psychiatry in Edinburgh. On completing these he then had a personal analysis with Ernest Jones, and hence was firmly rooted in Freud's approach. He began psychotherapeutic practice in Edinburgh some years before Fairbairn started to see him. This was an unusual step for Fairbairn at that time, which suggests a strong pressure from his own conflicts. Sessions were continued throughout a period of about two years, daily at times though with some breaks. Thus, in March 1922 he went to Paris to attend clinics. Within a few weeks, however, he had contracted pleurisy. The condition worsened with the result that he spent the next two months in hospital, a rib resection having to be carried out. This was an anxious time for his parents and his father journeyed to Paris to ensure that everything possible was being done. In the autumn the analytic sessions were resumed daily for most of the next year.

EMPLOYMENT AND MARRIAGE
After graduating in medicine in 1923, he had a spell in general practice near London. He then spent most of the next two years as an assistant in the Royal Edinburgh Hospital, the chief psychiatric hospital and the centre for training. In the middle of this period, his father died quite unexpectedly from septicaemia following the extraction of a tooth. Fairbairn seems not to have been upset by this event and to have scarcely mourned his father's death. He had long felt a considerable resentment against his father because of the latter's opposition to all schemes whereby his son would be getting opportunities that he (the father) thought unnecessarily costly or otherwise undesirable, as when he vetoed a proposal that Ronald should go to Oxford. For the father, this was a place of dubious morals and, of course, a hotbed of Episcopacy. Ronald appeared to become freer in various ways following his father's death, and he dealt expeditiously with the business of getting his widowed mother resettled into a new home. A sign of this greater freedom is that he joined the Anglican Church, to which his mother had originally belonged. From adolescence he had been sensitive to the contrast between its services and the rather grim, forbidding atmosphere of the Presbyterian Church which his father had attended with dutiful patriarchal regularity.

By the autumn of 1925, Fairbairn began to see private patients for psychotherapy in his own consulting room, with the support of the senior psychiatrist in the hospital and also of his own analyst Connell. In the following spring he rounded off his general psychiatric training by obtaining the University Diploma in Psychiatry.

To work as a whole-time psychotherapist in Scotland was inevitably going to bring a high degree of professional isolation, and the desirability of moving to London had to be considered. In 1926 he discussed with Dr J. R. Rees, the future Medical Director of the Tavistock Clinic, the possibilities of work and training there, but with no feasible financial prospects the whole issue was shelved. He now accepted two part-time appointments in Edinburgh. One was a purely medical one as a general physician to a hospital dealing mainly with terminal illnesses. He enjoyed this work as it kept alive his keen interest in medicine, and he gave it up with regret five years later when the pressure of his psychotherapeutic practice became too great. The other appointment was to the staff of the Psychology Department in the University. Here his duties were to include teaching psychodynamic psychology to medical and non-medical students plus the postgraduate trainees in psychiatry. Almost immediately after he had made these arrangements a quite new preoccupation developed.

From his student days, his social life had included a few girl-friends but with no serious attachment. In the somewhat formalized ways of the times, especially in his circles, he had attended many dances, the main occasions for young gentlemen to meet young ladies. Now almost thirty-seven, and perhaps again from the freedom felt after his father's death – though more probably from his personal analysis and the completion of his credentials for starting out on his psychotherapeutic career – he had begun a friendship with a medical student. The relationship blossomed rapidly and in the early autumn of 1926 they were married.

Mary More Gordon was a tall elegant woman who came from an old Scottish landed family. She thus had an appeal to Fairbairn's love of the old-established social order in addition to her personal qualities. She was musical and fond of the sophisticated social scene in which she had been brought up. As a result, she and Fairbairn went out a good deal in their early days – rather more often than was his wont – to the theatre, concerts, dinner parties, and so on. She was soon absorbed, however, in different activities. From the flat in which they began their married life, they moved into the house in which Ronald had his consulting room and which was now to serve also as their home, an arrangement that continued for many years. Then in the summer of 1927 a daughter was born.

Following the change in his choice of career, there was ample evidence of the deep and unswerving dedication Fairbairn brought to psychoanalysis. He now maintained, alongside the commitments to his family, his active investment in its theory and practice and he wrote his first clinical paper soon after the birth of his daughter.

From the record of his development, there is no doubt that Fairbairn fuelled his psychotherapeutic work with a powerful dynamic interest. The mysteries of the inner world had preoccupied him from early boyhood. They were closely connected with the Victorian taboos maintained with great strictness by his parents, and which were also preserved by a barrier of silence in the contemporary academic world. Sexuality and its aura of guilt and sin were almost unmentionable, a phenomenon in puzzling contrast with their universal everyday manifestations. The presence of his own conflicts could be inferred from his inhibited sexual development, the choice of his career, and from his embarking on a personal analysis – an unusual decision in the early 1920s – when he was half-way through his medical training. The analysis had ended as he finished the latter, and its liberating effect was reinforced by his father's death about this time, an event that gave him a sense of taking on the fuller responsibilities of manhood.

From his early years he had acquired the habit of wanting to tease out what was basic in the understanding of complex phenomena. His academic training in philosophy had then developed this trait into a sophisticated capacity to identify, to conceptualize, and to appraise explanatory principles. (An early instance of this attitude is described in his diary. As a young man he saw the first aeroplanes to visit Scotland, which included both biplanes and monoplanes. Having been duly impressed by their potential he observed that the monoplane would be the model for the future because it derived from a 'principle' which had survived in nature after a long evolution.)

This intellectual characteristic is of particular importance in studying his writings because there has long been a persistent attitude amongst psychoanalysts that the stature of Freud's intellect put his theories beyond criticism. Such an attitude was often justified in the early phases of his work because of his unique experience and knowledge, though he himself stressed that, while the phenomena he exposed were incontrovertible, his theories were highly dispensable. There is in this connection the peculiar nature of psychoanalytic data, which makes it a lengthy process to test theory against observations. One consequence is that analysts can have to contend with periods of uncertainty and inner turmoil when struggling to assimilate the nature and origin of phenomena which do not fit into existing conceptions. Furthermore, the unconscious links with the latter usually entail an inner working through of the new material, and the authoritative status of Freud tends to be a reassurance at these times.

Fairbairn's thinking is unusually well disciplined, with its careful state-ments about existing theories, his reasons for suggested amendments, and the data exposing the need for these changes. A second consideration is that of personality features, especially unconscious ones, that might distort objective thought in the highly subjective psychoanalytic work from which observations are made. I believe Fairbairn had no less a capacity for objectivity than most analysts. One factor, however, should be referred to, namely, his emphasis on the therapeutic aim of psychoanalysis. His first solution, to get help for his own conflicts from religion, was associated with the simultaneous desire to be able to use what he received for relieving stress in others and hence his decision to train for the ministry. In his later professional life he would frequently remark on what he thought to be a progressive lessening in the adherence to the primary aim of psychoanalysis, namely, the relief of suffering. It was not so much that analysts were indifferent to this aspect in practice, as that its implications for the understanding of the dynamics of the relationship between analyst and patient could be overlooked. The accelerating accumulation of information, with an associated focusing on technique, carried for him the danger of distorting the study of the whole person and his or her needs. Nevertheless, it was his firm conviction that help for psychological stress could only come from knowledge and understanding based on sound explanatory principles. It was this belief that led him to abandon the Church for psychotherapy. Later he records (Fairbairn, 1955) that he chose to follow Freud rather than Jung because Freud's conceptions offered a better prospect of solving psychopathological problems. His patients were going to be a very active challenge from which he might contribute to human welfare in a realistic way. The influence of such motives upon his work can best be judged with this factor in mind.

2 The emergence of the psychoanalyst

THE FIRST CLINICAL PAPER

AFTER TWO YEARS of analytic experience, it is not surprising that, in view of Fairbairn's earlier religious interests, its first major by-product was a paper entitled 'Notes on the religious phantasies of a female patient'. Though written in 1927 and presented to the Scottish Branch of the British Psychological Society in that year, Fairbairn did not seek to publish it until it appeared in his book *Psychoanalytic Studies of the Personality* in 1952. By that time, he could recognize its place in what he termed in his Introduction, 'the progressive development of a line of thought'.

The patient, a spinster of thirty-one, was treated at first for only a short period. She had had a series of breakdowns during the previous ten years, and the one that had brought her to treatment had the same features as the earlier ones, namely, prostration and inability to face the demands of life along with sleeplessness and disturbing dreams. There was thus a regressed state with marked anxiety. She attributed her troubles to sexual conflicts around masturbation, though she stated she had no sexual knowledge when the breakdowns started.

There had been distressing conflicts since childhood about religious themes accompanied by visions and phantasies. In spite of her conscious lack of sexual knowledge, the visions were frequently of infantile male genitals. Fairbairn selected for consideration the phantasies clustered around three identifications: (a) with the Mother of Christ; (b) with Christ; and (c) with the Bride of Christ. In keeping with the psychoanalytic standpoint, he relates these religious needs, first, to the early childhood attitudes to parents persisting in the unconscious, and, second, to the need to relieve the guilt deriving from a repressed Oedipus situation. Of the latter he remarks that there is no doubt of its exaggerated proportions. The phantasies are fulfilments of her oedipal wishes for her father, or, particularly in the third group, for her brother as a substitute for father. When we turn to his account of the patient's childhood attitudes to her parents, there is a strong impression of the incipient formulation that foreshadows his subsequent theoretical development. The classical oedipal situation and the libido theory are highlighted in relation to the patient's sexual feelings towards her brother and father underlying her compulsive masturbation. Yet there is throughout a tendency to give a primary and independent status to the effect of the actual relationships of the patient with her parents, especially of the influence of a dominating mother/sister combination and the totally absent father. The split between the parents had been caused by the father's destructive alcoholism which led the mother to take the patient when a baby, along with the large group of older siblings, to a new home. The father subsequently became a taboo subject. Although the patient had no contact with him, he remained a powerful figure whose existence constituted a threat to the family. In his description of the initial analytic work with her, Fairbairn focuses on the significance of the religious phantasies as attempts to satisfy a longing for a missing personal relationship with her father. The distinction between a need at the personal level and a more restricted instinctive sexual drive is unmistakable, although Fairbairn does not pursue this theme. What he points out, however, in the religious phantasies is the personal significance of the identifications. Thus, to be the Mother of Christ makes her the woman upon whom the Spirit of the Father descends, and this holistic personal aspect is also seen in her being the Son of God. The phantasy of being the Bride of Christ he sees as a symbolic fulfilment of the libidinal wishes towards her brother. The grandiose character of the phantasies differentiates them from the ordinary Christian experience, for, when possessed by each, she really feels herself to be the principal figure to the point where there is a failure to distinguish phantasy and reality. There is thus a markedly schizoid state underlying these intense activities of her imagination. The sexual longings are inextricably merged with highly complex organizations within the personality, each of which is capable of functioning like a separate person expressing the need for a specific relationship with another person.

The inclusion of this paper in his book over twenty years after it was written shows how much he recognized his early questionings. While these incipient notions are adumbrated, he was too aware of his limited experience, especially with longer-term intensive analyses, to presume to formulate such basic issues as he raised later when he asked whether the sexual interest or the need for the personal relationship was the primary motive. It was also a time when he was thinking of a move to London to gain more training. He had just completed his doctoral thesis on the theory of repression and dissociation, in which his grasp of classical theory had established his professional credentials in London through his contact with Edward Glover. Any disappointment over the failure to gain a suitable opportunity there was compensated by his new situation in Edinburgh. He was now happily married and with a daughter. He had been appointed to posts in the University, so that he felt his professional aspirations to be supported by academic father-figures. There were thus various influences that would reinforce his conservative caution about advancing views other than the standard ones. We can note, in addition to his placing the aetiological importance of the family relationships in the foreground, a more definite expression of his independent mind in relation to a quite different theme. As one brought up in a conventionally religious family and steeped in the evolution of classical and religious thought, he comments that he is against the reduction of the higher values in human culture to simple psychological origins. He adds, however, that 'psychological origins provide a legitimate field for investigation on the part of psychological science'. Here he feels sufficiently sure of himself to dissent from a psychoanalytic view common enough even before the appearance of Freud's *The Future of an Illusion*. (Interestingly enough, Freud was writing this work at the same time as Fairbairn was engaged on his paper.)

In a postscript added in 1952 when this paper appeared in his book, he describes intermittent analytic contacts with the patient over the next nine to ten years. Following some initial improvement, a progressive deterioration occurred until she became confined to bed on account of extreme exhaustion. No organic basis could be found for this state, which Fairbairn concluded was 'neurasthenic' from the addiction to persistent masturbation, and the weakness progressed until she died. On visiting her the day before her death, at which time her faculties were unimpaired, he was sure she was in a state of extreme sexual desire. Her last words to him were, 'I want a man.'

The postscript's ending presents a strange puzzle. Written long after he had adopted his object-relations theory, he advances three possible causes of her death. Did she die of an unsatisfied sexual desire, or of masturbation, or of a self-destruction by repression of unmanageable instinctive tensions? These questions suggest that Fairbairn himself had here reverted to the libido theory in its original form with Freud's notion of neurasthenia as the consequence of the frustration of normal sexual satisfaction. Her complete regressive withdrawal from life and its need for men, along with her surrender to the care of her persecutory mother/sister, would seem to require some consideration of the schizoid splits in her personality. We should have expected some comment, for instance, on an unconscious suicide to end the intolerable attacks of the sadistic rejecting object on her forbidden needy self, or on the frustrating father/penis with the breast/mother at a deeper layer. Reasons for this anomaly will emerge later in the light of what was happening in his own inner world at the time of adding the postscript. What can be mentioned at this point is a noticeable lack of comment on the patient's destructive phantasies although several references are made to these. At the time of his writing the original paper, aggression did not have such a prominence in psychoanalytic thought as it subsequently acquired. Melanie Klein was scarcely known. Nevertheless, the patient's hatred of her mother imago was linked to an obsessive fear of killing her older sister who assumed a dominating controlling attitude towards the patient. Again, from adolescence the patient recalled a fear that she would be hanged for some crime which would suggest that she had in phantasy murdered her mother/sister, since in her day in Britain hanging was the inevitable consequence of a conviction for murder. More directly expressive of her sadism is her experiencing the nails tearing Christ's flesh when he was being pulled from the Cross. These phantasies must have played a major role in her anxieties and probably in the regressive flight from her inner world. By the time Fairbairn wrote his next clinical paper there was a very different emphasis on such sadistic phantasies.

When we recall that this first paper was written after only two years' experience and with very little help – and certainly without the supervision any young trainee would get normally – Fairbairn shows an extremely good grasp of the unconscious processes within the person.

CONSOLIDATION

There now began in 1928 a period of steady analytic work, at first with six patients and with several more after a few years. His relations with his two academic seniors were good and he was involved in clinics conducted by each of them, one for adults and the other for children. In the Psychology Department Professor Drever involved him in the intelligence testing of deaf children in which Fairbairn co-operated quite readily, especially in investigating their vocabularies. Domestically, however, there were anxieties. His wife was admitted to hospital for a short period and four months later gave birth to premature twins, neither of whom survived.

The intensely subjective nature of psychoanalytic practice makes it difficult to preserve an adequate degree of objectivity unless the analyst has some trusted colleagues with whom to share the many doubts and questions that arise constantly, especially as his experience with patients gets deeper. Apart from Connell, who had been his analyst, there was no one specializing in analytical psychotherapy with whom Fairbairn could have an appropriate interchange. (One doctor who had trained with the London analysts had returned to Edinburgh. Daunted perhaps by the unsympathetic climate of opinion, especially in medicine, along with the difficulties of the task in relative isolation, he had changed from trying to make the unconscious conscious as a livelihood to the less demanding role of the opposite process by becoming an anaesthetist!)

It was fortunate that after he began his analytic practice, support was forthcoming from the British Psycho-Analytical Society. Introductions from Connell to Ernest Jones and Edward Glover were particularly helpful in introducing Fairbairn to the members. As a fellow Scot, Glover could readily sympathize with the compatriot battling alone against the granite-like resistances of Scottish Presbyterian culture. It could not have taken long for the analysts in London to feel that, though Fairbairn had emerged in psychoanalytic work from rather restricted experience, he was a colleague who could be trusted – even by the exacting standards of Glover and Ernest Jones. He was transparently a man of culture, of great personal and professional integrity, as well as having a thorough grasp of Freud's writings, so that there was no question of dealing with some 'wild' analyst who might discredit the relatively new movement. There was a revival of the possibility of a move to London, but he was unsuccessful in his application for the post of Director of the newly established Child Guidance Training Centre there. Any disappointment over that event did not appear to have been unduly disturbing, and he was soon immersed in preparing various papers. For the next few years he would occasionally express regret that he was not in London, since he wanted to have colleagues with whom he could discuss issues as they arose. He was not by nature a solitary person either professionally or socially. Subsequently, he was glad to have remained in Scotland, away from the passions that led later to the divisions amongst the psychoanalysts around Melanie Klein's work. In his view these were inappropriate reactions within any scientific or professional body.

From 1928 to 1930, in parallel with his increasing practice, he devoted a good deal of time to securing a thorough knowledge of psychoanalytic principles. He read several papers on aspects of psychoanalysis to a wide range of audiences, from student societies to various mental-health bodies. His more specialized papers were given to the Scottish Branch of the British Psychological Society or to meetings of staff and postgraduate students in the Psychology Department. Topics in these contributions included reviews of McDougall's *Abnormal Psychology* and Freud's *The Ego and the Id* (after the English edition appeared in 1923), general discussions of 'The super-ego' and 'Adolescence'; Fairbairn also described 'Impressions of the International Congress of Psycho-Analysis' (1929).

Two contributions on theoretical issues are of particular interest, because they contain in embryonic form a few of the ideas that were developed in his later theories. First was an address early in 1929 on 'Fundamental principles of psychoanalysis' to the historic society of the medical students and published subsequently in the *Journal of the Royal Medical Society of Edinburgh*. Because of its limited circulation, it was unlikely to have been widely noticed, but Fairbairn may well have sent a copy to Glover to inform him of what he was doing. His interest and competence in formulating essential theoretical assumptions are well demonstrated. He stresses the fact that psychoanalysis was a method of treatment, although he was not taking up its therapeutic status on this occasion. The classical principles are presented in a carefully reasoned way and his only reservation comes over Freud's use of the term 'sexual'. Here Fairbairn's familiarity with the current theorizing of the British psychologists McDougall and Drever on instincts leads him to suggest that sexual satisfaction is only one form of the general class of appetitive or bodily satisfactions described by them. A better term for the general class would have been 'sensous', which would have allowed a specific quality to the early satisfactions, for example from sucking, while not precluding a readiness amongst the different sensuous feelings to merge as when becoming 'sexualized'.

It was then, as now, the custom in Britain for those aspiring to professional advancement to proceed after the first medical degree to obtain the postgraduate Doctorate of Medicine. For this examination a thesis had to be submitted, and Fairbairn chose as his subject to contrast the views of Janet and Freud. The title for his dissertation was 'The relationship of dissociation and repression, considered from the point of view of medical psychology', a substantial 30000-word essay.

Summarizing, he states that his object was to consider the relationship between the two conceptions because of the prominent part they have played in modern psychopathology. At the outset he comments upon the unnatural divorce between medical science and psychology, and he is clearly imbued with a strong wish to undo this division for the benefit of both. From a historical perspective, he proceeds to the views of McDougall and Rivers, the early British medical psychologists, which he finds inadequate. The main discussion centres on Janet and Freud, with a careful, meticulous appraisal of their contributions. His well-argued conclusion is that dissociation is 'an active mental process, whereby unacceptable mental content or an unacceptable mental function becomes cut off from personal consciousness, without thereby ceasing to be mental – such mental content or mental function being regarded as unacceptable if it is either irrelevant to, incompatible with, or unpleasant in relation to an active interest'. Having rejected the tendency to use the terms as interchangeable, he takes repression as a special form of dissociation of the unpleasant, without those repressed mental elements ceasing to be mental. Repression is possible only at the highest level, the 'rational' or 'conceptual' level, of mental development. What is dissociated is part of the mental structure which is felt to be unpleasant because of its relation to the organized self. It is only here that we can properly speak of 'conflict', the term used to describe the state which provides the essential condition of repression. Thus the source of what is repressed is of *internal* origin whereas in dissociation of the unpleasant, the dissociated material is of *external* origin, i.e. determined by events. The internal origin of the repressed has it roots in the instinctive tendencies whose satisfaction would be pleasurable in themselves but intolerable to the organized self, i.e., tendencies not organized into the hierarchy of sentiments and ideals which form the self. Repression, as Freud described, is thus a defence (MD thesis, p. 88).

It is noteworthy that, in contrast with the British medical psychologists who used Jung's term of 'complex' for minor unconscious organizations of instinctive tendencies out of relation to the main personality as equivalent to 'sentiment', Fairbairn prefers to regard the organizations that are repressed as more extensive and so more akin to a 'secondary personality' as investigated by Morton Prince and others. As other writers had done, he refers to two characteristic features of the repressed, namely, its relative permanence and the high degree of activity involved. These features can be readily understood from their origins in the instinctive tendencies. Here, as he is ending his thesis, he makes a statement of great interest as foreshadowing the later developments of thinking.

> Freud picturesquely describes the source from which these (instinctive) tendencies spring as the 'Id' (*The Ego and the Id*, 1923a, p. 28), but this term merely exemplifies the confusion which results, when attempts are made by medical writers to explain mental processes in independence of general psychology. The 'Id' is an unnecessary and redundant term for what are familiar to psychologists as the innate instinct dispositions. It is the permanence of the instinct dispositions which gives rise to the impression of the relative permanence of the effects of repression. (MD thesis, p. 73)

It is because these instinctive tendencies are, biologically speaking, the dynamic of all action, that, when any of them is repressed, repression must necessarily involve a degree of activity which is found in no other form of dissociation.

Fairbairn wrote at the start of his thesis that, in contrast with medical science, the subject-matter of psychology is the behaviour of the organism; and its aim is to interpret behaviour in terms of inner experience. 'The "mental processes" of which the psychologist speaks are the laws of behaviour interpreted in such terms, and the study of these processes constitutes the science of Psychology.' Fairbairn's philosophical training had certainly given him a clear conception about levels of discourse and he was firmly decided about keeping the psychological free from resorting uncritically to the physical.

He was awarded his MD degree in 1929. (In his brief autobiographical note (*Brit. J. Med. Psychol.*, 1963) he gives 1927 in error). His thesis was graded 'highly commended' which, though not winning him a gold medal, nevertheless indicated an appreciation of its quality, especially when it was not centred on the usual objective data with appropriate statistics that characterized research studies.

His output of work was now at a high level, with his general life situation going well. His first son was born in 1930, thus constituting for Fairbairn the larger family he himself had longed for in his own childhood. He also enjoyed the friendly attitudes of the professors of psychiatry and psychology along with the contacts he was maintaining with the psychoanalysts in London. He was invited to attend the International Congress of Psycho-Analysis in the autumn of 1929. Fairbairn valued the breadth of outlook to be had from keeping good relations with the allied disciplines of general psychology and anthropology. It was almost certainly in this mood that he contributed a brief theoretical paper in 1930 to the *British Journal of Medical Psychology* (Vol. 9). Ernest Jones had suggested in an article entitled 'The psychopathology of anxiety', that 'morbid anxiety is a perverted manifestation of the fear instinct, which, in the case of neurotic conflicts, has been stimulated to activity as a protection against the threatening libido'.

Fairbairn criticized this view on the grounds advocated by the general psychologists McDougall and Drever, namely, that fear was the emotion characteristic of the instinctive response to danger which could be that of fight or flight. He was again showing in a carefully considered manner that, while identifying himself with the psychoanalysts, he was ready to chide them for confusions which might have been avoided had they not ignored some of the recent thinking amongst the psychologists. It must have been very encouraging to the relatively unknown outsider to have had, as a reaction to these papers from the formidable Jones and the London group (of which Melanie Klein was now a prominent member), an official invitation to present a clinical paper to the British Psycho-Analytical Society. This occasion, probably initiated by Glover, was expressly to give the members an opportunity to appraise his analytic competence. He chose an unusually complicated patient of whose treatment he gave an impressive account, which, as with his first clinical paper, was not published until it was included in his book twenty years later.

THE SECOND CLINICAL PAPER

The title of this second clinical paper, 'Features in the analysis of a patient with a physical genital abnormality', indicates the nature and origin of the patient's difficulties. The patient, a single, middle-aged woman, was referred by her family doctor, who described an examination he had carried out when she was twenty because of the absence of any menstruation up to this time. He found no genital organs with only a pin-head opening as a vagina, which led nowhere. Fairbairn accepted this opinion at first and decided to take her on for analysis for her neurotic symptoms that consisted of recurrent breakdowns. After treatment had gone on for some time, he doubted the accuracy of the doctor's opinion and a gynaecologist concluded from a fresh examination that she was essentially male with male gonads accompanied by secondary female sex characteristics. When a still later laboratory examination by a geniticist established the excretion of gonadotropic hormones as within the normal female range, the patient was left with her conviction of gender identity as a woman.

A schoolteacher, she pursued her work with excessive zeal until general tension and anxiety developed to the point at which she had to give up in a depressed and despairing state. Her stress arose from a relentless striving to obtain perfect control over the children by keeping them absorbed in work, a goal which inevitably proved unrealizable in spite of her energetic efforts. When she stopped work, a remarkable change to mild elation would immediately occur, to be followed by depression soon after she had driven herself back to work, and this cycle was frequently repeated. As the depressive states approached, she felt a sense of struggling against a nameless overwhelming force with mounting anxiety almost to the point of suicide. In a crisis with floods of tears she would feel humiliated and crushed and would allow no one into her room except her mother, to whom she surrendered unconditionally. The salient oedipal situation involved a mother who readily induced the establishment of a 'titanic super-ego', a rather insignificant father and an exciting and indulgent grandfather. Memories of the latter brought back what she described as her 'infantile self', followed by the recall of early sexual sensations. There was then a release of pent-up libido, which led her into many casual flirtations with men in the train on her way to analysis. This infantile self progressed to an omnipotent one with delusions of grandeur, in a manic phase which receded after a few months of analytic work, to be succeeded by a dominance of anal material which then moved to intense oral-sadistic impulses towards father's penis. The absence of a normal vagina, however, seemed to reinforce, rather than compete with, her intense penis envy. She gradually came to see the connection between her depressive attacks and the unconscious guilt over her sadistic destruction of the grandfather's penis. With the schoolchildren representing her sadistic self, she sought to pacify her super-ego by attaining a complete subjugation of them. This omnipotence, Fairbairn suggested, was typical of obsessional and paranoid states because of its aim to control the repressed sadistic phantasies, in contrast with the omnipotent gratification of libidinal longings seen in mania and schizophrenia. He was thus separating from the latter what Melanie Klein later termed the use of projective identification to permit control over the bad self and its objects.

After the oral-sadistic wishes had been recognized, the patient's interest in men changed to experiencing acute self-consciousness in their presence. Fairbairn notes the resistance to the repressed wishes as infinitely less than to the realization of the guilt which drove her to exploit paranoid techniques with ideas of reference. Here we can see the embryo of his later theory of repression as directed primarily to the object rather than to the impulse considered apart from it. Two aspects of this patient's personality particularly impressed Fairbairn. First there were the unusually labile movements amongst the full range of the various defensive positions which led her to exhibit manic and depressive as well as paranoid and obsessional states. Defences had thus to be seen as a repertoire of manoeuvres to cope with the intolerable unconscious guilt over the destruction of her objects. They were, moreover, linked with the second impressive aspect, namely, the personification of various aspects of her psyche, that is, a distinct structuring into virtually separate selves. The two most persistent were: (a) 'the mischievous boy' who represented a childhood self, playing endlessly, and who, by possessing a penis, could secure limitless enjoyment; and (b) 'the critic', at times a male in authority, but much more characteristically an aggressive woman, often undisguisedly her mother.

In dreams, the 'I' could be herself as 'the critic', or as the 'mischievous boy', though more usually the dreamer was herself as an independent onlooker sometimes on the side of one or the other personification. These personifications appeared to confirm Freud's tripartite structures, but there were others as well, so that he notes the accepted trio does not necessarily encompass the total personality. Thus there eventually emerged a charming 'little girl', always about five years old, who had none of the 'mischievous boy' attributes. This figure was interpreted by the patient as how she would like to have been in childhood, completely acceptable to her super-ego.

Another personification that appeared late in the analysis was 'the martyr'. In this figure the patient dealt omnipotently with her guilt by the grandiose phantasy that the punishment for her defiance would benefit humanity. These relatively subordinate figures of the 'little girl' and 'the martyr' nevertheless carried the same quality of personification, that is, they took over her self at times.

While the multiplicity of these personifications made Fairbairn question whether Freud's tripartite formulation did justice to the complexities of the structuring within the psyche, this is not merely an issue of numbers. He is drawing attention to the fact that Freud's structural theory is not based primarily on purely psychological considerations but partly on bridging the body and the mind. This frame of reference, in Fairbairn's view, leads all too readily to an insidious attachment to Freud's divisions as the component entities of the mind, perhaps because the id, with its close links with the body, plays into the general tendency to treat the physical as of a different order of reality, a more 'real' one, than the mental. From the purely psychological angle, Fairbairn's patient gives ample confirmation of functioning structural units corresponding to the ego, the id and the super-ego. His point, however, is to emphasize that these structural units, which operate as persons or actors, are neither mental entities, nor are they inherently restricted to three, as his data show. Furthermore, their boundaries do not conform to those of Freud's divisions. He also comments on the fact that these personifications are not, as Freud suggested in relation to the origins of multiple personality, confined to the products of various identifications of the ego. 'The critic' can be regarded in that way, though the others are best seen 'as functioning structural units which, for economic reasons, attained a certain independence within the total personality', that is, they could operate as though separate selves. In this patient, the personifications were largely unconscious until analysis exposed them, although they could invade the conscious field at times to produce a multiple personality.

With this view of the differentiation of sub-personalities which could be in conflict with each other, Fairbairn then concluded that the same processes producing them could lead to the differentiation of the ego, id and super-ego. He also noted that while this differentiation is maximal in severely disturbed individuals, analytic experience suggests a wide range in the degree of differentiation and, thus, that a degree of such differentiation is a feature of the normal personality.

The chief significance of this patient for Fairbairn was that in spite of the prominence of the genital abnormality, the symptoms could be understood in psychoanalytic terms. The fact that some of her sisters also had the same physical deformity without having become neurotic proved it was not the cause of the psychological disorder. The development of her sexuality was naturally affected by the abnormality, but for him the specific features she presented raised quite fundamental questions about the conceptualization of the structuring of her personality from her early experience. Unconsciously the clitoris was equated with a penis, and her envy of the penis was much more prominent than of the vagina of which she was deprived.

The latter symptom led Fairbairn to ask whether penis envy might be a consequence of the repression of female sexuality rather than the converse. Were that to be so, then penis envy would have relatively little to do with anatomy and much more with the psychological origins of the repression of female sexuality. It is here that the essence of his future standpoint emerges, because he saw such repression originating from the interpersonal conflicts of infancy and childhood aroused by parental attitudes. The sub-personalities established from these struggles varied in their mode of operation. One could 'take over' for a period of days or weeks, as in mania, with an almost exclusive dominance – though more transient phases were usual. The patient, in fact, said she felt a different person when that self was in control. The super-ego appeared to operate for the most part in a more complex way, though it could predominate at times like the others. The 'layering' of the structures within the totality of the personality from successive developmental stages is a striking feature of the super-ego; and its establishment during the earliest phases of development is clear in this case.

Compared with his first clinical paper, the analytic work described in this one is of a notably 'deeper' level. While the patient brings out her classical oedipal situation in the first phase of the analysis, she is soon immersed in the earliest levels of development, particularly in intensely sadistic phantasies. Fairbairn notes, however, that, though the resistance to the emergence of these impulses into conciousness is strong, it is not nearly so strong as that against the unconscious guilt over the destruction they have caused to their objects in her inner world. Her desperate defensive struggle against depression highlights the position of analytic theory in relation to manic-depressive states at this period. As compared with the first patient, even allowing for the differences in the clinical material brought by each, there is a much greater emphasis on the sadistic phantasies, directed to the 'bad' figures of the inner world. Here we can see the influence of Melanie Klein's early views, with which he had become familiar since writing his first paper. In these, a phase of maximal oral sadism in the second half of the first year was one of her central themes.

The emergent struggle between two theoretical approaches is now much nearer the surface. Klein's oral sadism derives from Freud's energic concepts, with the biological force of the death instinct as its source. At occasional points Fairbairn seems to be thinking in these terms (with their neurophysiological roots). For instance, he refers to the 'release of the patient's libido'; and ascribes her freedom from anxiety during a prolonged physical illness to 'a narcissistic investment of libido'. He treats her oral sadism as though it were, like the libido, a biological entity which fluctuated in amount. The way in which he refers throughout much more often to the part object, the penis, as the target of this sadism and only occasionally to the whole person with whom it was associated, may also be thought to be in keeping with the concept of an impersonal destructive energy. Melanie Klein's great step forward lay in her understanding of depression as the consequence of the cognitive development of the child, whereby the mother began to be perceived as a whole person. The critical integrative role for the future development of the person was the successful working through of the guilt and anxiety engendered by this development – but this theoretical advance was a few years away. Despite this trend to orthodoxy, what is impressive is his description of conflicts in the patient as amongst the different relationships sought by these highly personalized structures.

These divisions within the person are such that the properties of three of them match closely the tripartite structuring of Freud. Fairbairn, as mentioned already, stresses that there are more than three divisions and, when they are conceived as originating in incompatible relationships, there is no inherent reason why only three should emerge. Indeed, he describes two other structures that carried different parts of the patient's self, though these were not so conspicuous as the others. Here he is again, as in his MD thesis, airing the possibility that the id is an inadequate concept, one derived from the speculative neurophysiological assumptions of Freud, rather than from the phenomena of the neuroses at the psychological level. He considers that to see the primitive self of his patient as evolving structures corresponding to the mischievous boy or the ideal little girl, constituted as separate dynamic subsystems, fits better such clinical data as the fluid boundaries of the personalized structures in the psyche. More important for him is the fact that her behaviour is almost invariably a compound from the activity of all the structures in Freud's scheme. Freud's id must be conceived, not as separate impulses impinging on the ego, but as the first organizations that embody out of early experience the most primitively impelled parts of the person and which operate like sub-selves. The savagery of the earliest super-ego includes as much id as any other structure.

Expressions of the classical oedipal situation and the libidinal stages are dealt with (this paper was, after all, his first presentation to the British Psycho-Analytical Society), yet there is here an independent mind moving forward in a careful academic fashion, that is, respecting the theory being challenged and describing clearly and convincingly the data on which he rests his questions about the established concepts. The paper as a whole has the imprint of high-quality analytic understanding and competence. The discussants included Jones, Glover, Sylvia Payne, James Strachey, Joan Riviere, Melanie Klein, J.C. Flugel and Marjorie Brierley. The most satisfying expression of the appreciation of the senior analysts in London was their recommendation, shortly after Fairbairn presented this paper, that he be elected to Associate Membership of the British Psycho-Analytical Society – a notable tribute to someone who had not undergone the usual training programmes.

Apart from its impressive technical quality, there is, as with his first paper, a marked sense of his responses to the patient's difficulties coming from unconscious resonances as well as from the symptoms of a most unusual case. Both patients had sexual conflicts in a major role. The father was either absent or lacking in impact, and both patients felt their mother to be unduly intrusive and controlling. The family situation produced in each a strikingly dramatized set of figures in the inner world. For Fairbairn, in both cases it was the urgent striving from early childhood to find qualities of personal relationships that would make up for what each patient felt deprived of within the family, that gripped his attention, rather than the compulsive need for sexual gratification.

The 'instinctive interest' in the father's penis is closely merged for Fairbairn with the longing for him at a personal level. Even in the first patient's eventual obsessive preoccupation with masturbation, it was the creation of the personalized relationships between herself and the deities in her inner world to meet her desperate needs for actual relationships that formed the original content of her neurosis. The intense conflicts amongst these incompatible relationships of several selves, like a multiple personality, reflected closely the family figures as she felt them in her childhood.

This paper constituted a landmark in Fairbairn's development. It fore-shadowed his future line of thought about how the personality was structured. As Otto Kernberg was to write many years later (Kernberg, 1980), it 'demonstrates the subtlety of Fairbairn's clinical understanding, his highly sophisticated treatment of an enormously difficult and complicated case'. Its immediate importance, however, was that it established formally his associate membership of, and his status within, the British Psycho-Analytical Society. He was now entitled to attend its meetings, which he managed to do a few times each year throughout the 1930s, contacts that were of critical importance for him. One result of these contacts was that he could learn about Melanie Klein's work and the reactions to it at first hand, an opportunity which must have helped him to make his own appraisals after allowing for the many pronounced personal reactions it aroused.

3   External stresses

I N 1932 the all-round supportive environment Fairbairn had enjoyed for the five years since his marriage and his embarking on his psychoanalytic career began to deteriorate.

The first major change, in sad contrast with his recognition in London, was in the academic and professional scene in Edinburgh. When he had completed his formal psychiatric training in 1926, he accepted a University appointment in the Psychology Department, whose head was James Drever. This post was sponsored jointly with the University teacher in Psychiatry, G. M. Robertson, the Superintendent of the Edinburgh Royal Mental Hospital. Amongst British psychiatrists Robertson was unusually sympathetic to the new 'medical psychology'. He had neighbouring his own hospital, for the later stages of the First World War, the unit already referred to in which W. H. R. Rivers and William McDougall, the well-known English psychologists, were treating officers suffering from shell-shock. (Two of their patients were the poets Siegfried Sassoon and Wilfred Owen.)

Fairbairn's post was to include in its duties the teaching of 'medical psychology' to students taking courses in general psychology and to the medical students. There were also the few psychiatrists studying for the postgraduate Diploma in Psychiatry. Drever's psychological views were not as arid as much academic psychology later became. He had been trained in the philosophical tradition which encompassed theories of the total personality dealt with in a personalistic way. Important psychological figures for him were William James, G. F. Stout and the more recent McDougall, who brought to the fore social behaviour and instinct theory. Drever had made a notable contribution in his book *Instinct in Man* (1917) in which he put forward his theory of the bipolarity of emotion. In this view, each instinct did not have only one specific emotion associated with it, as McDougall had suggested. Instead, Drever maintained that, according as the instinctive aims were furthered or thwarted the corresponding affect was quite different. This bipolar theory impressed Fairbairn by its importance to psychodynamic understanding in that it did not make an entity of emotion, as had happened in psychoanalytic theory. (It was this theory that Fairbairn had adopted when he criticized Ernest Jones's 'instinct of fear'.) Here emotion was a specific affective colouring which accompanied instinctual activity. There was no doubt about its regulative function, but it was not an independent primary motive force comparable with that of the instincts.

Through his early contacts with the leading analysts in London, Fairbairn had drawn their attention to the importance for analytic theory of the writings of McDougall and Drever, and thereby shown the value of collaboration between psychoanalysis and general psychology. Drever was never able to reciprocate this open-minded attitude, even though Fairbairn had from the start of his appointment gone a long way to co-operate in the work Drever instigated. Thus, Fairbairn's time was largely used either in teaching students to carry out psychophysical experiments or in participating in some of Drever's investigations, for example on the intellectual capacities of deaf and dumb children or young delinquents. Fairbairn was the kind of person who found interest in a wide range of psychological investigation, and in 1929 he read a paper on the 'Comparison of the vocabularies of deaf and hearing children' to the annual meeting of the Scottish Teachers of the Deaf and Dumb. Nevertheless, to be as patient as he was with his involvement in Drever's projects was perhaps, as he described in his later personal notes, a reflection of the passive role he was too prone to take up.

Fairbairn, however, was not entirely accepting of this overall position, for he got Robertson to give him more teaching of the psychiatrists doing the Diploma in Psychiatry. This satisfaction was short-lived, for when Robertson retired in the summer of 1932, he was succeeded by D. K. Henderson, the co-author with R. D. Gillespie of the standard textbook of psychiatry in Britain for many years, and a very different type of person from Drever or Robertson. An autocrat in the preservation of his psychiatric hegemony, he quickly made it plain that Fairbairn was *persona non grata* within his professional empire. Though an enthusiastic disciple of Adolf Meyer, who emphasized the current psychological stresses in the causation of the patient's illness, he clearly felt psychoanalysis as an intolerable threat.

An entirely different and unexpected stress appeared at about the same time as the academic troubles. This was the much more painful one of growing tension in his marriage. His wife began to resent his work, because it isolated him during the day and absorbed him for much of the evening when he was writing. She had been used to a social life in which the male members of the family had created the main interests. She now appeared to be increasingly frustrated by the lack of this provision. Although she was a cultured woman and gifted musically, and was freed from most domestic constraints by having servants as well as a nanny for the children, she must have lodged a considerable degree of dependence on her husband, for she never established a significant life of her own. She wanted her husband to spend much more time with her socializing, or, at least, to be in one of the branches of medicine that she could more readily identify with and which would tend to take their practitioners into a more active social life. Her frustration showed in outbursts of aggression against Fairbairn.

The effects of these stresses were almost completely hidden from the outside world. Good manners with well-controlled expressions of feelings had been an essential aim of his whole upbringing. There was in his personality the much more powerful dynamic of his ideals and the dedication to his scientific aims to keep him steadfastly on course. Fairbairn was also deeply attached to his wife and children, as well as being profoundly tied to his moral principles, with an enormous respect for the preservation of the loyalties and obligations they entailed. Marriage was a sacramental bond for one who had continued to be a practising member of the Anglican Church. The situation was accepted by him as best he could, and he tried to meet some of his wife's needs.

Countering the negative changes in the academic scene, there was his dedication to psychoanalysis. He had from the start of his practice studied Freud's writings assiduously. This knowledge had not constituted a set of fixed principles or rules by which his practice could be controlled, but had been assimilated into a stimulating force with which he appraised the phenomena presented by his patients in a perpetually creative interplay. If the accepted theory did not satisfy him, he would go back to Freud to consider again the nature of his dissatisfaction. If he then considered he had to amend the classical theory, this was done with the greatest caution and respect. Freud's whole psychoanalytic approach and the knowledge it had brought had a very great significance for him. In a core part of his self he lived psychoanalysis. Along with his practice and his theoretical studies, he responded readily to societies and groups which showed an interest in learning about it. He also corresponded with a wide range of writers on psychoanalytic topics.

Without any trace of fanaticism, psychoanalysis had deeply imbued him with an almost missionary zeal to share the 'good news' of its contribution to mankind's understanding of his own nature. Moreover, his basic trust in people had led him to believe that, when assimilated in depth, this knowledge would enable others eventually to fashion their own ways of using it constructively. It was very much against the grain for him to tell others what they should do. He had no illusions about the resistances aroused within individuals and groups towards psychosocial change. Any effects of psychoanalytic knowledge on society in general would be part of a long-term process.

The sustained impetus of his conviction about the importance of psycho-analysis clearly came from an essential dynamic core of his self, as was seen in his constant creativity. Moreover, he bracketed with psychoanalysis a wider attention to the broader scene of the human sciences. He was a regular attender at the meetings of the Scottish branch of the British Psychological Society. The psychology of primitive cultures was another interest that was expressed in the maintenance of active contacts with the Royal Anthropologi-cal Institute, of which he was a Fellow. Amongst his interests, art occupied a special place. He visited art galleries whenever he could and saw most of the major exhibitions in London during the 1930s. This had been an interest of his father's which he acquired from early years, and it was reinforced by his having a few artists in analysis. He also enjoyed discussions with Herbert Read, the Professor of Fine Art in Edinburgh University, whose writings impressed him. He kept a notebook with pages headed with topics on which he could jot down ideas that occurred to him. These covered a wide range of individual and social psychological issues, many of which were later developed into papers in his own creative way. A few months after Henderson arrived in Edinburgh, Fairbairn gave a talk to two of the University societies, and before the end of the year he addressed the Odonto-Chirurgical Society of Scotland on 'Psychological aspects of dentistry'. In this address there was his usual lucid concise account of psychoanalytic principles; then, as a help to the understanding of their patients' reactions, he illustrated some of the anxieties from unconscious sources that are particularly liable to be aroused by dentists. He avoids any attempt to give practical hints and, instead, hopes to allay some of the dentists' concerns by enlarging their understanding of the origins of anxiety.

The person that the outsider met at this period when I first got to know him remained remarkably unchanged for the next few decades, that is, until he was well into his sixties. He was a tall, lightly built man, bald but with his reddish fair hair showing at the temples and in his trim moustache. There was a natural aristocratic ease in his bearing and speech, yet with no trace of condescension. Though not a sports enthusiast, his movements were lively and vigorous. In his dress he was conservative, invariably wearing a brown suit with the waistcoat cut in the double-breasted style favoured in the Edwardian period. On informal occasions there were casual tweeds. Until into his late fifties he was a heavy cigarette smoker, and he enjoyed wine. His consulting room was furnished with a fastidious conservatism, yet it was clearly his study and used as his own work place. A few unobtrusive photographs of his family and parents gave a personalized feeling to it. The other rooms of his home had beautiful Georgian furniture, traditional paintings, including a few old masters, and *objets d'art* inherited from his father. Modern art interested him for its psychological origins, but for aesthetic pleasure he kept to the traditional.

His manner, while retaining the reserve in his personality and some of the formality of his social background, was essentially welcoming and friendly, courteous and kindly. (Dr W. H. Gillespie told me recently that when he was doing early psychiatric training in Edinburgh, Fairbairn was a junior assistant. The trainees thought he kept aloof, because he did not want to be 'one of the boys'. They never realized he was then married and had a young family.) With his family he was an attentive husband and a devoted father. When in congenial company he was a ready and good conversationalist with wide interests. He followed the current social and political scene with the attitudes of the cultured conservative gentleman, tolerant of the views of others without concealing his disbelief in modes of change that were not of a cautiously considered evolutionary nature. One matter he never raised was his continuing religious convictions. Though forsaking the career of a clergyman, he had remained a regular churchgoer, especially to its main festivals.

From all his colleagues and others who were in contact with him I have never heard anyone say other than that Fairbairn was 'a gentleman'. In later years, when he was being attacked destructively as a representative of psychoanalysis, I felt this benevolent exterior was perhaps an over-powerful reaction formation and one which could well have been abandoned at times to release some of the justifiable anger that must have been there. That, however, was not possible against the layered inhibitions from ingrained politeness, the good Christian and, at deeper levels, the little boy terrified of retaliatory parental disapproval. There was clearly a great deal of his self that was kept behind the visible person. Nevertheless, what was apparent in his warm responsive concern with others was an authentic part that did not vary.

With no outward change in the relationship with his wife, the family situation was maintained sufficiently well in the next few years to allow Fairbairn to continue his work along with his constant involvement with his family. In 1933, he and his wife went on a holiday cruise to Norway, and on Christmas Eve their third child, a second son, was born. Some weeks before that event, he gave an address to the National Council of Women on 'Medical and psychological aspects of the problem of child assault'. The scope of his points here draws widely on general psychological, social and legal aspects with psychoanalytical references limited to Freud's views on the sexual instinct. In view of the academic hostility, itself a symptom of the strength of the cultural hostility in Scotland, there is an unusually forthright criticism of an earlier report from a Government Committee in Scotland on 'Sexual offences against children' which had recommended as the treatment for victims that they should be encouraged to forget as completely as possible the traumatic experience. Such a pronouncement in an official report would have come from the academic psychiatric and psychological establishment, and there is a distinctly acid tone when he states in relation to the assumption that banishment of a highly emotional memory from consciousness is equivalent to its banishment from the mind: 'All recent advances in the understanding and treatment of neurotic disorders are based on the discovery (by Breuer and Freud, over forty years ago) that nervous symptoms can be relieved by bringing to consciousness highly emotional memories which have been completely "forgotten" – or banished from consciousness.'

Domestic tensions seemed less disturbing in the first half of 1934 when there was an increase in social visits and outings with friends. At the end of July he and his wife went to London where he attended the International Conference of the Anthropological Sciences and they saw several of their old friends as well as some of the analysts. When it ended they set off on a second holiday cruise, this time to the Northern European capitals. A young woman had now come to live in the household, primarily to be a secretary for Fairbairn, but also to be a general companion-help to his wife, particularly with the two older children, now aged seven and four. She was remarkably successful in this complex role, being much liked by the whole family. The situation strongly suggests a re-creation by Fairbairn of his early family life, with his nanny relieving the constraints of his mother.

With the lessening of his time at the University, Fairbairn was now almost whole-time in his consulting room/study in the house. The increased number of analysands, however, isolated him from 9 a.m. to 7.30 p.m. daily except for a brief break for lunch. He was also habitually at work in his study on most nights from about 9.30 till after midnight and he must have been busy in this way soon after he and his wife returned from their summer holiday, for he wrote a substantial paper at that period. As he mentions in a postscript to this paper added when it appeared in his book, he had been stimulated by a book dealing with the evolution of social groups in Africa, and there may very likely have been some reinforcement from his attendance at the anthropological conference.

THE SOCIOLOGICAL SIGNIFICANCE OF COMMUNISM

This essay, on 'The sociological significance of Communism considered in the light of psychoanalysis', was presented to the Scottish branch of the British Psychological Society early in December 1934. It is the kind of paper that has been habitually attacked on the grounds that psychoanalysts' attempts to 'explain' highly complex social phenomena are almost irrelevant because of their grossly over-simplified extrapolations from the psychology of the individual. Whatever else might be raised in criticism of this essay, Fairbairn's thinking about social psychological topics was neither naïve nor simplistic.

Recognizing that the social pressure to increase the cohesion of larger groupings must inevitably work to lessen the influence of the family as the primary formative setting in the development of social attitudes and attachments, Fairbairn is struck by the resilience in the capacity of the family to survive. Indeed, for him, any attempt to encroach too far into its role would compromise that system rather than eliminate the family. The survival of the family he relates to its biological functions, but he adds from his psychoanalytic experience a conviction about its necessity for the psychological development of the personality. If he loses his mother the child has to have a substitute figure in reality. When, however, the father and any substitute is missing, the personality creates one imaginatively, as though the individual cannot shape his own self without an inner imago to fill what he experiences as an intolerable void, a space in which a model of a father has to be inserted. Here he seems to imply that the family is the only means we have of creating the individuals who will be able to make effective members of the group. That the nuclear family, as it is in Western societies, can distort and inhibit the potential of its members by excessively constrictive attitudes has been proclaimed noisily in recent years, and Fairbairn's comments on its fundamental role are perhaps even more timely than they were originally. The malfunctioning of such a persistent institution has to be examined with a view to getting it right rather than to its abolition (without due appraisal).

Guntrip, amongst several others, queried the value of this paper being included in his book. The more I have considered it, however, the stronger becomes my conviction that this paper was not a diversion from his main engrossing purpose. Fairbairn at this period was wrestling with the contribution of the family in the establishment of the personality, especially through the quality of the relationships between the child and both parents. The political situation in Europe in the early 1930s was disturbing enough, and he was far from uninterested in what was happening, socially and politically. It was a matter of principle to him to participate in such political action as would be expected from the responsible citizen. In discussions when left-wing views were advanced, common enough in academic circles at this time, he invariably preserved an objectivity which derived from his personal make-up, reinforced by his historical perspective from which the vagaries and excesses of populist movements were all too familiar. For him, as for Freud, the processes covered by the term 'group psychology' did not reside in some intangible location in 'the group' but were what went on in the individual minds of the members. He might well have added here what he noted in a later paper on schizoid factors, about group ideological movements *originating* only in the minds of individuals. He commented then on the frequency with which schizoid personalities left their mark upon the page of history, as when Hitler's influence later led to the blotting out of so much of humanity; and it would be idle to deny that unconscious forces exerted a great influence in both the creation and the acceptance of these ideologies. His two clinical studies had shown the way in which distortions in the attitudes of the adult personality were a direct reflection of abnormal early experience of family relationships.

Thus, on his apparent neglect of the economic factor in this instance, he states that extensive knowledge of historical and religious movements, 'supplies us with good grounds for believing that it is only when economic factors become harnessed to motives of a different origin that they become socially and historically significant'. The criticisms rankled a little because of this lack of objectivity about what his actual aim was. He made it explicit he was not appraising Communism or Fascism as political systems but was considering the evolution of human groups and what happened psychologically to the individual, and especially the family, in these social changes. To reflect upon such evolutionary changes from a psychoanalytic point of view was to him an important task because of the implications for the individual. Taking the family as the original biological group, he used the concepts of the classical theory to account for the cohesion it requires. The disruptive aggressive forces inherent in the oedipal situation come under control by the making of taboos on incest and parricide along with the adoption of exogamy as groups get larger. This evolution, that brings about the ever larger groups such as the clan, tribe and nation, then needs the cohesive bonds that draw upon religious sanctions and other belief systems. Although the movements establishing larger groups have consciously accepted the institution of the family, his interest is in the unconscious conflict between it and the ties demanded by the group, and signs of this opposition were not far to seek in the current political systems of Communism and Fascism.

Towards the end of the year, the tensions with his wife were exacerbated again, possibly by the degree of his absorption in work on this paper, in addition to the long hours with his analysands. This engrossment would be difficult for many wives to accept, and more so when she had no parallel investment of her own. Psychoanalytic work, furthermore, is not easily shared. Added to this frustration was constant friction over money. Their life style needed a larger income than Fairbairn could provide, especially when several of his analysands paid only limited fees and he had little in the way of private means. The whole situation could not but build up intolerable tensions, with the result that his wife's aggressive outbursts about it recurred with greater intensity.

The strains at this time were further increased by the hostility from the University side. The threat to Drever from psychoanalytic concepts had been much intensified by the contribution of Fairbairn in the discussions of the cases seen in the Child Guidance Clinic that Drever conducted. His anxiety was now prompting him to pursue a campaign to discredit psychoanalysis in the academic world and in the eyes of the general public. That Drever's attitude was not personal to Fairbairn was brought home to me two years after Fairbairn left the University appointment. Stimulated by Melanie Klein's writings about young children, I read a paper to the Scottish Branch of the Psychological Society on the phantasies of a few children I had been treating in his Child Guidance Clinic. The next day I received a note from him to say I was not to teach psychoanalytic ideas to his students as long as I was on the staff of his Department. Henderson had shared this attitude quite independently, but for Fairbairn I felt he was essentially an irritant rather than emotionally disturbing. He did not possess the intellectual depth of Drever and so evoked less respect. Fairbairn rather despised him, especially when he learned that Henderson's antipathy to psychoanalysis led him to breach the usual professional etiquette, as when he expressed low opinions of it to the relatives of Fairbairn's patients.

Fortunately, Fairbairn's standing with the London analysts helped him to maintain his modest financial position by never being without a waiting-list. It was encouraging, too, that support for his work, as mentioned earlier, was now coming from those who carried authority in psychiatry in Glasgow. Drs Angus MacNiven and T. F. Rodger, who had responsibility for the psychiatric teaching in the University there, were free to express their interest in psychoanalytic thought – and indeed they enabled this to survive in Scottish psychiatry when it could well have been lost for the next few decades. By the mid-1930s, the Psychology Department in Glasgow University also became well disposed to Fairbairn's work. The chief there was R. H. Thouless, who was in no way hostile, although his own special interests were in general psychology. A new member to his staff was R. W. Pickford, who was training in analytical psychotherapeutic work in an eclectic tradition. There had also arrived in Glasgow a refugee from Germany who built up a private practice in Glasgow without any formal appointment in the University. He was Karl Abenheimer, a cultured man who had had training in the Jungian tradition in Europe and who commanded the respect and high personal regard of several members of the Glasgow academic world as well as of Fairbairn.

From all that was happening in his outer world, there was little or no indication of the profound upheaval that was taking place internally. Neither I nor his close friends suspected it, and I learned about it only after his death from the members of his family who had all been confronted with it. He had begun to be 'possessed' by an inhibition of urinating in the presence of others. This symptom eventually interfered with his freedom to travel and it troubled him for the rest of his life. To understand something of this development it will be helpful to go back to the influential forces in the formation of his personality.

When he adopted the Church as his vocation, he wanted to be the good Christian devoted to helping others, yet not to be the emasculated type he felt was too common amongst the clergy. His wartime experience had changed the mode of realizing this reparative psychological masculinity from that of being a clergyman to that of becoming a medical psychoanalyst, and his effectiveness in this role had been liberated by his personal analysis. For this choice to be realized, he owed a great deal to his mother, who advanced his career against the rather grudging attitudes of the Scottish Calvinism ingrained in his father, who was financially as well as morally constrictive. His choice of career could permit him to explore the mysteries of sex, sin, guilt and conscience against the barriers his parents had created around these topics. His mother had forbidden his interest in them in a terrifyingly aggressive way, as will be described later, yet neither parent was likely to recognize his way of overcoming their prohibitions. The success he had achieved professionally and in his Army experience had allowed both parents to accept his psychological masculinity, while his marriage had given to him a woman who could fully accept his physical sexuality. When his wife became destructive to his work she clearly threatened to castrate his psychological masculinity. There seemed to ensue a regression to a defensive identification with his father, who could assert himself against being controlled by his wife. Unfortunately, his father's masculinity, as mentioned earlier, was deeply and mysteriously linked to his phobia of urinating in the presence of others, and Fairbairn began to manifest this symptom during 1934. It then became entrenched early in 1935 after a traumatic experience. There had been an unusually aggressive outburst from his wife, which was followed later that night by his having an acute renal colic with haematuria. He passed a stone with intense pain and was then off work for a few weeks.

Clinical experience would at once suggest that the symptom had arisen from a sharp splitting off in his self of a deep sadistic rage against his internal bad mother. Formed out of early experience and subsequently overlain by good relationships, this primitive structuring was now activated by its resuscitation in the external world both from his wife's close fit with the past and the loss of the good figure of his father. Not associated with strong conscious affectionate bonds, his father had nevertheless been a caring figure to him, one who later took pleasure in his achievements. Fairbairn seemed to need the closer personal affirmation in a deeper way than the more distant professional approval that the London analysts gave at the conscious level. Drever had been supportive when Fairbairn joined his staff, and he was a friendly person who inspired affection as well as respect. I believe the switch to his hostility, even though directed more to psychoanalysis than to Fairbairn himself, was a depressing experience for Fairbairn, although his growing friendship with MacNiven, the senior psychiatrist in Glasgow, was a good replacement. Correspondingly, the friendly attitude of his resident secretary, despite the disparity in their ages, also supported him, especially as she maintained a good relationship with his wife and family.

In the building up of the symptom, another external factor cannot be left aside. This was the expanding effect upon him of Melanie Klein's work. His contacts with Glover and the London analysts kept him abreast of her impact, and her contributions had appeared in the *International Journal of Psycho-Analysis* and the *British Journal of Medical Psychology*, at least one per year, since 1926. More immediately, her book *The Psycho-Analysis of Children* had been published in the International Library of Psycho-Analysis in 1932. Klein's views of the inner worlds of children being populated by relationships with highly emotional figures derived from their experience made a great impression on Fairbairn. Indeed, he had clearly made use of them in the early clinical papers.

Whether or not Fairbairn had any foreknowledge of the content of her current thinking, his illness prevented him attending the meeting of the Psycho-Analytical Society to hear Melanie Klein read her paper, 'A contribution to the psychogenesis of manic-depressive states'. It is essential in following Fairbairn's development to appreciate the nature of the impact this paper had, not only on him but on analysts as a whole.

History was to show that that meeting was a momentous occasion for the future of psychoanalysis. The paper had a far wider implication than the contribution to the psychopathology of one disorder that its title indicated. It was a new and profound insight into the development of the personality. Though Klein disclaimed any divergence from Freud in the status of her concepts – for her they were developments of Freud's work – they were in fact radically different in their basic implications. Thus, while she made great use of Freud's death instinct as the biological energic source of the dominant part played by oral sadism in the infant, it can be argued that this concept of the origin and nature of violent aggression was quite inessential to her developmental scheme. What she introduced was a structuring within the self from the start by the infant's relationships between its unitary ego and the caring family figures. At first, the objects in these relationships were the 'part objects' of the instinctual urges such as the breast, the penis, and so on, with the differentiation of external from internal being embryonic in these early stages. A world of internal objects was fashioned from experience, with each of these structures embodying the intense quality of the primitive affects which had cohered in their formation. Frustration could be felt as a violent attack from an object, and, with repetition, the latter was made into a persecutor because it was merged with all the rage originally evoked by it.

With all these violent feelings it became a permanent inhabitant of the mind, with a constant readiness to be activated and so to arouse acute anxiety as a terrifying retaliator. Conversely, experiences with the good breast/mother established an imago that brought security and bliss. Since frustration is in some measure unavoidable, anxiety-laden conflicts between these internal structures were universally built into the psyche, which became as a result an arena for intensely dramatized phantasies. Klein described the inevitable defensive process that went on to escape from the anxieties, for example, a splitting off within the mind of the bad object from the safe feelings of the good object, with a subsequent denial of its existence or else a projection of it on to parts of the outer world which might then be avoided, at any rate, in phantasy. Naturally, the internal objects lacked the definition that would come with the developing perceptual and cognitive functions, but they mediated responses to the outer world. A frightening persecutory breast/mother carried the expectancy of attack which was gradually lessened with good mothering. As intellectual development proceeded, the inner world became the scene for endless imagined manipulations of the inner objects, from sadistic murder of bad objects, or phantasies of being murdered by retaliatory attacks, to the elaboration of idealized objects created to give unfailing comfort and reassurance.

Klein showed that the ego (used at this time as equivalent to 'self') and the segregated internal objects were in constant interaction with the real parents. Much of the inner world with its primitive relationships thus operated like a dynamic template exerting conscious and unconscious pressures towards disproving its fears when the real parents did not behave like the imagos projected on to them, or coercing the outer world to match the objects that were longed for. Thus, in the adult depressive, loss of an important real object could stir up the anxiety and guilt from the feeling that the deep phantasied attacks on the original frustrating figure had left it a dead, murdered body inside the self. In contrast with Freud's fundamental assumptions of impersonal energies setting the pattern of the development through the phases of their biological maturation, here was a structured inner world being formed from birth out of the experiences with the mother which shaped the future person and his functioning in all his interactions with the world.

From the start, in a world dominated by the basic split into 'good' and 'bad' objects, a crucial developmental stage occurred from about the middle of the first year. Advances in cognitive functions entailed the mother being perceived as a whole person, so that splitting could not be maintained so readily. She became actually the same figure who could be 'good' or 'bad'. This began what Klein called the 'depressive position', a developmental stage in which the primitive destructive impulses with their phantasies of the destroyed mother had to be superseded by her restitution through the growing capacity for love and reparation. The reaching of this goal, the normal outcome of the ordinary good mother–infant relationship, constituted what was tantamount to Erik Erikson's later notion of an epigenetic phase, that is, one in which new integrated modes of relating to the world developed within the organism as the maturation within the ordinary good environment evolved new and more comprehensively organized structures out of its experience (Erikson, 1959). The successful working through of the depressive position freed the person for an effective development of his potential resources through increasingly varied exploration of the outer world. Conversely, a failure in this process left him prone to various interferences with his general learning and a specific proneness to the future emergence of depressive states should his environment fail to support the defences built up against this recurrence. A particular feature of the working through the depressive position to which Klein attributed great importance was the consequence of the infant's maturation bringing the father alongside the mother in a very close relationship. The father began to be felt unconsciously as another person whose penis could be a substitute for the deficiencies of the breast/mother. The infant's deprivations also gave rise to intense envy of the parental couple phantasied as giving each other in an orgiastic intercourse all the primitive satisfactions denied to and envied by him. Destructive sadistic hate towards this parental couple then became another source of anxiety that had to be surmounted by the experiencing of both parents as meeting his needs as well as their own and so reinforcing his conviction about the reparative power of his love. Failure here carried the threat of losing any good object and consequently of the loss of sanity derived from the integration within the self that only a good object in the inner world could sustain.

However much these concepts might be rejected, everyone at the meeting knew that Klein had given in detail over the previous years incontrovertible evidence in support of them. She had shown that with the use of the classical analytic method, young children in their spontaneous play revealed all their primitive feelings of love and hate towards their parents and others in the family. Freud had disturbed the sleep of the world by confronting man with his unconscious mind and the powerful role of infantile sexuality. Klein had now brought to the psychoanalytic world an even more threatening upheaval. It had been hard enough to get a professional movement established that could assimilate and use the unpalatable truths of the universal infantile sexuality and Oedipus situation. Now it was as if these were the mildest of introductions to our inner worlds, for here was nightmarish violence of almost unbearable savagery against the parents from the very start and only replaced by love and reparation as the result of favourable experience in the family relationships, first with the mother and then with the father. Castration was a later and more specific, less catastrophic, source of anxiety, compared with the constant threat of disintegration of the developing self before the infant had built up enough security and trust in the mother and later the father. The nature of these earliest conflicts and the anxieties inherent in them could only be described as psychotic in character. They could be defended against by massive splitting between the inner objects and the relations with them, in a strenuous effort to deny the existence of the bad and dangerous situations or to project them on to objects felt as outside.

One difficulty for some analysts was to believe the young infant was capable of the mental activity assumed by Klein. Fairbairn did not have this problem. Since he assumed the self (or ego) to be a unity from birth, and instinctive behaviour to be the ego in certain modes of relationship, he could readily envisage the unconscious phantasies postulated by Klein. Also, though the infant did not have the experience that added a rich content to these phantasies, his acceptance of the British academic psychologists' view of emotion as a specific colouring of such processes provided a basis whereby the earliest interactions of the infant with his mother could have the means of organizing patterns of relationships that preserved a continuity with later experience. The infant's emotional experience, in short, was quite adequate as a basis for the development of a varied range of relationships. Each of these would start with a specific affect dominating the pattern of a structure which would then assimilate the later experiences in which much more mature cognitive processes would operate. Thus experience in the early months could well shape the personality.

It may readily be thought I have given a somewhat dramatic account of the impact this paper of Klein's had, especially as it is now familiar history. That it is close to reality was manifested in what happened afterwards. (For a fuller account of events related to this issue see Pearl King (1983).)

The British Psycho-Analytical Society held a special meeting in October 1935 at which a full discussion took place, opened by Ernest Jones. Subsequently, groups began to be formed according to whether or not members accepted Klein's work as valid, and hence to be taken as a serious contribution to psychoanalysis, or regarded it as a 'deviation' from Freud's work, and a wild, dangerous one at that. There was not only the disturbing content of the infantile hate, there was implicitly a challenge to the foundations of Freud's theoretical structure. 'Deviation', the word used by some analysts, was a strange one in a scientific context. It ordinarily is applied by the members of a religious or ideological group to those departing from its beliefs, and its emergence serves to indicate the depth of the feelings aroused. Splits were soon to develop between the British and the Viennese analysts, which were actively perpetuated by the latter when many of them became established in the USA years later. For several post-war years Klein's views were consequently treated like an 'un-American activity'.

Fifty years later, we can now see the issue settling into one to be decided by analysts from their own experience, as any new scientific development should be. My purpose in recounting this piece of history is to convey how disturbing this paper was to most analysts, and why. Those who could tolerate its unconscious reverberations in themselves, that is, accept in some measure the violence of the phantasies in the earliest stages of development and their influence and persistence in the subsequent shaping of the person, considered that the phenomena with which Klein was dealing were of the greatest importance. For them, however violent and psychotic in character they were, she also showed they could be worked through. The degree of anxiety and hostility aroused unfortunately created groups whose members became either uncompromising opponents or zealous adherents. There were in the British Psycho-Analytical Society several notable exceptions, such as Ernest Jones, John Rickman, Ella Sharpe, James Strachey and D. W. Winnicott, who made use of her insights in their own independent fashion. In this category was Fairbairn who, although deeply impressed by her views of the child's inner world, retained his objectivity in appraising them against his clinical findings and in their theoretical significance. I have already indicated that her early papers had a notable influence on him, as seen in the way his patient with the genital abnormality had alerted him to the prominent part played by oral-sadistic phantasies in her conflicts. When he returned to Scotland after this meeting he spoke with considerable appreciation about the importance of Melanie Klein's paper. Once it was published he obtained reprints which he gave to the few Scottish psychiatrists he thought would be interested. Later he said he was disappointed by the way so many analysts were not able to treat her views as ideas to be weighed carefully in the light of their own experience and, instead, reacted to them as though they were heresies against a religious belief.

Following this crucial encounter with Melanie Klein's formulation of the developmental significance of the depressive position, there were five years in which Fairbairn seemed to be struggling internally with its reverberations. In his account of the patient with the genital abnormality he had referred to the prominence of the manic-depressive process and his understanding of it. Unconscious guilt had been recognized by him as the chief source of resistance. Klein was now saying that, to the assimilation of the guilt, there had to be added the satisfaction of the innate disposition to make reparation by love. Manic denial could take place when the destructive self and its object were split off and projected outside, and when the super-ego with its evocation of guilt was also banished from awareness. For the reinstatement of an integrated self there had to be an immersion in the depressive guilt as a prelude to the object being loved, cherished and made whole again. Although perhaps not sufficiently stressed by her, this process had to be fostered by the mother's manifest expression of her loving acceptance of the child as a whole for a sustaining attachment to the good object to take place. In the situation with his wife, Fairbairn could not effect an integration, because of her unchanging attitudes. His work and thought were deeply suffused with his reparative drive, and it was this that she was rejecting. There seemed no alternative to a deep massive split in his self, and with this becoming organized, he was able to maintain a manageable situation for continuing his life with his wife for the sake of the family. Though he kept up his long working hours, there was more life together, with social occasions and weekends from time to time visiting friends and another holiday cruise, for the third year running. A few visits to London were included in their trips and he would fit in a meeting with Glover and Jones. The *modus vivendi* was not unlike his later basic endopsychic situation with his central self managing the business of living, his libidinal self with primitive sadism aroused in response to the attacks on it largely locked up in the phobia, and his anti-libidinal wife placated at a distance. However, the situation was more complex than can be described in these terms and will be considered more fully later.

A few months after the special discussion meeting, Fairbairn read a brief clinical paper on 'The effect of a king's death upon patients undergoing analysis' to the British Psycho-Analytical Society shortly after the death of George V early in 1936. Three of his patients had intense reactions with pronounced oral-sadistic phantasies showing a marked tendency to oral incorporation of parental figures. The first was a young man referred to him from a psychiatric hospital to which he had been admitted because of intense anxiety states. His symptoms were: (a) an inability to tolerate separation from his mother; (b) a hypochondriacal conviction that his heart was diseased; and (c) recurrent violent palpitations along with an overwhelming fear of death. He had been in analysis for about four months, during which it was made abundantly plain that his need to be with his mother arose from his constant fear that she had been destroyed by his oral sadism. In parallel, his other symptoms stemmed from the dread of his internalized mother devouring his heart. These symptoms had been considerably ameliorated before they were brought back by the frequent news bulletins indicating that the King's illness was a very serious one. The night after the King died, the patient had a dream which represented him killing his parents and a younger brother who had died some years previously. This dream was followed by another in which his mother warned him against eating a jelly near which she was standing. She thus indicated the destruction to have been an act of oral incorporation from which the internalized figures embodied the patient's own sadistic urges in their persecutory retaliation.

The second patient was a bachelor of thirty-one who had been over two and a half years in analysis. He had had a severe chest illness at the age of five which had left him a semi-invalid dominated by anxiety about his chest. This concern had been replaced by a compelling urge to urinate which was so distressing that he sought analysis. Analysis lessened this symptom only to reinstate the chest one, which was accompanied by a fear of poisoning. As the intense oral sadism underlying these symptoms came to the fore the concern about his chest was replaced by gastric symptoms. The King's death greatly depressed him with its reminders of his father's death. He became very afraid for his own safety as a feeling developed that there was an antagonistic and dangerous force within his body. These symptoms emerged from analysis as a war between an internalized father-figure and his own oral-sadistic ego, so that the King's death was for him like an enactment of his oral-sadistic attacks on his father, leading to the retaliatory destructive force within.

Soon after these reactions to the King's death he had a dream which represented a restitution of his father by his giving him a sumptuous meal. This was followed by a dream in which urinary sadism could be inferred to have replaced the oral sadism of the previous one, for in it the King was restored to life and health after having been destroyed by a flood, presumably symbolic of his incessant urge to urinate.

The woman with the genital abnormality was the third patient, now over forty and in her ninth year of analysis. She had been replacing paranoid defences against her marked oral sadism by depressive attacks precipitated in each case by an actual incident. The King's illness was the stimulus for one attack accompanied by several dreams. On the night before she heard of his death, she dreamt that her own father died, and then on the next night there was a series of dreams. In the first she was filled with terrifying affect that had no specific figures though it made her feel hopelessly mad. Next she dreamt she was turning cold from the feet up and would eventually be finished. This was followed by one of showing her mother a perfect little house she owned and in which she was living. This idealized scene changed to one of a ferocious dog trying to get at an animal in a box she had. Then police came to question her about a dreadful disaster, which had apparently happened to a man she did not know and whose father had died. Fairbairn takes this dream to show her protecting her real father, the animal in the box, against her oral sadism expressed by the ferocious dog. She had actually had a depressive attack a few days before the King's death after she had stifled an intensely angry reaction to her father, a pattern she had shown on several occasions when feeling resentment towards her analyst.

In all three cases, the focus is on the release of oral sadism following the death of the King. The sadism, however, is conceived almost entirely in Melanie Klein's way as an independent urge, an expression of the energy from the biological death instinct, whose strength is an innate given rather than a reaction to frustration. Allowing for the fact that the paper was written less than a month after the King's death as a short communication to the British Psycho-Analytical Society, and so precluding any fuller consideration of the data, there is a distinct impression that the impact of Melanie Klein's paper has largely taken precedence over his previous thinking about dynamic personifications as a required conception for describing the primitive structuring in the personality (instead of that provided by Freud's tripartite scheme). Perhaps, too, he wished to substantiate her view following the disbelief and hostility she had encountered. There is, however, some uncertainty in his adoption of the energic origins of the independent, biologically given, oral sadism. Thus early on in the paper the young man had projected 'a considerable charge of oral sadism' on to his internalized mother, whereas the war inside the second patient is 'between his own oral-sadistic ego and an internalized father-figure, whom he had endowed with oral-sadistic attributes'. The urinary symptoms of this man are of interest because of Fairbairn's own urinary symptom at this time and his comments in later years on the tendency amongst analysts to underrate the extent of urinary sadism (PSOP, p. 76).

In view of the interrelatedness of the internal objects and events in the outer world which is brought out in all the patients, it is noteworthy that the theoretical implications of this are left aside. Fairbairn comments that Melanie Klein had early on in her observations noted the closeness of these interrelations, though he too did not pursue the issue. Most striking perhaps is that this relatedness points to a dynamic connection between 'outer' and 'inner' that requires a concept of the openness of the inner systems to the social field to maintain their stability by bringing supporting objects within their boundaries. It would seem that the ongoing existence in the external world of the King as its symbolic father-figure was needed against the inner destruction of the father, a presence in a supportive dynamic field even though an unconscious one. It is here that the question arises about events in Fairbairn's outer world that could have contributed inhibiting factors at this time. The persecutory academic father-figures, although not now in his immediate environment, were nevertheless very much around: unconscious death wishes would thus not be far to seek. He himself, as shown in his diary, held the monarchy in great esteem for its symbolic function in stabilizing the structure of society and the family. In the Anglican Church there was also a close bracketing of God and the King. The death was a highly significant event to him as was the growing involvement at this time of the King's son with the American divorcee, Mrs Simpson. Apart from not belonging to the appropriate social class, she was widely felt by the nation to be an inappropriate person to support the dignity and the responsibilities of a king. Some of the feelings on this issue may have reinforced those about his wife's lack of sympathy with his work. His own reaction to the death of his father thirteen years previously had indicated a rather defensive belittling of his significance for him, for he always had a photograph of his father in his consulting room/study. Towards Mrs Simpson, Fairbairn was decidedly negative, and I recall his saying with some feeling that she was unlikely to become the wife of the heir to the throne as she was so clearly associated with the figure of a 'bad sexual woman' and hence to be avoided. History, however, showed this thought to be related more to his inner world than to that of the heir-apparent.

The acceptance of the virtual reification of oral sadism by Melanie Klein is particularly striking because of the way in which the inner world of his patient was responded to in the earlier paper. There the oral-sadistic attacks were given ample prominence, yet the inadequacy of these conceived as originating in drive energies was what had been aroused in his mind by the dramatic personifications in her inner world. It seemed that these theoretical questions had receded under the impact upon him of the vividness and concreteness of the violent destructiveness in the primitive relationships within the inner world. Theoretical considerations could not proceed until the phenomena had been assimilated more completely and with their unconscious implications reconciled.

The extent to which Fairbairn's early reactions to Klein's paper were apparently to identify with her adoption of Freud's life and death instincts is to be seen more directly in a short paper he wrote a few months after the previous one. Having addressed over the past years some of the national bodies concerned with mental health, he had his attention drawn to an article in the *Liverpool Quarterly*, a journal published by Liverpool's Council of Social Service. In this article, Lord Hurtwood, a prominent socialist writer, and a member of the executive of the League of Nations, had suggested that, amongst the factors predisposing nations to war, aggressive attitudes acquired in early childhood from family stresses might well play a part. In his response, Fairbairn, while recognizing the complex social factors underlying wars, agrees that the surest hope for peace rests in the long run on the quality of family relations. Aggression, however, is an innate instinctual urge and so a biological given that cannot be removed. Doing something effective to avert war is possible by facilitating the love instincts which minimize the factors that stimulate and foster aggression, especially by the assurance of a mother whose love satisfies her child's deepest emotional needs and which is not a masquerade for her own conflicts. There are some conflicting resonances in this statement, for while he supports the concept of an innate aggressive drive, he nevertheless stresses the quality of the actual relationships with the parents as of critical importance. The reference to the mother who masquerades as a good mother while really expressing her own conflicts arouses one's suspicion that a personal chord is being struck here. Two years later he again expressed this view about aggression and later admitted some pressures in his life prompting him not to differ from the orthodox analytic view. Thus though he is impressed at this time with the independence of the aggressive drive, his acceptance is not whole-hearted.

The papers that followed in the next few years can be seen as reflecting a series of unconscious reactions that preceded his creative synthesis from his assimilation of Freud, the impact of Klein's work, and the turbulence in his inner world from the stressful events in his inner and outer worlds. The outstanding feature is the tenacious thrust from his central self to make sense of the complex clinical phenomena he was encountering through sound explanatory principles. From adolescence his curiosity about the puzzling secret areas of human behaviour, the phenomena of conscience, guilt, sin and sex, was at the heart of his being. Knowledge by itself was not enough. To this drive was added all his urge to find, from a greater understanding, ways of relieving the human suffering associated with the inner torments to which these issues gave rise. It seemed, in Klein's new formulations, that this overall dynamic was his reparative drive to counter what he must have sensed in himself as the outcome of highly destructive phantasies. His history and his work pointed to the presence of a severe anti-sexual mother-figure and a father whose sexuality was confused by his having a strange urination phobia. His wife's hostility, like a release of this persecutory mother, had evoked in Fairbairn his father's symptom and, from psychoanalytic experience, this would be almost certainly derived from urinary-sadistic phantasies. His interest in Klein's emphasis on the intense sadistic phantasies of the infant had evoked a preoccupation about these, with a conflict about them coming from a 'bad innate impulse', like an original sin, and perhaps arousing unbearable guilt, or arising as a reaction to some of his mother's attitudes, in which case he was absolved. It seemed that the excessive badness of his internalized objects and his hate led to a splitting off of them from his central self. In it he was then safe to assert his autonomous self through the growing competence and confidence in the private world of his ideas.

He appeared to need a period for working through these conflicts with some indirect approaches to them in the first instance. He had long been interested in the psychology of art, and at this period he had a few artists in analysis, at least one of whom suffered from spells of marked depression. As a clinical paper was not feasible for professional reasons, he became for most of the next year immersed in a general consideration of the subject. Klein's paper on 'Infantile anxiety–situations reflected in a work of art and in the creative impulse' had been published in 1929. There she had described the function of the artist's production in undoing destruction of his inner parents; and she stressed again the making of reparation in her paper on the manic-depressive states. This theme now became the topic of Fairbairn's next two papers. As well as drawing the stimulation from his artist patients, he visited the Surrealist exhibition in 1936 in London in which Dali's paintings aroused considerable reverberations. He saw them almost as illustrations for Melanie Klein's writings, especially on the oral-sadistic destruction of the mother's breasts and body, along with attempts to make restitution.

Fairbairn may well have felt that the artist's inner task might help him with his own, and so he took it up in the first of the two papers, 'Prolegomena to a psychology of art', which he read to the Scottish Branch of the British Psychological Society in 1937.

TWO PAPERS ON ART

His opening stance is that artistic activity must be regarded as like play, something undertaken at the behest of the pleasure principle, that is, 'for fun' or for the joy of artistic creation, in contrast with work, a 'serious' activity determined by the reality principle. Artistic activity differs from most play activities in that its aim is to 'make something for fun'. Supporting this conception he adduces the puritan hostility to art because of the pleasure-seeking motive. As Freud had done, he then draws on the closely allied activity of dreaming (though here no motor activity is allowed). Using the analogy between art and dreams, he sees the art work as corresponding with the dream work in transforming the artist's repressed phantasies into the creative phantasy that can be embodied in the work of art. And in both cases, a failure in the transformation work leads to a functional failure. In the dream, sleep is not protected and in the work of art, without an appropriate amount of repression – which the Surrealists aim to minimize – then the common view is that the art produced is not of a high order. Taking the two great human urges of libido and destruction, and Melanie Klein's discoveries about the compensatory phantasies of restitution, it can then be suggested that artistic activity is pursued to relieve the inner tensions from intolerable anxiety and guilt over phantasied destructive attacks on loved objects. In Surrealist art, such as Dali's paintings, we see the artist portraying the development of his symbols as well as reconstituting the parts of the destroyed object into the unity of the composition. To be successful, art work must convert unacceptable phantasies into a form which in the first instance meets the inhibitions of the super-ego and, second, which pays a tribute to its ideals. Positive values are thus created by art in the act of restitution of the good parents by the ego, and though the role of the super-ego is characteristic of later stages in the cultural development of man, the creation of the work of art can still be regarded as 'making something for fun'. He finally comments on his choice of the 'solitary activity' of the artist for his starting-point as apparently dismissing the need for an audience. Artistic creation requires an audience, but this essentially consists of the inner objects (super-ego) which have to be made good again after the attacks upon them.

The feeling of incompleteness that this paper evokes was partly amended by the second paper, 'The ultimate basis of aesthetic experience'. It was written in the course of the following year, in which he had again visited some of the exhibitions in London, particularly those devoted to Surrealist objects, to Picasso and to Cézanne. This paper was read to the Psycho-Analytical Society in London early in 1938. The experience of the beholder is now considered in the light of the conclusions drawn in the first paper on the nature of the forces in the artist from which he creates his work.

A unique feature of some of Dali's paintings is, as mentioned, his depiction of the symbolizing process that created the work. This interest led to the Surrealist idea of the 'found object', that is, an object discovered in the external world having an immediate expressive appeal and so carrying a symbolic significance which bridged outer reality to the inner world of the dream. The 'found object' thus represented 'an immediate point between the attitude of the artist and that of the beholder'. As Fairbairn puts it, it is a work of art approximating quantitatively to a zero value on a scale for the amount of art work. The 'found object' has features enabling it to represent for the artist a fulfilment of his needs, and is hence created by the discovery itself as a creative act of the artist. For the Surrealist, however, his aim is to unite the world of reality with the unconscious in contrast with the more traditional artist whose unconscious destructive phantasies are denied and therefore disguised. Aesthetic experience is thus the experience of the beholder when he finds an object which symbolically satisfies his unconscious emotional needs. Within the world of art, 'found objects', have been specifically created by artists for the spectator who must therefore approach a picture, for example, with a perfectly open mind as the pre-condition for discovery. Works of art may fail in this role because of excessive censorship depriving them of symbolic significance or because of under-symbolization so that they repel the beholder. An optimal amount of symbolic significance is necessary to give a release for the emotions of destruction of the object together with an impression of its restored completeness and perfection. Beauty is thus determined by the beholder's particular needs regarding restitution.

Whilst confining his analysis to the motives of the artist in producing the work of art, Fairbairn recognizes art, like religion, as a universal need of the individual because it represents experiences of the destructive manifestations that endanger the existence of the good object being counteracted by the re-parative activities of creative love. Intended merely to outline the fundamental factors underlying the psychology of art and aesthetic experience, processes which he thought had been so profoundly illuminated by Melanie Klein's contribution, these papers nevertheless leave us dissatisfied. His general thesis of the artist making restitution of his inner, destroyed objects carries all the conviction and power of Klein's insights, and Fairbairn was one of the earliest analysts to write about their explanatory value in art and aesthetics. In later years he thought these papers contained an essential theme, yet he had a sense of something about them that was inadequate, and so he decided against including them in his book. For myself his categorizing a work of art as something made for fun has always struck a wrong note for the introduction of his theme. 'Fun' lacks all the serious resonances that we feel are needed by the application of the dedicated artist in creating his work. 'Fun' is taken by Fairbairn as describing activities undertaken for their own sake in contrast with 'serious' activities which lead to satisfactions not inherent in the activities themselves. This distinction he puts in psychoanalytic terms as resting on that between play, or activities motivated by the pleasure principle, and work, in which the reality principle is prominent. Even after he has described the relief of tension from the undoing of the destructive impulses by acts of restitution in the creation of the work of art, he seems to keep to the non-specific aspect of the tension as justifying his classification of the activity as 'making something for fun', whereas it must be the specific content that is releasing. By referring to the pleasure principle and its association with the relief of tension, his own involvement in the theme becomes attenuated – as if his thoughts at some level were being written in fun, a denial of the deeper agony, and often tragedy, inherent in making restitution for the destruction of something highly valued. Yet he specifies this aspect in his final paragraph. Can we make 'fun' understandable in this general way? Can we make it a primary end in itself like pleasure, without referring to what gives it the quality of its specific 'pleasure', that is, to the aims of the associated activities? We do make many things for fun and a common implication of the term is that the fun label for any activity or product is to indicate to those concerned that there is no intention to be destructive or to cause pain. The aggressive element in having fun with others, or at their expense, as in games, is usually obvious, and we ensure that such activities are not to become 'serious' by subordinating them through appropriate controls which are understood and accepted. Their aim, too, is often the acquisition of skills with the need for recognition of achievement.

The ignoring of an essential social reference to the transience of 'fun' was perhaps reinforced by his starting from Herbert Read's statement (1931) that art begins as a solitary activity, to which Fairbairn adds the qualification 'on the part of the artist'. All purposeful activity begins with the individual mind and what is intended here is presumably that, in addition to the unconscious motives, a considerable amount of reality thought has to be given to the situation before others become involved. By taking 'the others' to be solely the internal objects, an essential part of the artist's activity is left out. The notion of 'internal objects', as Klein used the term, was relatively new at this time, and the term covered structures within the mind one of whose functions was to be the objects of repressed instinctual drives. But the systems that contained them were closely connected with Klein's introjective–projective process so that external objects could take on some of their role. Thus, while the depressive position in its origin is primarily an internal process fuelled by the need to cope with guilt and anxieties, there is always the involvement of the outer world as it proceeds. The boundaries of the conflict spread to encompass relations with the external objects. It is here that the focus on the 'solitary activity' detracts from this essential external reference in the 'serious' element of good art. While there may often be pleasure in creating it, it is hard to imagine many artists feeling that their work is something made merely in fun. The product quite apart from its production has to prove the restitution. There is too much intense conflict, and not a little suffering, before their aim is accomplished for that categorization to do justice to what they experience. The destruction–restitution thesis without the manifest product of its transmutation into the shareable realities of the process within the individual mind leaves us too much in the familiar territory of the philosophers, poets, writers and religious thinkers, namely the antinomy of good and evil. Freud's life and death instincts with their generalized functions and speculative basis are also more metaphoric than explanatory when it comes to the need to penetrate the specific nature, origin and modes of operation of man's struggles with the two great antagonists. Without some precision and articulation in our formulations of both processes in action we cannot achieve the kind of advances in our understanding that we seek. The inextricable linkage between them in the very nature of life might impose the severest limits to what we could actively change in a radical way, but at least we might manage their effects better.

The Enlightenment of the eighteenth century had left man with the emptiness that followed the banishment of his relationship with God as the enlivening and cohesive essence of his soul or spirit. The nineteenth-century Romantic movement that followed had exposed the impasse man encountered when he turned inwards to explore his self. Subsequent attempts to advocate art as providing the supreme meaning to life were felt by the turn of the nineteenth century to be a rather feeble foundation for an ideology that could combat the frightening scale with which the modern technological surge was facilitating Eliot's 'walking death' of the individual and the destruction of the world. The Expressionists and the Surrealists were, nevertheless, motivated to confront man with what he had to face if he looked inside himself. The importance of the current state of the culture of the artist's society in regard to what he creates cannot be ignored. Artists have long been prominent as 'the first debunkers', with their 'Bohemianism . . . a refusal of the uneasy disguises of conventional living' as Adrian Stokes puts it (1955).

While Fairbairn allows their aims, we note his reluctance to accord to the modern artists a claim to 'great art', because of the naked way the unconscious forces are presented. Hitherto, men had acknowledged these forces only with generalizations that were so vague in regard to their nature and origin that they could be too readily ignored. The Expressionists and then the Surrealists were grasping intuitively, yet vividly and urgently, what man's destructive forces were doing to himself and his world. Far from being solitaries responding to reclusive inner worlds, these artists were in close sensitive contact with the culture of the outer world and imbued by powerful urges to provide some insight into what was happening as a challenge to which to respond. Their creations evoked the same frightening and repellent feelings in a wider public by the visual concreteness of inner realities as did Mrs Klein's precise verbalizations, distilled from her direct observations of children's inner worlds in their play, amongst the contemporary psychoanalysts, psychiatrists and psychologists. It was the same truths that were being proclaimed simultaneously, yet independently, by the artist and by the psychoanalytic research workers. It was equally unpalatable whatever its source, and just as the new works were 'not art', so too was her work dismissed as being not psychoanalysis, and certainly not science, that is, not acceptable knowledge for the cultural establishment.

The difference between the creative endeavour of the artist and the work of the scientist is that the latter wishes to get articulated knowledge and understanding into a form which can be applied through specific measures to 'improve' the environment. The Cartesian scientific philosophy, with its reductionism to depersonalized atomistic forces and objects, had created an unbridgeable gap between the artist and the scientist, with the loss of the common ground in their aims and activities. The artist shows that, however threatening the inner forces, they must be, and can be, faced and an integration achieved. This he does in the form given to the actual object he is driven to create. But if, as Braque says, art disturbs and science reassures, this requires sufficient exposure of the nature and origin of these inner forces by the artist to be followed by the analytic research of the scientist to secure measures of control.

Dali's paintings attracted Fairbairn because they depicted the violence of the infant's attacks on his mother's breasts and body along with a symbolic restitution. We have to ask, however, if Dali's reparations are sufficiently personalized to be felt by the viewer as undoing the guilt of having, in phantasy, destroyed his mother as a person. At Klein's primary level of part objects, that is, before the mother is fully *personalized*, a chest of drawers, even when full of things, may be felt as a restitution of her body; but, to put it into adult terms, gifts of things are but a part of love. It is the essence of the resolution of the depressive position that the new holistic feeling of being a person with the capacity for personal love has to be expressed in the giving and taking at this new level. The restitution for destruction at the personal level entails two tasks. First there has to be worked through a full experience of the concern and the despair about being able to restore and preserve the good mother, internally and externally. The second task is the reciprocal preservation of the emergent self. The self now carries the feeling of being identified not only with its good objects, but with life itself and so with responsibility for them. The threatened loss of them is equated with annihilation. Successful separation and individuation from the primal matrix has to achieve the confidence and security that the self needs to manage its growing powers and relationships with the real world. Mere restitution of damage is an inadequate statement of what becoming a person means. A whole new range of motives and purposes develops with the individuation of the autonomous self, and the new development has its own maturational impetus.

All great art has this enlivening and uplifting feeling of the spirit, as we commonly refer to it. It is presumably this feature that evokes the wish to preserve for all time the objects made from great art. The primitive characteristics of what Melanie Klein called the part object, or pre-personal, relations have to be adapted to the new importance of the 'persons' in the family. That is the essential resolution of the depressive position. The magic and omnipotence of the phantasies of the inner world in the new-found self have to be exchanged for the joys and satisfactions of outer reality and real people. When their external world provides the facilitating environment, that is, when the parents manifestly enjoy a child's giving responsiveness, the self is then structured for its development and enrichment within the world as maturation moves on. If this critical progress is blocked or distorted, from deprivations or traumata in the environmental input required, the self is left to find a mode of survival – as in an excessive introversion, a life centred in its own inner world with varying degrees of detachment or withdrawal from people. Severe threats from whatever cause to the integrity of the self arouse the terrors of disintegration and madness, or a degree of withdrawal and apathy that is equivalent to death because it cannot sustain the psychic metabolism necessary to life.

There can be little doubt that the artist is driven from within to master the anxiety arising from a degree of failure in resolving this basic developmental critical phase. Many poets and writers have expressed this view. For Adrian Stokes, who had a long analysis with Klein, the artist is a person whose depression is far more acute than in the normal person. He becomes possessed by his need to resolve it, which he does through the achievement of uniting in the formal integrity of the work of art his unconscious conflicting tensions.

He need not effect a radical change within the unconscious structuring of his own personality. Indeed, it would seem that a too-direct contact with these conflicts threatens him seriously with madness and so his restitution of his good object has to be external for it to survive. His own personal life may be, and often is, chaotic. He places greatest emphasis on the survival of his work, so that art can demonstrate his inner mastery and at the same time serve the world as an affirmation, not only that restitution can be achieved, but also that in this achievement there can be the realization of the ideal of reverence and truth and the reaching of a new level of 'beauty' or integrity in relation with others. The great artist is deeply concerned about the acceptance of his achievements by his society and by posterity, and posterity reciprocates its appreciation of his work by safeguarding its survival as an eternal reminder that love can be greater than hate – and that it can be ever aspiring to new and wider synthesis.

There is no question of the richness and depth of his thinking in this paper. Ernest Jones opened the discussion from the chair, and amongst those taking part were Matte Blanco, Ella Sharpe, J.C. Flugel, Joan Riviere, Melanie Klein, Melitta Schmideberg (Klein's daughter) and Winnicott. In the archival records, the paper is noted as 'Full of observations and ideas that need to be considered in context. Short summarization would only distort.' The gap I felt in his considerations lies in an insufficient stress on the artist's products as gifts in perpetuity to fellow men. It is perhaps this aspect that starts him off on the 'made for fun' angle. Although he includes all the experience of making the restitution from the agony of emptiness and despair, the achievement of the satisfying object from intensely exacting work is what gives the artist and the appreciator the excitement of hope and creation surmounting the destructiveness. One cannot but speculate that what is missing is the creative work still to be done in his own inner endeavour, the work that would produce the satisfying theory whereby the nature of the restitution process within the self could be fully understood and thus made possible for others to achieve through work on their self.

At the time he was empathizing with the work of the artist, Fairbairn's environment was far from facilitating his own work. He had demonstrated to his academic seniors his readiness to further integrative approaches when splits were hardening between psychoanalysis and general psychology and psychiatry. Instead of being appreciated, he was treated by the prominent father-figures in his immediate intellectual world as something evil, danger-ously seductive and disruptive to the naïve. He was thought unscientific as well by the guardians of the allowable knowledge of the mind. At home, his wife was attacking his whole attempt, because of his absorption in it, to facili-tate man's need to understand and control his hate. Melanie Klein's views on the depressive position had stirred up disturbing forces in himself. The patients impinging most notably were schizoid artists, amongst whom was one, mentioned earlier, who was markedly depressive, and it was their struggles with which he appeared to be most closely identified. Their involvement in their creativity closely paralleled his preoccupying concern with producing his own 'art work', albeit he had not yet achieved an adequately integrative form for the theory he was seeking. We can assume his block to be the essential depressive one, that is, how to make restitution of the inner parents destroyed by sadistic attacks when it was the invasions of these phantasies in his own inner world that were troubling him.

Melanie Klein had described how the child's interactions with his parents, their manifest acceptance of his good self as well as his destructive one, gradually changed the highly polarized good and bad feelings associated with the early internal, and in her view, partial objects. Left with the excessive segregation of good and bad feelings of the earliest stages in which part objects play a dominant part, the adult can only undo a severe split within a relationship if the analyst provides one in which the hate can be expressed towards him. The ensuing transmutation only occurs through the analyst's understanding acceptance of it, without retaliation and with his survival as someone still concerned about, and caring for, the patient by his consistent attention. With no analyst in Edinburgh, a disturbing exacerbation of unconscious sadistic phantasies in his current situation could only be split off if his creative thrust was not to be denied, and his whole record showed that it was an urgent vital part of his self.

After his resignation from the University posts the academic persecutors were now more of an irritant and a disappointment than immediate tormen-tors, although their hate was there in the background. His wife's hostility, however, was actively close all the time. All his ideals and principles led him to contain this situation, though the stress was expressed in the urinary-retention symptom which constituted by now a more persistent manifestation of his serious conflict. In an entirely negative environment, it is doubtful if he could have kept his creative self active in any other way.

There were two ongoing relieving features, namely, the support of the London analysts and a growing friendly appreciation of his work in Scotland outside Edinburgh, but they were not a constant reassuring presence. More influential, perhaps, was the personal support he got from a 'good woman friend' as he later recorded, identifiable as his secretary. There were no obvious indications of an affair – an almost inconceivable situation for one with his powerful super-ego. Yet her great interest in his work seemed to provide enough to counter the effect of the change in his wife's attitude. It seemed that there was a revival of his early family, with his father made alive in himself and his hostile mother counteracted by the good nanny/secretary. The split allowed him to maintain a relationship with his wife and to keep the profound investment in his work from his central self actively in being. He must have been painfully aware from the symptom that things were not right in himself and that his non-clinical essays were not drawing upon his most pressing feelings. Certainly the aspects that are missing from the papers on art make them, despite their high quality, not fully representative of his usual powers. Their exclusion from his book expressed his dissatisfaction, and in fact he wrote many years later to Guntrip that, while there was an important core to them, he would prefer to rewrite them for any publication.

In these papers we see clearly an assimilation of Klein's views on early development and, in particular, the acceptance of her emphasis on oral sadism. There is a strong impression that he found the concept of the inner world built up by the formation of internal 'objects' very facilitating. His first two clinical studies had shown how much he felt a need to structure the internal world in terms of personifications and the relationships they sought. He then had to raise doubts about the notion of the id with its unstructured energies as a foundation for the development of the person and his conflicting relationships. There is thus a question as to why he had so readily accepted Klein's oral sadism as virtually an entity directly derived from the innate death instinct. Klein's apparent emphasis on structuring in the person from the start and her recognition of the role of the relationship with the mother as fundamentally important are not paralleled by enough attention to the full theoretical significance of her views. She departed radically from Freud in her views of the very early structuring of object relations yet she constantly stresses her convictions about the independence of the death instinct in shaping these relationships. She saw no problem in using a concept of an energy without structure, yet having an aim, as an explanatory basis for organized behaviour at a personalized level. It was this emphasis that contributed to Edward Glover's view that what she was propounding was a doctrine of original sin with an associated solipsism in regard to the infant's relationships.

Fairbairn was too taken up with the reality of the sadistic phantasies in his patients and the fit between the clinical manifestations and her views at this stage to question them more critically. The need to do so emerges in his art papers where we feel that, while the resolution of the conflict between the residual structures of the earliest phases and the later personalized relationships must play a prominent part in what is an epigenetic phase for the development of the self, Klein's description of the depressive position has left us without an adequate account of what the new personalized self entails. Its creation and its subsequent creativity involved more specific understanding to be given of this process of restitution of a damaged object within a closed system.

The strong inner urges that led to the two papers on art contrasted with the next two essays, which were more reactions to persecutory attacks. Apart from their cogency, their careful construction, the lucid development of the argument, and the elegance of his thinking along with the gentlemanly manner in which he expressed his critical appraisals, Fairbairn's general bearing conveyed the stamp of the scholar in whom intellectual work was balanced by a considerate objectivity towards the views of others. For his students and colleagues he was manifestly someone who brought to his work a seriousness which engendered a reciprocal respect. His thought was based on findings which could not be lightly dismissed. These aspects naturally added to the anxiety that psychoanalysis had evoked in the local academics. Both professors of psychiatry and psychology were active in trying to keep their departments free of psychoanalytic influence by making Fairbairn the target of a campaign to discredit it. Drever had attacked the unscientific status of psychoanalytic ideas at a meeting in St Andrews the previous year – one largely confined to psychologists. Henderson's hostility was expressed informally in the medical and psychiatric worlds, and it was goaded by what he was hearing of Melanie Klein's writings, which he had tried to read and dismissed out of hand. 'That woman writes like the Book of Revelation,' was one of the remarks he made at this time.

AGGRESSION

Fairbairn responded to this situation by accepting an invitation to read the opening paper in a symposium on aggression arranged for the wider membership of the British Psychological Society as part of its annual meeting in St Andrews in 1938.

Since the other papers were to be devoted to specialized areas, for example aggression in childhood or in social life, Fairbairn commented by way of introduction that he would consider the general question of aggression as a primary instinctive tendency. He then singled out Drever's contribution to this subject as distinguishing one group of instincts, the appetitive tendencies, from the commonly listed reactive tendencies, because these instincts were evoked by inner states. This view thus linked the current academic conceptions of McDougall and Drever with Freud's theories. Taking Freud's final formulation of the two groups of instincts, the life instincts or libido and the death instincts or destructive instincts, he stated that these views were increasingly confirmed by psychoanalytical research. In regard to his immediate purpose, he noted that British psychoanalysts in particular tended to accept aggression as the primary psychological manifestation of the death instinct, a view recently reinforced by the uncovering of the enormous part played by aggression in infancy and childhood. For psychoanalysts, the instincts are sources of inner tension, biological drives, which urge the infant, for instance, to suck the breast. Special confirmation for such a concept came from the phenomena of phantasy. Phantasies were the dynamic psychological manifestations of the instincts in the inner world and in seeking their goal they exploited experiential data for the satisfaction of these inner needs. In any given behaviour aggression and libido could be fused in varying proportions. Libido and aggression, however, in all psychoanalytic experience, were not mutually convertible. Aggression had to be regarded as an irreducible force in man. For applied psychology, the critical issue was then whether or not its amount was amenable to environmental controls. It clearly varied with degrees of frustration. The stimuli of frustration were inner states as in different degrees of hunger in animals. Similarly, the analyst was confronted daily with fluctuating intensities of aggression in his analysands, directed towards himself, which he attributed to the changing degree of frustration associated with different phantasies from early childhood.

Fairbairn remarked at this point that no child could avoid the experience of almost intolerable frustration and it was 'in relation to the satisfaction of his more highly charged libidinal needs and of his craving to be loved that the child feels frustration so intolerable' (1939, p. 169). In later life the external control exercised by the parents was replaced by the inner control from the super-ego, that is, the structure derived from the phantasies created from the experience of the parents as frustrators. It was to be noted, too, that the frustrated libidinal desires of infants and young children inevitably fused a good deal of primary aggression with the libido. The resultant phantasies became highly sadistic and therefore had to be repressed. Fairbairn then added that this repression of infantile sadism was the factor that raised serious doubts about the modifiability of aggression, doubts which were strengthened when we kept in mind the inevitability of infantile frustration. Furthermore, these earliest established endopsychic situations appeared to become perpetuated by enduring modifications of the endocrine balance.

On the basis of these views (which he had expressed in the Liverpool paper), aggression could be controlled by regulating its channels of discharge or by lessening the frustrations which provoked it. The former had a dismal historical record largely because the methods used had involved increases in frustration. The latter would seem to have greater potential essentially if such lessening of frustration could be carried out in the earliest stages of development when frustration had its greatest influence. Even so, such effects would not alter the inborn fundamental instinctive force of primary aggression.

In the light of hindsight, the surprising thing about this paper is its presentation of Freud's classical views at a time of his growing dissatisfaction with them. When Guntrip was writing his book *Personality Structure and Human Interaction* (1961) he was puzzled by the support Fairbairn gave in this paper to Freud's theories. In reply to a query about this, Fairbairn wrote to tell him of what he could not know, namely, the personal vendetta Drever was conducting against him, as well as Henderson's hostility. 'I fancy these circumstances combined to deter me (unconsciously) from risking my position with the psychoanalysts, when I was already suffering considerably at the hands of the enemies of psychoanalysis.' He then added that Guntrip might venture to say, in partial explanation of his defence of the psychoanalytical theory of instinct in 'Is aggression an irreducible factor?', 'that he may have been led to defend accepted psychoanalytical views of which he had already become critical'. The presentation is essentially a statement of the current 'received views' with support for Klein, and there is not much in it to indicate that it is other than a *pièce d'occasion* with little of his own recent thinking in it. (I have a strong suspicion that Glover or Ernest Jones might well have suggested his participation following a request for someone to put the psychoanalytic standpoint. Several of the London analysts took an active role in the British Psychological Society at that period.)

Loyal as it is to his analytic colleagues, it nevertheless exposes sharply the situation in which Freud's formulations had continued to be adopted uncritically. The death instinct had been rejected by most analysts, but that was only a part of the metapsychology founded on the nineteenth-century philosophy of science. There must have been some strange intellectual strains in Fairbairn to have written it, because he was customarily acute in his perceptions of conceptual anomalies. As with his suggestion that the work of art was something made in fun, there seems to be a very great deal thrown out with the bath water. Thus in contrasting the analytic view of inner states determining behaviour with the common emphasis on reactions to external stimuli, the whole question of where phantasies get their content from is dealt with in the brief reference to them as an exploitation of experiential data. In Klein's scheme, the infant's mind is full of the products of proactive phantasies through which the objects in the outer world acquire significance from the affective quality that is projected on to them. Realistic knowledge of them is achieved as a result of the to and fro of projection and introjection.

Klein had crystallized for Fairbairn the importance of internal objects from birth; but by focusing on orality and oral sadism as the salient instinctual influences in the experience with the object, she gave the impression of neglecting the influence of the actual behaviour of the object as the first determinant of the experience with it – and, above all, of the behaviour at a personal level. It was this factor that was prominent in his early clinical papers when he drew attention to the realities of family relationships from the earliest stages. Captivated at first by the dramatic nature of the infant's inner world as she portrayed it, he then seems to have accepted her early emphasis on the central role of oral sadism as tantamount to establishing its autonomous status in the negative attitudes to the object. Nevertheless, there soon emerges some of his concern for the fundamental role of the whole or personal object when, in referring to the inevitability of frustration of the infant's oral needs, he adds the intense craving to be loved as a source of intolerable frustration.

Ethology and adequate analytic studies of mother–infant interaction were, however, some years ahead. It was thus in keeping with his general exposition of aggression as conceived by the analysts that he should end sharing Freud's pessimism about reducing the strength of the instincts. Frustration, however, and hence the release of aggression, might be minimized by more understanding of the psychological development of the infant.

Early in 1939 he addressed the National Council of Mental Hygiene at its biennial congress in London on 'The psychological aspect of sexual delinquency'. As on all his visits to London, he met some of the analysts individually. These contacts kept him informed of the psychoanalytic world and especially with what was going on in the conflicts within the British Psycho-Analytical Society. A few visits to Glover were the rule, and on this occasion he saw only Glover. His remaining in good standing with the London group was important and especially so in view of his isolation in what had been for some years a highly persecutory world. He admitted his paper on aggression had been confined to the standard theory because of his fear of losing their affirmation of his professional self. In this paper he maintained his association with the orthodox views of sexuality.

In his address to the Edinburgh medical students in 1929 on the fundamental principles of psychoanalysis, Fairbairn suggested that Freud had extended the meaning of 'sexual' too widely. It would have been better had he kept 'sexual' for those activities related to the sexual act while using the more common word 'sensuous' for the full range of the appetitive feelings. Freud's position was that the various bodily feelings of infancy and childhood had to be regarded as sexual, since the later manifestations of adult sexuality were best accounted for by seeing these as a development from infantile stages. This view had become so ingrained in psychoanalytic thought that the libidinal stages of the erogenous zones were 'facts' taken for granted rather than a theoretical inference. Fairbairn's questioning the use of 'sexual' for all the infantile manifestations had largely rested at this time on his acceptance of the McDougall–Drever views of instincts with their separation of reactive and appetitive tendencies, and with each one having a specific emotion attached to it. His early clinical papers had then raised his questions afresh about the status of Freud's structural theory, especially of the id. His doubts had now receded and he founded his comments on sexual delinquency on the classical terms. Sexual development had little to do with object-relationships. It was determined by the biological maturation of the libido. Hysterical symptoms had been shown by psychoanalytic research to derive from conflicts over tendencies to perversion that had clear links to childhood activities which could only be understood as sexual. Normal development leads to the transformation of the sexual interest in parts of the body, the part objects of childhood, to whole persons. The failure in such development leaves the adult with urges leading to the perversions. Also, because sexual interest is so regularly frustrated in early years, it becomes commonly fused with a great deal of aggression. Hence the marked sadistic quality of the perversions – the end-product of such early deprivations. Most people with failures in their sexual development deal with the latent urges of the infantile sexuality by various character defences or by the emergence of 'symptoms' that is, actions alien to their main personality over which they have relatively little control – as is the case with the delinquent in whom the urge continues to take charge and so to be expressed directly in its immature sexual form. On the control of such urges he notes the development of the super-ego from a very early age, as Klein had suggested, to which he adds that by far the most important control of the impulse is 'the ego or central core of the personality or the self in the strictest sense'. Furthermore, the capacity of the ego to exercise control, its strength, as this issue was termed when it later came to the fore, rests on the structure it acquired.

The theoretical line was strictly orthodox throughout, and only in his concluding observations are there the resonances of his deeper gropings. His early clinical studies showed a complexity in ego structure from various personifications derived from object-relationships. As so often described by scientists when struggling with a pressing theoretical issue, the clarifying steps only occur when some unconscious resolution takes place. Pondering these last two papers, the reversion to the classical standpoint with the manifest inadequacies of its energic assumptions strikes one as rather more of an intellectual block than a creative breakthrough. There was a sense almost of atonement for harbouring guilty heretical notions, or perhaps some relief of guilt because of the depersonalizing of the origins of hate.

On his return to Scotland, there were indications of some overstretching of his resources. Although the tensions between his wife and himself were unchanged, the overall external relationship was maintained, and his wife was with him on the London visit. They met various friends and saw a second Surrealist exhibition. The latter, however, was counterpoised with a visit to the traditional art in the National Gallery. He must have been rather pressed in the weeks preceding this visit, for there was another lecture to be given shortly after it. Whatever the origins of any stress affecting him, two days after his return he contracted a very debilitating influenza which kept him off work for ten days.

PSYCHOANALYSIS AND SCIENCE

The occasion of this next paper was an invitation to speak to the St Andrews University Philosophical Society early in February 1939, and he took this opportunity to discuss the widespread academic hostility to psychoanalysis. The title of his paper was 'Psychology as a proscribed and prescribed subject'. In selecting a title, as in his writing in general, he was most particular, almost pedantic, in his choice of words. His theme was essentially the proscription of psychoanalysis by academic psychologists, and he obviously chose in this instance attack as the best form of defence. He was clearly making a reply to the academics' charge – one in which Drever had played a prominent part at the meeting in St Andrews almost a year before – that psychoanalysis could not be recognized because it was not a scientific discipline. For him it was in the same category as alchemy and astrology. In his relatively short paper, Fairbairn asserts that it is the academic psychologists who are really the unscientific ones, as for example, in the extent to which they ignore the most significant psychological phenomena in man such as the unconscious, sex, love, conscience, sin and guilt along with almost the entire range of the manifestations of hate and aggression: war, persecution, revolution and fanaticism. Moreover, their attack on the scientific status of the psychoanalytic method was similarly unfounded. He then states that the real reason for the hostility to psychoanalysis is the fear of what it uncovers in man, a fear that had recently been greatly intensified. It now reveals, in addition to the dark urges of primitive sexuality, man's dangerous destructive forces plus the rather insecure defences with which he protects himself against these through his culture. In the course of history, such dangers from increased self-knowledge have often been referred to by religious leaders, who as well as destroying the heretics have thereupon offered a message from their gospels containing the methods of coping with them, usually by reinforcing their repression. Psychoanalysis does not provide any such remedy; it hopes, instead, that by increasing our knowledge and understanding of the nature and origin of these unconscious forces, man will achieve some control over them.

Many of the issues taken up are as relevant today as they were when he commented upon them, and this paper is still a useful one in the current conflicts about the status of psychoanalysis in theory and practice. As Fairbairn puts it: 'The fact is that, the higher the cultural value of a subject in our university curriculum, the less freedom of thought and inquiry is permitted.' The traditional role of a university is to safeguard the culture of its society and it was thus inevitably in conflict with another of its functions, namely to advance knowledge by free scientific inquiry, for the latter inevitably 'has had a disintegrating effect upon the prevalent culture'. Here he does not make this latter term as specific as he might, for 'the traditional culture' to be preserved by the academics was essentially the scientific materialism which had dominated science progressively since the middle of the nineteenth century. The assumptions, moreover, about what was 'real', and so the only proper object of scientific inquiry, were increasingly trivializing the whole research endeavour in the human sciences.

The situation that surrounded the writing of his paper was eminently real. Ironically, the grip of materialism, with the reification of concepts, was almost as powerful on psychoanalysts as on any other scientists, and it was this reality that Fairbairn was beginning to feel more clearly. To revert to the deeper activities of his inner world, it is perhaps not too fanciful to see merging with the conscious considerations of his paper the echoes of the boy protesting against the parents who prohibited the pursuit of his natural curiosity, especially when there was so much evidence all around of the human phenomena that he was adjured to ignore. To be a proper scientist and avoid messy subjects had a close fit with earlier experience. At the risk of overstretching some speculation, it might be asked whether or not there had been in these last papers a change from his preoccupation with the depressive position to an assertive one in which he was attacking the persecutory castrating parents. In this stance he was now supported by more obvious affirmation in the professional field. Glover had visited Glasgow several months earlier to give an address on psychoanalysis to the mental-health professional groups including the academics. There was a large audience who showed considerable interest, a marked contrast to the Edinburgh scene.

A few weeks after he read his attack on the psychologists, he was elected, despite some lobbying against him by Drever, as President of the Scottish branch of the British Psychological Society. Within the week following, he was back in London to be accorded full membership of the British Psycho-Analytical Society. He also attended on this visit the twenty-fifth-anniversary dinner of the Society, so that he could feel there was no doubt about his status with those who mattered most to him professionally. Again he saw Glover a few times, contacts which he maintained in two further visits during the summer. A visit to Edinburgh by Michael Balint brought a feeling of the international significance of the psychoanalytic movement to which he now belonged. In keeping with a greater confidence, he played cricket for the fathers at his daughter's school in England before the summer break.

4 Prelude to creative articulation

THE SWELL of encouragement in the first half of 1939 to his psychoanalytical self seemed to fire Fairbairn's resolve to pursue the line of thought that had been gestating over the previous years. Possibly, too, the threatened outbreak of war was bringing back the assertion of his independence as had happened twenty-five years before when the First World War began. He then had to stand out against his mother's pressure to keep him from volunteering to join the Army. At any rate, he remarked when writing his paper on the war neuroses a few years later, he was beginning to formulate his new theoretical framework when war broke out early in September 1939. This event inevitably brought great changes for everyone in most areas of life. An immediate one for him was the evacuation of the children away from home, in keeping with the national policy. His daughter, aged eleven, was at boarding school in England and his elder son, aged nine, went off to a residential preparatory school some miles away from Edinburgh. The younger son, aged six, went to stay with relatives in Scotland. In response to the formation of the volunteer force of Air Raid Wardens, Fairbairn enrolled immediately. Fortunately, the duties proved fairly light, although there was a 'hit and run' raid by some small German planes aimed at the naval base a few miles away. One small bomb landed not far from his home – an incident to which reference is made in the first chapter of his book.

Fairbairn and his wife, along with the resident secretary, continued to live in their home and he carried on until the following spring with his usual list of about eight to ten patients daily.

Throughout 1939 he had been increasingly stimulated by his schizoid patients, some of whom were very demanding in their dependence. His urinary symptom must have been causing increasing concern at the same time because of its persistence. Sadistic urination phantasies were prominent in one of his patients in his reaction to the King's death. In his own symptom there seemed to be a link between it and an identification with his father, whose symptom was well known in the family. Obviously, all that led up to the symptom cannot be known. Our concern is with the prominent features of his inner world that led him to turn the traditional preoccupation away from impulses to personal relations. There are good reasons to assume a highly ambivalent relationship with his mother. She had clearly established a severe inhibition of the expression of his sexuality, and much of the affect in this early situation had been resuscitated by his wife's hostility to his work. His religious investment had apparently been a transformation of his early conflicts over sex, conscience, guilt and sin into the strong ambition to satisfy his curiosity while preserving a close inner tie to an idealized father equated with God. A sense of injustice about being denied help with these conflicts would readily become, from his religious upbringing, an urge to help others with personal problems, and when welded to a strong feeling for what was substantial in dealing with actual experience, he had no doubts about his eventual choice of medical psychology (as it was then called) rather than the Church, as a career.

As an only child with parents who held strongly moralistic attitudes, he had a profound division in himself. Analysts would expect to find in one part intense infantile rage against the frustrating aspects of his parents, repressed and kept unconscious by a combination of pressures. There was a severe super-ego and a well-developed ego that could rely on the intellectual strengths he possessed for pursuing knowledge that now incorporated his early curiosity. There was also the active backing of mother who consciously conveyed her conviction to her son that he was unusually gifted and with a special future which she wished him to realize.

From his interest in the family relationships of his analysands, his own early experience with his parental attitudes must have puzzled him and certainly left in him a disbelief that the natural self of any child would be filled with impulses as bad as they made out. His later personality expressed convictions of a very different order, and we note in his case descriptions and, in his addresses to mental-health groups, the recurrent theme of the mother whose love meets the deep emotional needs of her child in contrast with the one who presents her child with a masquerade of her own conflicts. The recalcitrance of his own symptom could only stem from powerful unconscious conflicts to which he could not apparently gain any useful access. What he sensed as a creative breakthrough against the rather stultifying position in which Freud's metapsychology was keeping psychoanalysis was manifestly pressing forward. Looking back from my own experience of working with him during the early years of the war, the latent excitement about his views was striking to his close colleagues, especially in a personality in whom control and reserve had been deeply ingrained. To pursue his line of thought was clearly the assertion of his very life, there was almost a degree of being possessed by it, yet joyfully so.

Whatever the inner forces were, they gave rise in the months just after war broke out to a systematic study of his own childhood. He wrote careful notes of a self-analytic nature and it is to these I wish to turn, as he did himself, at this point. They begin with early memories and an account of a traumatic incident which had a clear connection with the symptom. He then records various aspects of his personality and their history which he felt to be related to the development of his urinary difficulty.

SELF-ANALYTIC NOTES

The notes were written for the most part between late October and mid-November 1939, that is, in the period when the uncertainties about what the war would bring were enforcing an uneasy lull in most activities. They fall readily into groups in the order in which they were written. Some are in the form of the thoughts as they occurred, while others are in a narrative form. Most of the earlier material I quote in full as readers can thereby get their own pictures of the inner world that was the well-spring of his later ideas. As the notes go on there is repetition in places and I have therefore abridged slightly the later sections.

Following this first impetus, there is a gap of over eight months before he describes a dream. I have included the account of this dream as there are enough notes about it to convey some of its meaning. There is then a gap of about twelve years before some additional notes are recorded. These, however, are not illuminating as they consist of a tabulation of factors that might have contributed to the symptom, most of which are mentioned in the early notes. I have given a paragraph summary of those points that seemed to be new. Along with these later notes are some crude drawings of dreams. There are no notes about them, and so I have not introduced them. They are, however, vivid indications of some of the early anxiety situations.

The subjects of the notes are as follows:

1. **Early memories**: These are undated but apparently written as the first group of notes in the early autumn of 1939.
2. **Traumatic incidents which left a permanent effect:**
   a. *Dramatic incident in a railway carriage.* Description of a highly traumatic incident in childhood.

    b. *Three childhood traumas.* These are referred to frequently but not
    described.

3.   **Notes on the urinary-retention symptom and
related early conflicts:**
    a. 29/10/39. Notes.
    b. *Summary of further notes on this theme.*

4.   **The family situation.**

5.   **A dream on** 4–5 August 1940.

6.   **Summary of further references to the symptom
written in** 1950–55.

7.   **A brief note on drawings of dreams in the same period.**

The first notes are of special interest in that they are recorded free associations. All the other notes are written as organized narrative or as organized tabulations of relevant factors.

1. Early memories

Making mess in high chair at a meal in nursery. Mother angry. Being in go-cart and feeling cold and bored while nurse stood talking to a man (? soldier) on pavement outside a neighbouring house. Feeling annoyed with nurse. Knew mother would be angry with nurse if she found out. Being in cot with croup (? as a result of catching cold in last incident), feeling terribly hot, unable to breathe and gasping for breath. Father holding umbrella over me to keep in steam from steam-kettle.

There was fire in grate: and cot was in front of fire in parents' bedroom. Father appeared a good protective but rather ineffective figure. Waking up in cot beside parents' bed on Xmas morning and looking at parcels (Xmas presents) at bottom of cot. Parents were still asleep: and I felt impatient for them to wake up so that I could start opening the parcels. Perhaps I felt I could not do this without their permission; or perhaps parcels were on floor out of reach.

Waking up in cot after having wet the bed. Aware of smell of urine, wet feeling and mackintosh sheet. Mother coming and telling me not to touch myself and warning me that boys who touched themselves were liable to get awful diseases like paralysis when they grew up and saying something happened to men who went with bad women.

Mother coming when I was in cot and putting her hand under the clothes to see if I was touching myself and warning me about awful consequences to such a practice.

Having irritation of foreskin and telling Mother who put vaseline on foreskin. Wondering why it was all right for Mother to touch my penis and not for me to do it. Wondering also why it was right to touch my penis when I took it out and held it to pass water and not to touch it for the sake of touching it. Finding these problems an insoluble mystery. Evidently it was a case of touching penis being all right when authorized by Mother, but fatal otherwise.

Being in bath and being told by Mother to wash between my legs. Wondering why it was all right to touch my penis when washing between my legs (which Mother represented as almost a moral obligation) and wrong to touch it for the sake of touching it. Unable to understand what magic constituted the difference.

Being in Midland Railway train going to Yorkshire. Eating strawberries and then being sick.

Being in bath with Cousin E in Yorkshire. Her mother, who was bathing us, went out of bathroom. Cousin E making 'water-wheels' with her hands between her legs and touching as she did so. Feeling self-conscious and inhibited, but envious of her for her lack of inhibition. Perhaps she invited me to follow her example and I felt too inhibited and guilty to do so. Perhaps she invited me to touch her between her legs and I refused. Perhaps she made attempt to touch me and I would not let her. Her mother returned in the middle of the 'performance': and I felt very self-conscious and guilty and wondered if her mother would notice this.

Being in bed with Cousin E (? grandfather's house). She suggested a game of mutual masturbation. I refused to participate remembering Mother's warnings against touching between legs. She said that she touched herself and her mother had never stopped her. She also said that there was another game she played, viz. putting her finger up her bottom. She suggested that we should take it in turns to put our fingers up one another's bottoms. I reflected that I had never been told not to do this by Mother. I was rather casuistical about this as I knew it was the same sort of thing but argued that I had never been told not to do it. So I agreed: and we played this game. I found it very exciting: and her putting her finger up my bottom gave me an intensely pleasurable sensation which I recognized as similar in quality to the sensation caused by touching my penis. We went on till I felt satiated.

Being put to bed by Cousin K at Aunt L's. Cousin E was also being put to bed. She and I begged Cousin K to let us sleep together: and she eventually allowed us to do so. I fancy we hugged one another till we fell asleep. Waking up later to find that Aunt L was lifting me out of bed. She carried me to another room and put me to bed there. I heard her telling

Cousin K that she ought not to have allowed us to sleep together. This made me feel there must be something wicked about it.

Visiting London at an early age with parents [he was eight years old – J.D.S.] I remember the Pullman car we travelled in, also the train stopping at York for half an hour to enable passengers to have a snack in the refreshment room.

Remember that the house we stayed in was Uncle A's house. Remember the nursery and the nurse. Remember that Cousin W was a baby. Remember playing with Cousins L and A at crucifying a toy monkey with a long tail and our being scolded by the nurse.

Remember going to the Zoo with parents who had difficulty in finding the way. Remember getting a fright when a llama stretched its neck over the fence and snatched off my balmoral [The Scottish hat that went with the kilt worn by many boys at this time, especially in private schools where it was frequently the school uniform for dress occasions. – Ed.] with its mouth and threw it in the middle of the cage. Father gave the keeper a hand to retrieve my balmoral. Remember crying when we left Zoo because I had not seen the snakes. Parents said we hadn't time to see them because we had to be back at my uncle's for a meal and we were late already. Felt inconsolable. Had wanted to take our dog to London but was told by Father that we couldn't take it. I asked why not and he invented the excuse that men stole dogs in London. I asked how men could steal a dog when it was with you in street. He said they might put a box on top of it. This seemed to me improbable. Remember being on top of a horse bus in a busy street in London (? Oxford Street) with parents. I said to Father, 'Father, I don't see any men stealing dogs.'

If we regard these notes as the free associations in an analytic situation, albeit on this occasion a self-analytic one, we can make a picture of some of the deeper relationships in his early inner world that is independent of possibly more rationalized accounts. First there is a mother made angry by his not taking his food without making a mess, so from this early stage a dominant internal figure is of a severe mother attacking 'dirty' or disorderly behaviour. There are then several scenes in which is excluded from a couple and then from the parental couple in their mysterious relationship. With the nurse, it is Ronald who resents the frustration of being shut out in the cold. This anger is expressed by his mother taking it over, but with the proviso 'if she found out', which suggests that Ronald has a guilty interest in the nurse. Next he moves to a feverish state which may link with exciting phantasies about the parental sexuality. We are then struck by his father appearing as a comforting and protective figure. More obvious links with the parental intercourse follow with him in the cot in his parents' bedroom. Here there are 'goodies' for him in the form of Christmas gifts, but he must not touch them until his parents give permission. Ambivalent attitudes in phantasies of the parents' sexual relations emerge in the common reaction of young children to them, namely, bed-wetting. There is some condensation from later years, for mother is now suspicious about what he is doing with his penis and he is given dire warnings about playing with it. Puzzlement is next. It is an insoluble mystery that it can be touched only in circumstances authorized by mother. There is thus a very early and dominating structuring in his mind of this stern super-ego mother controlling his relationship to his penis with an intimidating threat against any sexual feelings for 'bad women'. To the young boy it must have been difficult to separate this mysterious group from other women. While we are obviously in a highly speculative area, the relationship patterns that appear in these early memories do gain in significance when we learn some of the later experiences. Thus, his mother's reaction to the nurse talking to the man is similar to what happened after an incident when she suspected sexual advances from a man who took Ronald for a walk. In short, there may well be in this memory the condensation of an early identification with the nurse/mother in the parental intercourse and later phantasies and memories.

The significance of the train journey and being sick from eating strawberries is too obscure for it to be linked to earlier incorporative phantasies, though he does specify the journey as one to Yorkshire where his mother's relatives lived, that is, where the sexual behaviour with his young cousins took place.

The memories that follow are of openly sexual play instigated by his little girl cousin. Although he resists touching his penis, he feels very guilty when her mother appears. Later he yields to a suggestion from his playmate to let her put her finger up his bottom. His mother's prohibitions did not cover this game from which he gets an intense, almost orgasmic pleasure. In these incidents, although the adults stop the games, they do not adopt any of his mother's frightening anger and severity, either to him or to the 'bad' seductive girls.

Castration themes follow upon the memories of these sexual indulgences. The sexual games proceed to crucifying a toy monkey with a long tail. When he goes to the London Zoo his hat is snatched off his head by an animal, but then given back when his father gets a keeper to rescue it. The phallic interest is again blighted when he is not allowed to see the snakes, at which he became inconsolable. This brings out the deprivation he felt at not being allowed to take his dog on this trip. This dog, though not often mentioned, seems to have been an important object to him because, in drawings of dreams made ten years later, he frequently depicts himself as a little boy wearing his kilt and balmoral and with his dog on a lead. The feeling expressed in the notes suggests that the dog was a vehicle for his secret (sexual) self, and he is very mistrustful of the excuses his father offers for not allowing him to have it. The dominance of the severe anti-sexual mother has thus become shared with his father as a castrator, who arouses Ronald's resentment without producing any pronounced fear of him.

An overall impression from this first group of notes is of the little boy having internalized the perpetual closeness of the only child to his parents and with a mother excessively driven to eradicate 'bad' sexuality. The constant presence of his parents' relationship seems to have fostered a strong curiosity about what went on between them sexually. His frustrated feelings were apparently increased by the rather inhibited physical contacts his parents made with him, making him resentful and envious of what they gave each other. Against all these negative feelings the basic quality of the mother–infant relationship must have had much that was developmentally good, for we have no indications, nor any record of behaviour problems nor of undue clinging or detachment. There was little room for the expression of any assertive protest or aggressive behaviour, though we have to allow an important unconscious expression of such feelings in the bed-wetting. Presumably it was this problem that emphasized the mother's attention to his penis, and there was a degree of phimosis to heighten this concern. The outcome was an imaginative child driven more than usual into his inner world and who could use his intellectual gifts well, provided there was no explicit sexual interest. It is as much the absence of references portraying his mother as a good object along with her repressive attitudes, however, that give us the picture of a dominating, frightening, controlling mother who must be complied with at all cost. Father is a comforting figure when Ronald is ill, but he too becomes a castrating parent, though not so frightening as mother.

2. Traumatic incidents which left a permanent effect
a. Dramatic incident in a railway carriage

This experience happened when Ronald was eight years old (according to entries in a record of holidays he kept from an early age). His description conveys vividly its significance for the urinary difficulty.

28/10/39

Incident on Highland Railway in old days. No corridor; train very late; stopping at every station. Father's bladder very full. Ladies in carriage – all ladies except father and me. Father conferred in whispers with Mother. Mother whispered to her friend and the other women. Then

Father urinated at his end of compartment, while Mother and perhaps her friend, held up newspapers as screen. I was on same side of newspaper screen as Father. It was [an] appalling experience. Father seemed in great pain and had the greatest difficulty in passing water. It took a tremendous time for him to pass it; and it only came in driblets. He 'sweated blood'. It was like seeing Christ on the Cross. I was closely identified with Father in the experience. I was on his side of the newspaper screen, and I wanted to urinate very badly too. I watched the scene aghast. I was terribly sorry for Father. It seemed awful to be unable to urinate when you wanted to so badly, and to be confronted with [the] danger of [one's] bladder bursting (a danger which Father had often dwelt upon to me). It seemed bad enough for him to be placed in a situation in which he could not go to [the] lavatory when he required to; but it seemed even worse that the presence of women imposed a barrier upon his urinating in the carriage. I believe that first of all he tried to urinate out of the carriage window or through the slightly open door; but he failed and had to urinate on the carriage floor, which eventually was swimming with urine. I remember the sound of the urine trickling down on to the floor. I wanted very badly to urinate too; and I think that, after Father had succeeded in urinating, I urinated through the door, which was held slightly open by Father. It may have been on another journey on the Highland Railway that I did that; but I think it was the same occasion. The train swung about terribly and I was afraid of the door shutting and trapping my penis – which it nearly did. I think I had a bit of difficulty in urinating myself. I felt pretty anxious and worked up after watching my Father's performance. Journeys on the Highland Railway in the old days always raised the urinary problem in a more or less acute form, as there were no corridor carriages and the trains were painfully slow and lost time all the way. I remember another occasion on a Highland Railway journey when my bladder became very full and I got out at a wayside station to go to the lavatory. I was afraid all the time that the train would go off before I managed to urinate; and I was very anxious about the situation. I was also afraid of having to rush back to the train before I had urinated. It seemed a desperate situation. I think I had a bit of difficulty in urinating on that occasion, but eventually I succeeded just in time to get back to the train before it started. It was a great relief to feel I had been saved from an intolerable situation. Being unable to urinate when the bladder is full seems to be almost the most intolerable situation conceivable. I fancy that, when Father had that awful experience in the train, I must have held myself responsible for his suffering – quite irrationally. Guilt over secret hostility towards him probably made me assume responsibility. I think I must have derived a secret satisfaction from his suffering, although I was [The notes break off here.]

This incident at once strikes us with its highly traumatic feeling. Its immediate links with the urinary symptom make it an early section of his notes, and as a traumatic incident it is described as something by itself, something that stood apart in his mind, powerfully present yet not really assimilated. Although he makes no comment here, his father's difficulty gives every indication of being an established neurotic one. He did describe to some of his own family how prominent his father's problem over urination became in his boyhood. The absence of toilets on the train was allowed for by the frequent stops so that his father may have withheld his urine unconsciously to release it in the presence of the women. Ronald was put alongside his father behind the newspaper screen and he too then shared the need to urinate. His castration fears quickly followed. When he recalled the incident, he felt that although there was the identification with father in his distress, he must have had a sadistic pleasure in seeing his father in this impotent position – and presumably the crucifixion theme in the childhood play was related to a retaliatory punishment.

b. Three childhood traumas

The three incidents to be described are not given a separate status in Fairbairn's notes. They are dramatic enough, however, to have stamped themselves on his development and they are repeatedly referred to in subsequent reflections about his symptom. There are enough details about the first two to describe the situations, but with the third one the references to it, though frequent, are bare. It seems to have occurred before the others, probably when he was six or seven.

(i) His mother's attack on his sexual curiosity

There is a bitter gnawing resentment associated with this incident in contrast with the mixed feelings for his father in the train.

On this occasion he had gone into the house by a back door where he saw some blood-stained diapers in a pail. His curiosity prompted him to ask his mother about them as he had a vague feeling, according to his later recollections, that they were connected with female genitalia and what went on in his parents' bedroom. To his astonishment she got into a frenzy of rage, gave him a beating and then locked him in the parents' bedroom for several hours. He felt this punishment was extremely unjust, and his bitterness gave rise, even at this early age, to thoughts of suicide probably in part as a revenge. It played a prominent part in many of his subsequent phantasies that it would be better to be a woman, relieved of his bad penis, and it certainly contributed to anxieties about penetration.]

(ii) Encounter with a homosexual man
Again the incident is primarily associated with his mother as the frightening anti-sexual super-ego.

He was walking by himself in a park near his home when a man made sexual advances to him. He 'put his hand up my clothes [his kilt] and started touching my penis'. When he protested the man said it did a boy good and made him strong to play with his penis. Fairbairn told him of his mother's warnings to which the man said that was all nonsense; it made a boy strong to touch his penis. He then became afraid of the man doing something dreadful to him and was greatly relieved to escape when some people approached. On returning home he was pounced on by his mother who was very suspicious when she learned about a man speaking to him. She asked him if the man had touched his penis, then accused Ronald of lying when he said 'No'. He stood his ground against her persistent questioning but went to bed feeling miserable and in disgrace. Nevertheless, he thought he started to touch his penis in a spirit of bravado and wondering if her warnings had deprived him of enjoyment arbitrarily. He thought she came later to renew her warnings about touching his penis, and he referred again to his mother's attitude having created the feeling that he'd be better without it.

(iii) The little girl run over and killed
Like the other incidents this one is referred to frequently in the later notes as a contributing source to the phantasies underlying the retention.

He called to a little girl-friend across the road outside his home whereupon she darted towards him without seeing a horse and carriage rapidly approaching. She was fatally crushed, and the memory stayed with him, including his feelings of responsibility for her death. (His family noted the persistence of this distressing experience, which never lost its pain for him.)

3. Notes on the urinary-retention symptom and related early conflicts
The next notes are specifically headed as related to the retention. They were written in three parts over about two weeks following the account of the railway incident and show a progressive attempt to get at some of the underlying unconscious forces. The first part is given as written. The other two have been slightly condensed because of some repetition in their contents.

a. 29/10/39
Difficulty in urinating before other men. Urinating before other men seems to have become a phobic situation. The same difficulty is liable to arise if I enter a WC to urinate and anyone is waiting outside; and even this

situation has a phobic quality. The fact that I am expected to urinate, even if no one is actually present, seems to create anxiety. The result is that I tend to take precautions about having to urinate away from home or away from some other equivalent place of safety; and this necessity tends to circumscribe my life. It leads me to avoid ordinary social life and to live within a rather narrow circle. Having to urinate in the presence or in the vicinity of anyone seems to be a danger situation and I tend to avoid such situations owing to the anxiety they occasion. I don't think I explicitly experience anxiety over the anxiety involved in such situations; but I certainly feel anxious about being exposed to the anxiety situation; and perhaps it is almost a case of 'being afraid of the fear', since I am very much distressed about the fact of being anxious in urinary situations. The position is very much the same as in the case of my fear of heights.

Sense of being tested all the time – not only in exams but in almost every activity in life (except in my professional work which has been thoroughly mastered, and in the setting which I have established for chosen activities in the interests of security). Sense of being tested manifests itself in public appearances, social contacts and sexual life, as well as in act of urination before others. Sense of being tested showed itself in school life (1) in comparison with other boys so far as libidinal activities were concerned, (2) in relation to demands of parents (super-ego) – demands which seemed to make presence of libidinal desires bad. Sense of being tested was thus accompanied (1) by sense of inferiority compared with others in libidinal sphere, (2) by sense of moral inferiority (guilt) owing to presence of libidinal desires.

Self-Consciousness – (1) Sense of inferiority in libidinal sphere, (2) Guilt over libidinal desires, (3) Projection of aggression upon others, (4) Adoption of passive attitude. Self-consciousness in adolescence which struck me as strange since I didn't masturbate; though I didn't there was conflict over desire to do so; and when I felt self-conscious with the headmaster, I felt he would think I masturbated. I thought it odd that boys who did masturbate should be free from self-consciousness. I felt out of it with these boys – libidinally inferior presumably. I felt safer with older people, towards whom I tended to adopt a passive role. I was always wondering 'what people would think'. I was afraid to make demands to do anything unusual and I was afraid to be legitimately aggressive. If I did allow myself to be aggressive I tended to lose control and become excessively emotional and make a fool of myself; and afterwards I felt remorseful and bitterly conscious of having made a fool of myself; and I would dwell on what had happened for ages and feel sheepish. Presumably I was afraid of my own aggression. I think I was conscious of the weakness of my ego and its inability to cope with my aggression. I lacked personality and capacity to assert myself with others and take the lead. What seemed natural in other boys in the way of self-assertion and leadership seemed out of place for me. All this points to (1) a sense of inferiority, (2) anxiety and guilt over my aggression. There seems to be a connection between my self-consciousness and the constant sense of 'being tested'.

The sense of being tested seems very much bound up with the demands made upon me by my mother as a super-ego figure. I am sure I felt she didn't like my penis; and this led me (1) to wish I hadn't got a penis and to adopt a castrated attitude, (2) to regard my penis as a bad object which ought not to be made a source of pleasure. The result was (1) the adoption of a rather female attitude and (2) considerable sexual inhibition. The situation favoured a regression to the position of treating my penis as an essentially urinary organ and extorting what pleasure I could get out of it in a urinary capacity. I recall that, when I lay awake at night with erections, I often tried to relieve tension by urinating – which was a difficult process in the presence of an erection. Frequently the erection subsided after I had urinated. I was liable to erections when I went to the lavatory alone to urinate or defecate; and again urination tended to make the erection subside. Often, after urination, the unhappy desire persisted and I went on passing driblets of urine for a considerable time.

b. Summary of further notes on this theme

In further notes written a few days later, many of these adolescent feelings are again described. Some new aspects, however are noted.

Nocturnal emissions caused him grave concern even though he could not be held responsible for them. It was the *loss* that disturbed him. His mother had told him of the terrible disease he could get if he touched his penis, and he feared the emissions would do the same. He thought it strange that God should give one a penis when it was wrong to touch it and, above all, to get pleasure from it. He wanted to get this pleasure and to feel it was something good 'instead of a bad organ and a source of temptation, a delusion and a snare'. He would gladly have sacrificed it on the principle of cutting off one's right hand to enter the kingdom of heaven. The urinary difficulty, he supposed, was related to his wanting the forbidden pleasure from urinating.

The anxiety aroused by his penis gave rise to the fantasy that it would be nice to be a woman. Having something (presumably a penis but not formulated as such) would effect a release of the tension from a full bladder. Female masturbation seemed to him a better and infinitely more pleasurable act than male masturbation, which was so completely forbidden. It occurred to him that retention had behind it a desire to have this relief by the insertion of a penis into the urethra. Once, after an operation (the rib resection in Paris) he had a catheter passed, and he felt he would have no further difficulty, which turned out to be the case. The loss of semen in the nocturnal emissions was very deleterious, like a woman's fear of losing the treasure inside her; and having something put in was an important compensation for being emptied. It also seemed important that the retention was like filling mother's breasts as a reservoir from which he could draw good milk from a hoard of treasure in himself since her breasts seemed empty of good milk. This identification with his mother contributes to the retention, because women fear losing contents. The retention is caused and maintained by the anxiety of good gifts withheld by a love object. Retention, however, brought the anxiety of looking a fool, for example in a public lavatory and, much worse, the 'commanding fear' of his bladder bursting. Being unable to get rid of urine collecting under terrific and increasing pressure is appalling. It becomes something very dangerous and destructive. The actual situation is bad enough, but the great anxiety seems to be that one should have forces at work within oneself that threaten to destroy one and

> the anxiety when my bladder is over-full and I am unable to pass water is quite capable of giving rise to suicidal thoughts. Indeed it is the only thing (with the possible exception of fear of heights) capable of rousing suicidal thoughts in me. I fancy that, when my bladder is over-full and I can't pass urine, I identify myself with my Mother and identify my bladder with her breast bursting with bad milk. This, I think, must partly account for the suicidal ideas, because I feel my bladder is something alien and hostile on these occasions.

4. The family situation

About two weeks after the previous notes, he wrote an account of his early family situation which is given in full.

14/11/39

The actual family situation in my early life was in no small measure characterized by a combination of my mother and myself versus my father. My father had been brought up in a hard school and was very down on anything in the nature of extravagance. He was also rather narrow-minded in many ways. The result was that I felt he denied me a great many things which I felt it reasonable to expect or, at any rate, to want. My mother tended, on the other hand, to press my father to give me certain advantages which he saw no reason to give. My mother was more socially ambitious than my father, and she wanted me to have social advantages which my father thought unnecessary. This came out in the choice of a school for me, and later in the choice of a university. My mother wanted me to go to Oxford; but my father was bitterly opposed to this idea. I think he thought it unnecessary that I should want to go to a university at all; but, on the assumption that I was going to a university, he expressed the view that it was ridiculous for me to go to Oxford when there was a perfectly good university in Edinburgh. He regarded the Oxford scheme as involving unnecessary expense and as being a concession to snobbery. I think he was also afraid that Oxford would have a morally degrading influence upon me. He had been brought up in this atmosphere of Scotch Calvinism himself; and he regarded Oxford as a place where morals were less highly prized than Scotland – a consideration which he associated with the fact that it was a hotbed of Episcopacy. The question of Scotch versus English also came into it.

Although he was not a Scottish Nationalist to any extent in the political sense, he had a strongly nationalistic feeling, which allied itself with social, moral and religious prejudices. He tended to regard the English as (1) politically oppressive towards the Scotch, (2) socially snobbish, (3) morally lax, and (4) religiously unspiritual and insincere, not to mention intolerant (in conformity with the typical Presbyterian conception of the Church of England). As my mother was English, my father's attitude to things English heightened the contrast between my mother's ambitions for me (which I made my own ambitions for myself) and my father's inhibiting, frustrating and castrating influence. I think my mother's ambitions for me had the effect of strengthening my narcissism. They led me to feel that I was someone rather special, someone out of the common run and superior to most of those in my suburban environment, someone with a destiny and a future. Yet I think I must have felt a good deal of guilt about my rather grandiose ideas and ambitions, because there was always in the background a sense of my father's disapproval. There must have been a lot of guilt before him on account of my aspirations, which seemed to run so counter to his ideas of life. Not that he was without ambitions for me; for he was always pleased at any success of mine, especially as I grew older – almost childishly pleased.

Indeed his obvious satisfaction was almost embarrassing, especially when he displayed it before other people, as he was rather prone to do. I found it almost intolerable when he showed that he was 'proud of' me. It made me feel very sheepish and ashamed. I suppose I felt guilty about the exhibitionist situation into which he forced me in this way – and not a little resentful too about his frustrating attitude towards me. I didn't see why he should frustrate me so much, and why he should find it necessary to oppose me in so many things. I didn't see why my whole life should have to conform to his ideas – or rather prejudices as they seemed. I must have had terrific hate for my father; and indeed I had barely concealed death-wishes towards him. If guilt made me put away overt wishes for his death when they arose, I at any rate permitted myself the fervent hope that, if one of my parents had to die, it would be him and not my mother. The idea of my mother dying first and leaving me alone with my father was too dreadful for words. I felt that, in that event, I should be utterly cornered and finally prevented from realizing any of my ambitions.

When father did die in later life, I felt terribly sorry, as a matter of fact. In the last illness he seemed a very pathetic figure; and I am sure I had a lot of guilt about his death, although this guilt did not show itself very obviously. I was supposed to 'rise to the occasion'; and I think I got some satisfaction from feeling I was doing so. I fancy I identified myself with him fairly strongly and felt I was taking his place and perpetuating him in myself. Previous to his death, however, I had a good deal of difficulty in identifying myself with him. I just hated when people said I was like my father, as they commonly did. I much preferred [it] when anyone said I was like my mother – which didn't happen very often. I wanted to be like my mother. She was much better looking than my father; but my preference went deeper than that. I think I must have identified myself pretty strongly with my mother; and that may have to do with my adopting a feminine role – as I undoubtedly did.

In the early months of 1940, the clinical load of nine to ten patients daily continued with few interruptions. The children were out of town at their boarding schools and were visited frequently at weekends. At the end of March his wife became ill with meningitis. The condition worsened gradually so that by early May she was barely surviving, and for some weeks Fairbairn's clinical work was much reduced. An improvement began about mid-May, although it was several weeks before she was able to leave hospital and it was not until the later summer that she recovered fully.

It was in early June that he began his part-time work in the hospital for the 'war neuroses' at Carstairs, a small village, in moorland country twenty-six miles from Edinburgh. This meant that he had to spend time not only there but also on a car journey three days per week, so that his analytical patients were reduced in number by about half. The assimilation of the schizoid phenomena that had been proceeding actively during the previous year was greatly stimulated by this change of work. He did not undertake treatment of the patients, almost entirely men from the armed services who had developed incapacitating psychological disorders under stress of very varying character and intensity, but carried out careful assessment interviews. The splitting phenomena in these disorders became very striking to him, as also were the underlying degrees of dependent attachments to their family figures. The impact of this experience was now added to what had started five years previously from Melanie Klein's paper and then gathered momentum from his own patients, seen from the new perspectives that were emerging from the depths of his own psyche. The close interplay of traumatic changes in external relationships with those in the inner world had been brought vividly home with serious disturbance in his own inner organization, albeit confined in its expression to the urinary symptom. The efforts to understand what was taking place in himself which had produced the self-analytic notes in the previous autumn were continuing, and in August he recorded a dream, a summary of which follows.

5. A dream on 4–5 August 1940

He was looking for a rabbit in a burrow; a dog scraping at the mouth of the burrow reminded him of the early sex play in the bath, with his girl cousin showing delight when poking her finger into her vulva in clitoris masturbation. Perhaps she had urinated too. He visualised himself as embarrassed and perhaps tense. Had she asked about his penis or wanted to touch it? Perhaps she wanted him to show how he urinated. He fancied he was embarrassed about his penis and remembered his mother's prohibitions about touching it and urinating in the bath. He was afraid someone would come, and eventually his aunt did. Perhaps his cousin had asked him to put his finger into her vulva and perhaps he did. He envied her with a hidden penis inside her vagina like the rabbit in the burrow. Like his mother whose body was too big for his little penis. He was once in the lavatory with his mother urinating and the rushing sound of the copious flow of urine impressed him. He conceived his mother as having an enormous hole (? cloaca) between her legs – like the enormous burrow in which it was impossible to catch a rabbit in the dream. It was impossible to get at mother's hidden penis (clitoris) and he envied female sexuality with its clitoris pleasure and which was free of the 'dangers' which his mother warned him were attached to his possession of a penis. The difficulty in urinating seemed connected with a desire for the advantages of female sexuality, and so to tear away his penis and put his finger into his bladder to make a free passage for the urine – like his sense of needing to be catheterized. He thought his penis was like a cork in the mouth of his bladder and he envied the female's apparent freedom from anxiety over urinary retention.

Clitoris sexuality as enjoyed by his cousin was not only free of the 'dangers' of male sexuality but also seemed to be more enjoyable. The mutual poking of anuses initiated by his cousin was at first resisted then accepted with some guilt. When eventually indulged in, it was felt to be highly pleasurable, especially when done by her. Some little girl-friends at home had embarrassed him by referring to enemas. He had had constipation in childhood for which his father had administered enemas and suppositories. The constipation made him anxious, especially after the incident in the train when he went for five days without a motion. That incident had made a tremendous impression on him, with his father suffering like Christ on the Cross. He was tremendously embarrassed, too, with a sense of being on the 'wrong side' of the screen of papers.

He hated his father for putting him in such a position with its painful identification with him in his distress. Father's anxiety had been conveyed to him, so that he began to need to urinate with the fear he would be unable to. After his father managed to urinate he held the carriage door slightly open for Ronald to urinate, and the lurching of the train made him afraid of having his penis trapped. He was very relieved when he did pass urine. He wondered if he had had to hold the door open while his father tried to urinate. Perhaps he was afraid then of the door banging on to his father's penis. The women on the other side of the screen seemed so immune from all the anxiety over urinary retention. Some of this anxiety became displaced to the constipation and the incident had led to (a) his identification with father as a martyr; (b) a renunciation of male sexuality as displayed in father's exhibitionistic situation; and (c) a desire to be a woman so far as urination and sexuality are concerned, a desire which became prominent in adolescence when erections caused intense conflict.

The dream thus derived from the continuing unconscious activity related to his mother's hostility to his sexual curiosity. His wish to be a woman with a secret penis and the desire to get at his mother's secret penis constitute the main phantasy. When he turned his attention from the rabbit-burrow to a mole-burrow on a mound near by, his son, who was playing a ball game with another boy, lost interest. Perhaps, Fairbairn notes, his son was at this time deeply concerned over his mother's serious illness and so more interested in his mother than in his father. The place where he was playing recalled the place where the incident with the homosexual man occurred.

This part represented, he thought, his son going to play with another boy when he felt frustrated in his relationship with his mother and his desire to find her clitoris. This frustration creates the desire to turn away from the world of his mother to that of the boys:

> The part of me entertaining this desire is, however, in conflict with another (and more powerful) part of me which seeks to find a substitute for the world of mother in the inner world – narcissistically. This narcissistic part of me is the part which figures in the rest of the dream – the scene about the mole-burrow on top of the mound. In this scene my own penis becomes the centre of interest in place of mother's clitoris, which is the centre of interest in the rabbit-burrow scene.

6. Summary of further references to the symptom written in 1950–55

No notes are preserved from the next ten years, then some were added in the years 1950–1955. They are all tabulations of factors he thought were relevant to the symptom and add very little to what has already been recorded. There had been sporadic incidents of retention in the past, for example in a crowded men's lavatory at the time when his mother was trying to prevent him from joining the Army, that is, when she was an actively castrating figure. The retention developed into a symptom when his wife became an aggressive, castrating mother-figure and his significant father-figures became rejecting and aggressive. He was then driven to seek a good object in another woman (his secretary). It was aggravated, and began to occur even in privacy, when his wife was very ill in 1940 and following the departure of the secretary just afterwards.

Accompanying the tendency to the retention were heightened desires to urinate, to keep the urinary content low to avoid this excitement. There was also the feeling of people and even stimuli such as noises becoming hostile and menacing. Common to the circumstances provoking the retention was the feeling of being tied to a castrating woman (mother) who arouses aggression which then creates too much guilt to express. The feeling of it being impossible to escape from the castrating mother gives a sudden suicidal impulse at times. He felt strongly he was not treated by his mother as a person in his early years. The retention seems to be an expression of the compulsion to sacrifice sexuality and a sado-masochistic regression with his aggression turned against his libidinal ego. He notes, too, that it has a reactive component to the 'oral need' for love and the loss of mother's love. His oedipal situation had father cut out from it, with a consequent staging in relation to the good and bad mother-figures along with a desire for a good father as a support against the castrating mother.

7. A brief note on drawings of dreams in the same period

There are a few dreams recorded which I have not considered as they do not add significantly to what has already been described. Several crude drawings of dreams on scraps of paper, but without any text, are of interest even in the absence of notes on their content. They bring out vividly the frightening quality of the little boy's inner world. Fairbairn is represented in many as the little boy in his kilt and balmoral with his little dog on a lead behind him. The mother in several is a large terrifying woman with a carving knife poised in her hand, and the boy is chained to her in some. His father appears only a few times and then as a seated observer. In two, a boy, or a monkey, up a palm-tree is throwing coconuts at the mother. There is one, however, in which a large benign-looking mother has one arm around the father and the other around the boy, holding them face to face in front of her.

FORMATIVE INFLUENCES

From his history and other external sources a picture has been con-structed of prominent aspects of Fairbairn's personality when he began his psychoanalytic career. His upbringing and education had produced a tightly organized and almost obsessively disciplined intellect, notably controlled by a self with a sensitive courtesy and genuine consideration for others. There was an intrinsic strong morality in all his relationships, with an open-minded tolerance towards human beings in general. The stability of his family relations with their stress on moral principles and the care almost intrusively fed into him within the closeness of his parents' rigidly run home – albeit with a firm, and in its own way warm, attachment to their many relatives – had fostered within him a steadfast cohesion in his attitudes and behaviour that made a good basis for the thoughtful listening from which all his thinking started. Nevertheless, the puzzling and painful contradictions in some of his parents' ways had built deeply serious splitting into his self. The unwavering single-mindedness of his professional self, in which his intellectual questioning was a central pillar, was remarkable in the face of what had emerged as a symptom with an obtrusive and tenacious vitality. Whatever its sources, the eruption of the symptom was effectively separated from interfering with the dedicated commitment to his work.

The self-analytic notes have provided evidence from which we can now add to the first description an account of some unconscious forces that would have influenced his clinical perceptions and reactions. We want to know the constituents of the self that was the agent of the remarkable work which began in the later half of 1940 with a power that stayed undiminished for several years and then subsided into a more subdued though steady level of consolidation.

Turning to Fairbairn's earliest formative experiences, the origins of the conflicts underlying the symptom were evidently in the earliest stages of the relationship with his mother, in the precursors of the oedipal role she played when she terrified sexual exploration and activity out of his mind by what can only be described as a savage attack. Her behaviour had wider effects than the inhibition of genital impulses. What he describes in his adolescence is a pervasive sense of being inferior to other boys, of having been deprived of the more general confidence from the possession of a secure masculine identity, a condition pointing to general anxieties in this primal self. Although derivatives from failures in the earliest relations with his mother are inevitably speculative, there are indications of a fundamental layer of insecurity from this phase. Thus, in his references to the links between the states of his bladder and his mother's breast, which at first seem somewhat intellectualized comments from his analytic knowledge, there is, nevertheless, a feeling of early realities in them, as would be expected in one whose whole intellectual attitudes and endeavours drew upon his deepest sources. That they are unusually illuminating emerges in 'Schizoid factors in the personality', the paper that was gestating when these notes were written. In his discussion of the chief characteristics of the oral attitude, he places 'tremendous significance upon the states of fullness and emptiness' for the child when he is deprived. He assumes that, when hungry, the child feels empty; and, when fed, full.

Furthermore, the child must feel that he has emptied his mother after he has fed. Hence, when deprived he becomes aggressively needy, which results in an enlarged incorporation of the breast itself and the mother as a whole. This experience arouses the fear of destroying the breast/mother and, when the emotional relationship with the mother is unsatisfactory in the period after the early oral phase, this leads progressively to the loss of interest in the personal aspects and their replacement by bodily attitudes.

Resonating personal experience seems more specific when the mother most likely to evoke such feelings is singled out as the one who fails to convince the child by expressions of genuine affection that she loves him as a person. Moreover, the worst experience occurs when the mother is felt to be possessive and indifferent, as with the devoted mother who is determined not to spoil her only son. In addition to feeling unloved as a person, the child deprived emotionally in the early oral stage readily gets to feel that his love for his mother is not valued, and so his mother becomes a bad object. It is then better to keep his love inside himself, because love relationships with external objects are bad or precarious. Relationships are hence turned to his inner world, in which good objects can be imaginatively created.

From all the suggestive evidence, we can assume that Fairbairn did not feel freely, that is, unconditionally, loved and accepted by his mother in his autonomous self. With this deprivation there was consequently a representation internally of the breast/mother with limited supplies of milk/love. Alongside these experiences, however, the evidence also supports another clustering, around the devoted care of the mother who was available with other expressions of good feeling. In spite of his mother's obsessive concern with order (she did not like messes), and her intolerance of potential sexual behaviour, she did not discourage his later imaginative activity; and, along with his father, she does seem to have provided well for 'stimulus hunger' and the development of his interest in the external world. A split in his feelings about his mother was probably compounded by the reality situation in which she was bracketed with the nurse/nanny figure. The latter would be much more spontaneous in her contacts. The combined figures may well have secured for Fairbairn a successful foundation for the early development of his central self. There seemed to be here the situation he re-created with the residential secretary.

Within the unity of his self, which Fairbairn took to be a requirement for an organizing centre of experience, a degree of splitting must have started very early. The cohesive force amongst experiences would lie in their affective tone, with positive ones fusing in one part of the whole and negatively toned ones being segregated into another part in which they would also merge because of their similar affect. The first split would thus have begun to separate the imago of the 'bad' mother.

With a persecutory bad mother as an unduly dominating internal object, there must have been anxious states from fear of her retaliation. Since there are no reports of overt manifestations of such tensions in childhood, he seems to have controlled the bad objects in considerable measure. One primitive way was apparently through constipation, in which he equated bad objects with faeces and then imprisoned them. When this mode of control became excessive there was relief from father's administration of enemas and suppositories which, in turn, would suggest the common phantasies of father's good penis entering him, a link perhaps with some of the later phantasies of relief from his dangerous urine by catheterization. The retained urine could sustain for a time the phantasy of a good full breast/mother, but, with rising frustration, it rapidly became a bad object full of his own sadistic hate that eventually released a flood of destructive urine while he was asleep.

With the developing awareness of the father as a figure prominently linked with his mother in the constellation of his care, we should expect a turning towards him to make good some of his mother's deficiencies. This process is seen in one of his early memories, when his father brings comfort for a feverish cough. Unconsciously, the familiar phantasy of father's penis being wanted as a substitute for mother's breast does not appear to have played a prominent part. The most important significance of the father, however, is his role in giving a model for the masculine self whose biological substrate 'expects' it for effective personalization. The first relationship with the mother may thus be regarded as laying the foundation for being a person; being a male has then to come into action. Fairbairn does not seem to have developed optimally in this respect, a feature mainly attributable to his mother's later attack on his sexuality but also influenced by the rather ill-defined role of his father's 'power' in relation to his mother.

The awareness of the father as a separate person is also accompanied by the fact of father and mother being a couple whose relationship stirs unconscious phantasies, for example, of making babies as well as providing the necessary environment. Klein postulates the unconscious phantasy of the parental couple as being a highly active one from around the middle of the first year. In her view, this phantasy is essentially a sexual one of the parents gratifying each other in different ways, especially orally and incorporatively. The sexual couple is then inevitably the object of envious attacks, of unconscious wishes to break it up and also to incorporate it. Fairbairn appears to have had unusually intense phantasies of this 'primal scene'. Amongst his earliest memories are scenes of his being in his parents' bedroom waiting impatiently for them to wake up, of feeling excluded from a sexual couple outside his home, of wetting his bed, and his mother's threats if he touched his penis. This reaction of attacking the parents in intercourse by urinating on them is familiar enough in analytic work. It is of interest to recall here Freud's urinating when he went into his parents' bedroom, though he was then about seven or eight. From Fairbairn's memories and the subsequent conflicts over urination, these phantasied attacks on his parents' intercourse must have exerted a powerful pressure. In Klein's view, the appearance of these phantasies introduces the oedipal phase. For Fairbairn this was a complex situation, for his forbidding mother was joined by his father in his exclusion from their mysterious relationship, and there does not seem to have been an adequate relationship with his father in boyhood to counter the frightening mother.

Few dates are recorded by which we can time his development, and so the phase we have been referring to is stretching from early childhood until he is approaching ten years of age.

Turning to the positive side of his development, there is no question that, while his mother, and to a lesser extent his father, had established pronounced bad internalized imagos, especially in relation to his merging gender identity with normal self-assertiveness and sexual curiosity, they were also providing a great deal of conditional love and care. From what we gather about their personalities from Fairbairn's notes and the little information from those who knew them when he was a boy, Fairbairn was the constant object of their concern and interest. As an only child this might well have been irksome. He felt it to be at times a constant supervision against his sexual curiosity. In the earliest years, there was the more relaxed relationship with his nanny. After that, and especially when he began school, there was the expanding fascination with the outer world. Although not mentioned, he would, as was usual in his social class, attend a small private school at first. Then he would go on to the preparatory school when he was about eight years old before moving into the main school a few years later. With his intellectual talents, he had a great deal of interaction with his parents and their facilitating encouragement. He was also involved in many of his parents' social activities. Within these areas, he was very much the desired son, to be guided along the correct lines towards being the adult gentleman.

From the development of all these compensatory interests and concerns, he seems to have achieved a state of being the acceptable 'good boy' who was highly valued. The pressure of his sexual curiosity, however, was constantly reinforced by his own capacity to appreciate the mystification his parents brought to any expression of it, and the experiences with his little girl cousins added still more to the forbidden excitement.

The discovery of the blood-stained diapers had raised anxious phantasies about what happened between his parents. The mother who threatened frightening consequences to any sexual feeling then became the terrifying real castrator who savaged him because of what he felt to be part of his natural self. The unconscious anxieties stirred up by his phantasies were further exacerbated by the periodic illnesses of his mother when she took to bed and became the focus of worried concern in the household. There were also the constant reminders of the mysterious dangers that afflicted his father's urination. Did she damage his penis? His relatives all had children, and why no others in his family? The hate of this internal persecuting mother was not relieved by his father's support. He was felt to have joined with her as another castrator, presumably controlled by her into impotence. He had witnessed the destruction of his little girl-friend by the crushing horses. His inner destructive hate had to be disowned at all costs. It was not only dangerous; there was also an obsessive confusion about so much if he did not split it off.

The anxieties, despite the strength of some of the frightening unconscious phantasies, were effectively repressed until adolescence. Throughout his school years up to that stage, the stabilizing effect upon his ego of his family relationships, the care given to him within the closeness of its rigidly run atmosphere, yet with a concerned attachment to him and to their many relatives and friends, had fostered a cohesion in his central self that made him an interested observer with an objective curiosity of pondering what he noted. The somewhat excessive introversion in these formative years paradoxically gave to all his thinking a notably realistic contact with what he learned, as though the intensity he was finding in his inner-world relationships was giving a quality to them of what he needed in the outer world. It was mentioned earlier that in his pre-adolescent years he aroused a great deal of interest in his family and their friends from the remarkably detailed way he had created an imaginary country. One feature, however, that he told his own children, is of considerable significance – it was an island. It is perhaps, too, a measure of the degree to which he had become a habitual conformer outwardly, that, although never making a critical note in his diary of his inner feelings about school, he told his children that he really hated it all the time.

Inner strain became troublesome with the resurgence of his bad mother in the face of his intrusive adolescent sexuality. This phase may well have prompted the notion of his taking up the law as his profession, especially with the strength of his feelings about the injustice of his mother's attitudes. The low self-esteem, however, was countered by a remarkable topographic change in his inner world.

As he came towards the end of his school years his talents had made it plain that he would go to the University, and he had decided he wanted to become a clergyman. With this decision, he showed the powerful influence religion had exerted upon his inner development. Beneath the conforming exterior of the schoolboy, there must have stayed a vital secret aspiration of being free one day to include within his autonomous self his physical nature. For his mother, he had now become 'special', with unusual talents, and so to be given optimal opportunities. His Calvinistic father, however, was opposed to any expensive education, so that his mother's wish that he should go to Oxford was rejected by him. Oxford appealed greatly to Fairbairn, not only because of the attractive scholastic settings, but as a chance to get away from his father's narrow rigidities, which were becoming difficult to bear. It was his father who had been the devoted churchgoer, so this choice of career did not arouse antagonism in him. Although his father's parsimony was difficult to tolerate, hostility to him drew on deeper sources. The misery he suffered at times because of his masculine inferiority must have made him resent his father for being so feeble in relation to his mother's hatred of his sexuality. Much of his own inferiority seemed now to be projected into his somewhat despised father, while his mother's support could well buttress the deeper omnipotent trends which he noted in himself.

There was also the incident in the train with its profoundly traumatic impact. His father had appeared like the castrated man, and protesting his plight to his wife/mother. He had then been deeply sorry for his father and identified with him in his suffering, as if he were being crucified. As far as he was concerned, the incident seemed to have established his father as castrated by mother, and his mother as the one who had internalized his potency – now to be transmitted to her son, not sexually, but as the object of her ambition for him to be someone 'special', distinguished in what he was to accomplish. It was a highly complex legacy, since, from various references in his notes, there is a strong indication that he had developed a persistent phantasy of the woman, his mother, having secretly incorporated the father's penis. The first dream, for instance, that he records in his self-analytic notes is his searching for a rabbit in a large burrow. The dog trying to find it is linked with his self as owning his penis. These unconscious phantasies were reflected in the topographic change within his self, for we see a pattern there in which the anatomical genital content symbolizes a great deal of the structuring in the layers between this primitive level and his fully developed adult self. Before considering this issue, however, we have to go back to what was happening in the reverse direction so to speak, that is, to the building of a new ego linked to a secret autonomous self which was gaining power steadily from what he was incorporating from his external world. The unconscious 'plan' had to be filled out for the way he was going to live in it as a man.

Religion had played a large part in his family environment from the start. From early boyhood he had attended church twice on each Sunday with his parents, and from a quite early age he seems to have listened with an appraising attitude to the sermons. In keeping with the Scottish Presbyterian Church, the latter were long, highly moralistic and, as often as not, boring. The inculcation of the Bible stories, and especially the life of Christ, however, seems to have made a deep impression. Im my own experience of clergymen, and especially Presbyterians, whether in analysis or in seminars held to increase their effectiveness as counsellors, these men have frequently had an ambitious mother and a father who tended to leave the mother the dominant figure in the family. The resultant deep hatred of the mother for moulding their self is extremely difficult to release because of its intensity along with the idealization of the mother. A splitting off of all aggression takes place which makes for resistance to recognizing and coping with it in themselves and others. This situation arises from the highly ambivalent feeling towards the mother, who, though having been resented bitterly as restrictive on the ordinary expressions of the assertive boy, is almost excessively devoted to her sons with great self-sacrifices on their behalf. The Christian myths are particularly appealing to such boys, and a deep identification with Christ occurs. Christ is the son who abjures hate and gains the love of God, who is internalized as the unconditionally loving Father. Sexuality is allowed under prescribed conditions, so that God is not an inveterate castrator, but hate must be disowned. They can develop a male sub-self with considerable capacities although it often exists within the cocoon of the internalized mother like her secret identification with her father and his penis.

By the time he left school, Fairbairn had decided to enter the Church, that is, to adopt the Christian ideals and to take the Son of God as a model for the self that carried his autonomous thrust. Such a move was extraordinarily apt as a way of finding a pattern in his circumstances for 'being' with greatly enhanced self-confidence, though it could foster latent omnipotent trends from the integration of so many positive values. He was thereby at one with his dominating mother, while his father's denials and inadequacies no longer mattered. Both approved of this self, which was also eminently acceptable socially in their world. At the conscious level it gave Fairbairn a means of building what Chein has described as the essential quality of being a person, that is, a commitment to a developing and continuing set of 'unending, interacting, interdependent, and mutually modifying long-range enterprises' (Chein, 1972, p. 289). With Fairbairn this purposeful ideal self was one with great motivational power. He became imbued in a highly positive way with being in the world, with being someone who intended to have a future, and whose would be with people. Though one would hardly expect him to become 'one of the boys', he did become, in contrast with his earlier adolescent self-image, an active participant in peer groups of young men sharing his main direction.

His sexual curiosity had never left him in the deeper layers of his being. His choice of philosophy as his university course had the hope that he might learn something about the mysterious conflicts around sexuality, although in that respect the 'conspiracy of silence' was as marked there as in almost all other sections of society. Nevertheless, his pursuit of this knowledge was not now frustrated by his inner mother. To become a clergyman with her enveloping support meant that he could allow the forbidden areas as part of his new role. He was, moreover, not going to be like those clergy, as he announced in his diary, who seemed to him to be essentially emasculated, and not only with regard to their sexuality, but also as men who were actively and enjoyably 'in life'. Again, remembering what he had contended with in his early years, he was hardly likely to become the 'macho' man socially, but he was acquiring a confident masculine intellectual vigour in his enterprises, as one who was ready to challenge others for his autonomy. There was no advance towards close emotional relationships with women, though he made several friends at a superficial level.

When he proceeded to postgraduate studies in Hellenism it did seem that he wanted to get at least a wider experience of human nature, if only through reading about it. Joining the Army despite his mother's wish to keep him at home was an indication of a definite assertion of a more autonomous masculinity. As an artillery officer he was never in contact with close fighting, but the carnage from the destruction of war may well have strengthened his need to keep unconscious sadistic phantasies securely shut off. Within the masculine world at war he must also have been exposed to the prevalence of primitive sexuality. There had been enough contact with medical psychology for him to know that its practitioners were concerned with all that had mystified him in a way that intensified his curiosity. The visit to the hospital in Edinburgh was a turning-point, because he was so intrigued by the phenomena of hysterical conversions which the medical psychologists could explain and change.

The most striking feature of his self as we see it through his history is, to my mind, the continuity of the development after adolescence in the power and scope of this core commitment to the realization of the goals of his ideal self. The bad experiences and deprivations, with the phantasies arising from them, were successfully split off as serious threats, as though all the frustrated autonomy had been drawn into the dynamic of this core of his central self.

Far from being constrained by his bad mother, he now had another split with her inner presence as a matrix of support for the man who was going to understand the mysteries of human nature, who would marry and have a family, and who would fulfil the Christian ideal of loving others by helping them to free themselves from inner sufferings by understanding their nature and origin. The support from his inner relationship with God had, however, an aura of secrecy about it. He turned away from the ministry, in which it had to be declared more openly. The question is thus prompted of this relationship reflecting some continuing split between him and his parents. After his father's death, Fairbairn felt he was openly taking his place and circumstances put him in this role, yet without the usual anxieties from any internal retaliatory father. He referred later, however, to guilty feelings about his father having been denied by an effective split.

His decision to seek analysis is of great interest in view of it being an unusual step at that time, and of how he coped with the inevitable parental curiosity about it. In this latter connection, he was probably helped by the fact that Connell, his analyst, was an impressive man, both physically and financially, while socially he was manifestly a cultured Christian gentleman, greatly respected in his parents' circles. It almost certainly represented for him a major assertion of his autonomy, yet one to be undertaken without his parents being disturbed or becoming negative – in some ways like his private relationship with God. There seems to have been no suggestion of his setting up his own home during the years between his return from the Army and his getting married. To remain in his parents' home was, of course, not so unusual in those days.

While the strength of his autonomous core is impressive, and Fairbairn recognized this strength when he described feeling he had mastered his work, various manifestations of residual insecurities were noticeable. Thus the affirmation of the academic fathers seemed to be required if he was to enjoy his autonomous self to the full. Equally, the maintenance of his masculinity still had to be sustained by its loving acceptance by a good woman. When he had both of these supports he functioned optimally. When his wife turned into the attacking mother, a major shift occurred in his inner world, yet not in his core self, for he continued to function here with an increased output. This change in his wife's behaviour, which had been gradual in the early 1930s, culminated in the outburst that happened at the time he had planned to be in London to hear Melanie Klein present her paper on 'A contribution to the psychogenesis of manic-depressive states'. As far as I know, the contents of her paper were not circulated in advance to the members of the Psycho-Analytical Society except, probably, for a few intimates. From his later notes, there had been intercourse before his wife's aggressive outburst, which was followed later that night by Fairbairn's attack of renal colic and haematuria.

Whatever the significance of these particular happenings, there is little doubt that his wife's hostility was precipitated by her growing feeling of 'not being treated as a person'. From what is known of her childhood, she lived very much within the confines of her family with an unusually close attachment as an only girl to her only brother. It seemed that she needed a kind of dependent closeness of which she was being increasingly deprived by Fairbairn's absorption in his work. To give up, or to lessen substantially, his investment in his work was to take away the core autonomy he had managed to achieve and to enjoy the productivity that had followed from it. The strength of this central self was also what maintained the repression of his dangerous sadistic phantasies. The puzzle I felt was to understand why: (a) the urinary symptom had emerged at this time with such a grip on him; (b) in spite of its disturbing effects, his working self remained apparently unaffected; (c) for the five to six years following the eruption of the symptom his intellectual studies remained largely unconnected with his clinical work, especially after Klein's paper had been so stimulating to him, but so disturbing in its themes to so many analysts; and (d) the role of his unconscious relationship with his father was revived so specifically in the symptom. The incident in the train with his father's symptom obviously had a fundamental influence in that he now seemed to have identified with his father in dealing with some catastrophic phantasy. There were many indications in his notes of a major split, whereby powerful destructive phantasies of destroying his parents in the primal scene, by his releasing on them a flood of urine equated with rage and hate, were effectively banned from any emotional entry into consciousness. If he had murdered his father in these attacks, he had now reinstated him as constantly alive in himself.

Klein's earlier work had revealed the intense unconscious phantasies of infants and young children, which they enacted in their inner world amongst the figures they had created there to represent the good and bad aspects of the emotional instinctive relationships with parents. Fairbairn had described his analytic work with such phantasies in the brief notes on patients' reactions to the death of King George V. In her 1935 paper, Klein again referred to the violence of the early phantasies and stressed the sequel to these in the infant, namely guilt and depression over the destruction of the mother as she was with the maturing perceptual capacity, that is, the whole and the same person who was both attacked and lovingly needed. Although she does not deal with all the developmental implications of her thesis, she emphasized that the earlier destructive phantasies were now succeeded by powerful impulses to make reparation, to put the whole loving mother together. Such a perception of a whole person can only come from the development of a corresponding feeling in the self of becoming a person, for unintegrated parts can hardly perceive a wholeness as long as this is entirely outside their own experience.

The loving reparation that, in Klein's description, the child must make is almost entirely the 'responsibility' of the child, who has to produce, *sui generis*, responses that will make the mother feel good.

Fairbairn, although he had not yet stated his view, must have been sensing from his own bitter experience that the child had to be given the capacity to give love. The reparative feeling had to be established in the emerging structure of the self of being good and loving from experience of the mother imparting such an attitude. He had had a great deal of devoted care, without the feeling of being loved unconditionally as a child. He had in his adolescence come to feel his mother as good and his whole professional success was a reparation to her. In this reparation, his father was left out as he had become the bad or, at least, ineffective parent, and also the one who did not wish to encourage his son in becoming someone special. The patients he described in his first clinical response after Klein's paper had reacted to the King's death with intense guilt and with attempts at restitution. The man with the long-standing urinary symptom did this after a dream of drowning the King by finding his father alive and well in a luxurious railway coach.

A puzzlement about the onset and the features of the symptom stayed with me for several years. I then thought I should read Klein's paper again to see if there had been some other disturbing theme in it. What I found there quite astounded me. It felt so uncanny I could hardly believe at first that the paper had not been added to since I had last read it. The following extracts will, I believe, convey the impact of a particular section.

Dreams of a male patient well advanced in his analysis

He dreamt that he was travelling with his parents in a railway-carriage, probably without a roof, since they were in the open air. The patient felt that he was 'managing the whole thing', taking care of the parents, who were much older and more in need of his care than in reality. The parents were lying in bed, not side by side, as they usually did, but with the ends of the beds joined together. The patient found it difficult to keep them warm. Then the patient urinated, while his parents were watching him, into a basin in the middle of which there was a cylindrical object. The urination seemed complicated, since he had to take special care not to urinate into the cylindrical part. He felt this would not have mattered had he been able to aim exactly into the cylinder and not to splash anything about. When he had finished urinating he noticed that the basin was overflowing and felt this as unsatisfactory. While urinating he noticed that his penis was very large and he had an uncomfortable feeling about this – as if his father ought not to see it, since he would feel beaten by him and he did not want to humiliate his father. At the same time he felt that by urinating he was sparing his father the trouble of getting out of bed and urinating himself. Here the patient stopped, and then said that he really felt as if his parents were a part of himself. In the dream the basin with the cylinder was supposed to be a Chinese vase, but it was not right, because the stem was not underneath the basin, as it should have been, it was 'in the wrong place', since it was above the basin – really inside it. The patient then associated the basin to a glass bowl, as used for gas-burners in his grandmother's house, and the cylindrical part reminded him of a gas-mantle. He then thought of a dark passage, at the end of which there was a low-burning gas-light, and said that this picture evoked in him sad feelings. It made him think of poor and dilapidated houses, where there seemed to be nothing alive but this low-burning gas-light. It is true one had only to pull the string and then the light would burn fully. This reminded him that he had always been frightened of gas and that the flames of a gas-ring made him feel that they were jumping out at him, biting him, as if they were a lion's head. Another thing which frightened him about gas was the 'pop' noise it made, when it was put out. After my interpretation that the cylindrical part in the basin and the gas-mantle were the same thing and that he was afraid to urinate into it because he did not want for some reason to put the flame out, he replied that of course one cannot extinguish a gas-flame in this way, as then poison remains behind – it is not like a candle which one can simply blow out.

In a dream on the night after this one, the patient dreamt of something like a live creature being fried. He could not make his mother understand that to fry something alive was a particularly painful torture but she did not seem to mind. As a child he had read a book about tortures and had been especially excited over the story of the execution of King Charles. (Klein, 1934, pp. 299 ff.)

Klein's analysis of these dreams threw new light on some fundamental points in this patient's development.

The urination in the dream led on to the early aggressive phantasies of the patient towards his parents, especially directed against their sexual inter-course. He had phantasied biting them and eating them up, and, among other attacks, urinating on, and into, his father's penis, in order to skin and burn it and to make his father set his mother's inside on fire in their intercourse. Castration of the father is expressed by the associations about beheading. Appropriation of the father's penis was shown by the feeling that his penis was so large and that he urinated both for himself and his father . . . (Phantasies of having his father's penis inside his own or joined on to his own had come out a great deal in his analysis.) The impotent and castrated father was made to look on at the patient's intercourse with his mother – the reverse of the situation the patient had gone through in phantasy in his childhood. The wish to humiliate his father is expressed by his feeling that he ought not to do so . . . (pp. 301–4)

In further comments, she notes that the death wishes against the parents had led to an overwhelming anxiety about their death. Again, if jealousy and hate stirred by some real frustration are welling up in him, the patient will repeat, in his phantasy, attacks on the internalized father, and the parents' intercourse. These dreams are dominated by distressed feelings for the loved objects and are characteristic for the depressive position.

Klein's paper, as already described, had made a great impression on Fairbairn, who had assimilated it studiously. I cannot imagine this dream not making an especially disturbing effect upon him with its astoundingly close fit with his specific anxieties. It is striking that it is never referred to in his self-analytic notes nor did he ever mention it. His symptom had manifested itself occasionally before his wife's attack and the renal colic, so that the dream was not the precipitant. Its effect must have been to release anxieties associated with his own urination phantasies, although we can only speculate on the specific ways. Many of Klein's patient's phantasies were identical to Fairbairn's. The inhibition of urination as the means of destruction is central. What is of greater interest, however, is how the phantasies were being responded to at this time when a powerful reparative trend seemed to be engendering the theoretical work that began in 1940.

While the original object of this urinary expression of his hate seemed to be the parental intercourse, the development of the good internal mother who supported his career, and the masculine sexuality concealed within it, had led to his father becoming its target. His wife's attitude was now putting the inner situation back into its earlier form. The dream in Klein's paper focused on the male patient's reparation following the destruction of his parents by urination and one consequence of the symptom could be, as suggested earlier, the restoration of his father by an identification with him. The outbreak of the First World War had enabled him to break free from his mother's control, and with his wife now largely detached from his central self, he could feel the internal parents to be less persecutory. The hospital patients impressed him greatly with the strength of their deep conflicts over unresolved unconscious ties to mother, and they added to the cumulative impact of his schizoid patients. He could see, like Dali in his paintings, a frame of understanding that could encompass the hate and the love by bringing both parents and child into the picture as essentially interrelated figures needing each other. I mentioned earlier being struck by one drawing, amongst those that depict his negative relationships with his mother in his dreams, in which his mother enfolds his father and himself in her arms.

5 The creative step
An object-relations theory of the personality

THE CREATIVE PRESSURE of Fairbairn's thinking rose progressively throughout 1940 and was such that he completed its first expression by the early autumn. This paper, 'Schizoid factors in the personality', was read in an abbreviated form to the Scottish branch of the Psychological Society early in November. Although his many papers read there were listened to with respect, the audiences, apart from the very few Scottish psychotherapists, had little or no clinical experience from which to appraise his thinking. Also, in a relatively small group of about twenty to thirty, the lack of sympathy with his viewpoint in a few of the dominant academic figures tended to dampen the discussion. On this occasion, some of the English psychoanalysts and analytical psychotherapists, now on wartime service in Scotland, could appreciate his work, and there was a lively, informed and friendly discussion. Perhaps a deeper impact was also to be discerned in the subsequent 'joking' remarks such as, 'I wished he had not described me so openly.'

To analyse a group of schizoid patients was in itself a bold step, for in the orthodox view the pronounced narcissism of these patients, with the consequent inability to form transferences, was held to make them unsuitable for psychoanalysis. We have learned of some of the forces which in Fairbairn's own inner world would respond to them and make clear some of the factors responsible for their difficulties. His empathic understanding, however, was always well controlled. He never talked about patients in any way that suggested undue counter-transference. His still unresolved phobia could be kept aside while his insights functioned in most areas. The clinical findings and his understanding of these form the substance of this first paper in his book and it is a crucially important one. All his subsequent efforts to systematize his theory rest on it, and for this reason I have made fairly detailed reference to it.

At the outset he states his growing interest in schizoid phenomena and justifies his belief in their fundamental importance on the grounds that they offer a unique opportunity for study of the foundations of the personality and the most basic mental processes. The widest range of psychopathological disorders can be studied within one person, because all the usual defences have been exploited as a rule before the deep underlying schizoid factors are exposed. In other words, the latter are clung to underneath the cover of intensely obstinate resistances. Nevertheless, when regression has not gone too far these patients can show much greater insight than any others. Moreover, contrary to the common belief, they are eminently rewarding from a therapeutic point of view because of their ready transference manifestations. What Fairbairn concludes is that severe schizoid conditions tend towards the negative end of a hypothetical scale of integration of the ego with the normal personality nearer the other. In between are the lesser degrees of disturbance seen in the psychopathic personalities, character disorders and the schizoid states or episodes that constitute most adolescent breakdowns. He then asserts, also contrary to the current beliefs, that most of the familiar psychoneuroses, whether hysterical, phobic, obsessional or anxiety symptoms, are defences against underlying schizoid trends and not derivatives from specific libidinal fixations. The common disabilities that lead people to seek analysis such as social and work inhibitions, psychosexual difficulties and the phenomena of depersonalization and derealization, along with dissociative phenomena as in dual and multiple personality, also derive from schizoid factors. The comprehensiveness of the term obviously puts everyone into the schizoid category, and Fairbairn accepts that this is so because at the deepest levels of the psychic organization there is invariably a degree of splitting in the ego. The universality of dreaming proves this, because the figures in dreams are representations of organized parts of the personality or internalized objects with which some of these parts have a relationship. The figures are thus personifications of the split parts. Although there is an obvious correspondence between Jung's introversion and schizoid processes, he prefers the latter term because it is explanatory in relation to psychological development in contrast with Jung's purely descriptive term.

Adults with marked schizoid features have amongst others three prominent characteristics, even though these may not be overt. They are: (a) an attitude of omnipotence; (b) an attitude of isolation and detachment; and (c) a preoccupation with inner reality. As he subsequently points out, it is the last that is the basic feature since the others are derivatives of a situation in which relationships with the outer world have been accorded less emotional significance than those in the inner world. It has to be emphasized, I believe, that these characteristics have one common feature, namely, they are attitudes of a whole person, and since they have such very early roots, they point to the functioning of the ego as a whole from the beginning.

Having placed the organization of experience and its disruption as the fundamental issues in our understanding of personality, his next consideration must be how it develops. The current psychoanalytic language with its mixture of descriptive and explanatory terms here begins to hamper his exposition. He gives Freud's 'ego' the common status of an entity, the ego which operates as the main agent determining development. As stated earlier, had he been writing in later years he would certainly have used 'the self'. I shall therefore use this term in what follows when the reference is to the system of the sentient matrix of the individual's psyche which responds as a whole and within which development produces various divisions or subsystems. The ego and self are taken to be synonymous at the start. When separated systems such as the future super-ego have begun to form, then the ego will refer to the central system within the original matrix which copes with the impact of the outer world. In this task it operates in many ways, for example by assimilating experience or by deflecting it into subsystems.

Following Freud, Fairbairn takes the most important function of the ego to be the adaptation of primal instinctive activity to outer, essentially social, reality. For this purpose perceptions of reality have to be integrated and behaviour matched accordingly. The evolution of man's mental equipment, with its capacity to make imagined relations, introduces the further need to discriminate between his inner and outer worlds. These functions cannot be carried out except through a system operating as an organized whole, or at least through an organization that is comprehensive in its sentient capacity so that the environment can be widely scanned and sufficiently discriminated to direct information to the appropriate system. At the start, therefore, Fairbairn assumes this primal unity with splitting as a consequence of the clustering of experiences into sub-selves. Leaving for the present some of the implications of the concept of splitting, we can at this stage accept his adoption of Melanie Klein's view that splitting has a general damaging effect of distorting and inhibiting the intellectual and emotional development of the child. It is also to be noted that Fairbairn's statement about early splitting often not being overt in the adult implies a further feature of the personality, namely, the subsequent development of a more superficial synthetic layer of organization. In this way the self seeks to cohere as far as possible rival systems into common purposes and activities evolved from later social and other realities to fit with their goals.

Schizoid phenomena are fully recognized by Fairbairn as having long been a concern of psychoanalysts. In terms of the libido theory, they were held to originate in the early oral phase, and he therefore assumes that splitting of the self begins under its influence. In his considerations of the making of the infant ego he condenses much that has to be teased out. The first issue is his use of the word 'libidinal'. From all that he wrote in the past and in the later papers, he does not equate it with sexual or with libidinal phases. One of his early papers suggested 'sensuous' as a better term, and he used it in discussion to include the specific quality of affect attending the appetitive instincts, that is, those involved in bodily needs, as contrasted with the reactive tendencies related to dealing with the environment. Both classes of instinct when active are experienced as 'needs', though the appetitive ones differ in being satisfied only by much more specific bodily activity with feelings described by the term 'consummated'. In view of the direction he was about to take, the retention of the adjective is confusing. On the other hand, he had to take the current analysts with him, and the classical adjective perhaps helped to draw attention to the view that the psychological need for the mother was just as much an imperative incorporative demand as that from the body. His use of the term 'libidinal objects' in these early writings has therefore to be understood as including the classical meaning at times but also the objects of instinctual interest to the person as a whole. 'Libidinal' is therefore an affective quality characterizing certain needs, mainly in relation to bodily processes although in his view certain primary psychological needs have this hungry, appetitive quality, for example, the need to be loved as a person. He recognized later that it was quite inappropriate to use 'libido' as a noun implying an entity, a special kind of energy.

Fairbairn distinguishes four features of the early oral attitude that shape the adult personality. The first marks his departure from the classical libido theory, because the libidinal object, that is, *the primary object that is sought by the primal instincts, is in his view the mother as a whole person*. This is the crucial statement that separates Freud's theory, founded on instinctive energies internal to the infant, from one that views development as a creative emergent from innate factors that occurs only through the psychological factors in the mother–infant relationship. The infant's need for a person who treats him as a person is a highly condensed statement directed at factors in both parties, and it is one that cannot be explained by the libido theory. What is referred to is a clearly felt need in the infant to be recognized, accepted and responded to as a unique autonomous being, yet a being that can only exist through being in relationships. Whatever its metapsychology would be, this need, while being incorporative, involves something holistic at a distinctly psychological level for satisfactory development.

Fairbairn was writing long before the studies of infant development and of mother–infant relations showed that a great deal went on in the perceptions of the very young infant at the inter-subjective level. In retaining the term 'libidinal' he confuses us further by condensing a whole complex of interaction and development proceeding independently of libidinal zones by asserting that the ego of the infant is 'a mouth ego'. The holistic need at the whole-person level has to be separated from what might be mediated by the mouth, although the mouth is of the greatest importance. Every one of his patients brought out abundantly the continuity of experience of serious emotional deprivations and a strong sense of things never having been right in their earliest relationships in the family, with the conflicts and inhibitions in their personal relationships as adults. These factors also spread their influence to create disorders and incapacities in other fields, for example in work and in the general investment in, and enjoyment of, 'the business of living'. In short, what stood out irrefutably in his schizoid patients was the failure to develop a capacity to make normal relationships with others and within themselves, and this failure distorted the effectiveness of the person in relating to the world in general.

At this point there is no further elaboration of this statement about being loved as a person, which to some extent gets lost when he switches to focus on the breast. His findings now give rise to a further fundamental assumption that the breast becomes the libidinal object in proportion as deficiencies in the personal relationship with the mother as a whole have occurred. There is an agreement with Melanie Klein's emphasis on the prominence of the part object, but he takes an opposite view to hers on its origin. She takes the breast as the primal part object because the infant is not yet capable of perceiving the mother as a whole. If the suckling relationship goes well, that with the mother as a person will grow from that. Fairbairn assumes that, although the more sophisticated perceptions of later stages cannot be present at first, the mother's attitude is sensed nevertheless. If denied the experience of a warm maternal acceptance, the infant is driven to an excessive investment in the breast itself for the satisfaction of its more general longings. This interpretation of the earliest experience also reverses Freud's theory of the oral pleasures of the breast feeding as the primary aim whose adequate satisfaction establishes the right basis for future development. The recent findings showing perceptions to be innately much more holistic in character than was formerly conceived, as for example in the phenomena of transmodal perception, and so a simultaneous sensing of aspects of the mother by modalities other than in sucking can be understood as a reality from phases much earlier than hitherto thought possible (see Stern, 1985).

Fairbairn accepts the great importance of the breast itself. Here, however, he takes a broad biological view of the essential relatedness of the organism with its environment. What is quite unusual in the light of much future theorizing is the way he brackets the bodily needs with the psychological, thereby making the development of the psyche 'belong to biology'. Thus, amongst the early oral features, while regarding the infant's need for the breast to be one of *taking* rather than *giving*, the *incorporation* and *internalization* change the feeling of emptiness; and he stresses this pattern as equally applying to the personal needs. These are distinct psychological processes through which adaptive learning with internal structuring take place. The psychological frustrations of his adult patients had clearly contributed to these retrospective assumptions about feeding. Further points he makes about the suckling in a further feature are that (a) the infant's sensing of emptiness and fullness must include his mother too and so, when he is full, he has emptied his mother; (b) a potentially pathogenic situation can then arise when a sense of frustration and deprivation has been present. The incorporative need acquires an aggressive greedy quality so that he seeks to incorporate more and more from his mother. And since she usually leaves him after his feed, the experience of the breast becomes associated with the anxiety not only of emptying it but of destroying his libidinally needed object. It is these features that can become intensified and perpetuated and hence underlie subsequent schizoid characteristics and symptoms.

Having inferred these organized patterns of experience in the earliest phase of development, the future influence of each is now considered. There is, of course, a circularity here, as it was the schizoid characteristics in the adult from which he started. His more detailed correlation of the hypothetical early experience with later behaviour is valuable, however, because the original 'hunch' is inevitably only loosely attached to what it is going to develop into, and he now checks, so to speak, the goodness of fit. Taking first the schizoid tendency to treat people as less than persons with an inherent value of their own, he relates it to an unsatisfactory emotional relationship with the mother and later the father. The deficiency for the infant stemmed from 'the mother who fails to convince her child by spontaneous and genuine expressions of affection that she herself loves him as a person'. The sense of something missing forces the child to simplify the relationship by depersonalizing the object as was done in the regressive focus on the breast. Bodily contacts are substituted for the emotional deficit due to gaps in the mother's personal emotional input to the total feeding experience. The child cannot sustain a joyous personal attitude in the relationship when this has not been adequately experienced as coming from the mother and so never structured as a spontaneous pattern in his later relationships. Such people subsequently treat others as 'things' in relationships from which emotion has been permanently withheld.

In considering the significance of the characteristics of the early oral stage, there is again great emphasis on the bodily processes. The future capacity for relationships with the outer world is heavily influenced by the alimentary patterns of relationship because of the deep primal emotional equivalence between the bodily and mental contents. The influence of the incorporative tendency as a general mode of relating can be readily accepted if we assume the infant has to satisfy 'hunger' for experience and 'knowledge' of the environment, and that these emotional qualities are all structured within the holistic self. Taking, however, has to be considered in relation to giving, which is especially inhibited in the schizoid character. Freud had early on established a close connection between the excretion of bodily waste and later character formation, but, as with the oral phase, the significance of anal behaviour lay in the pleasure, or interference with it, from the bodily zones. The social relationships involved were mainly acknowledged in the notion of faeces as a gift. Fairbairn takes the earliest psychological significance of faeces to be that of creative activities. Their widely accepted symbolic function of representing bad or dangerous objects to be eliminated is for him a later development. The sense of giving in excretion is, of course, almost entirely dependent upon the mother's pleasure in the infant's achievement of beginning control. With the earliest anxieties about states of emptiness, insecurities in the infant–mother relationship tend to be defended against by storing up bodily contents, and the schizoid consequence is the great reluctance to part with mental contents.

This need to keep his feelings to himself creates a marked impression in others of the individual as being shut-in emotionally, or of being a cold fish when, in more severe conditions, the repression spreads to affects in general. With the growing pressure to be involved in social relationships, the schizoid individual may learn to play, consciously or unconsciously, social roles with quite a lot of feeling and apparently good contact with others. This behaviour is mediated by more superficial structuring of experience, as is seen when analysis makes plain the split between the role-playing self and the secret inner one.

Another important manifestation to emerge from the analysis of his patients is the prominence of exhibitionistic trends. For Fairbairn, such activities are taken as a means of avoiding the anxiety over giving by substituting 'showing' instead. He observes, too, that a common feature of such a defence is the breaking through of the underlying anxiety attached to giving. Noteworthy here is the restriction of his thinking to pre-phallic stages. Also, the specific motive of wanting, and, indeed, of needing, the self responded to with approval – as a normal feeling accompanying achievement – is given an inadequate status.

The regressive reactivation of the incorporative factor in the later 'greedy' attitudes to others he emphasizes again as rooted in the traumatic quality of the child's feelings of not being loved and of not having his own love for his mother accepted and valued. The consequences of this situation are therefore: (a) the mother becomes felt as a bad object for not loving him; (b) since there is so little regard paid to his own love, the child feels it must be bad and so he keeps it inside himself; and (c) love relationships with people are bad in general, or at best precarious.

Such a profound mistrust of the outer world leads, as with the earliest frustration at the breast, to a hypertrophy of incorporative attitudes with a building up inside the mind of a store of objects with which he can make relations in phantasy. In keeping, too, with the differentiation of external and internal being unstable in the early phases, the self feels strongly identified with its internalized objects. This aspect adds to the difficulty in giving because of the feeling of being emptied – a touching illustration being that of one of his artist patients who felt that virtue had gone out of him after he finished a picture. Various defences are used to mitigate this painful feeling of deprivation, one of which is a strong attraction to intellectual processes. Often the attempt is made to work out intellectually some way of making better emotional relations with people, but the deep anxieties attaching to that vulnerable activity soon emerge to stop them. The emotional investment in the inner world becomes highly intensified and so can offer great satisfaction to the self, either through creative activity with products that may be greatly esteemed by others, or by fusing auto-erotic satisfaction with the inner phantasied relations, especially in the perversions. Nevertheless, ideas and intellectual processes are here substitutes for the relationships whose natural expressions belong to those with others. There is thus a profound split between the part of the self that sustains these higher conscious levels and the parts in which the primal feelings of the earliest experiences established their patterns of relating. Fairbairn concludes that this split, the commonly described split between thought and feeling, arises from repression carried out by the later and more superficial part of the self. In the severe disorders such as the schizophrenias and the grossly schizoid personalities, the split is obvious. He returns, however, to his remarks at the beginning of his paper on the widespread incidence of splitting, often unconscious, which manifests itself in so many kinds of obsession and fanaticism, with intellectual creations substituting for the deficiencies in the relationships with the parents. This theme at the time of his writing was an intrusive one which Hitler was demonstrating so devastatingly.

The deep attachment to the inner world with the freedom to manipulate its relationships establishes a great sense of omnipotence and grandiosity. Not always revealed, these trends remain extremely resistant to exposure and change in analysis. The intensity of the clinging to them is paralleled by an equally intense effort to keep them secret – a situation all too understandable when we keep in mind their function of giving the highly vulnerable and frightened self an inner fortress, built on the security of possessing relationships, even if only phantasied, against the pains of 'narcissistic wounds' as the classical terminology put it. Fairbairn does not spell out the source of the greatest anxiety to the emerging self, namely its disintegration into madness, if these inner objects are lost. Nevertheless, he does observe that they are felt to be as precious as life itself. The development of a self is, in short, inconceivable without relationships.

The other early oral factor he discusses is the implication of the emptying of the mother following incorporation and the further consequence of her disappearing, namely, of being destroyed when she puts the baby down. This dilemma is illustrated by Little Red Riding Hood being left alone with her incorporative need in the form of the wolf in her grandmother's place. Normally this anxiety over the devouring of the loved breast/mother is worked through with the experiencing of mother's repeated returns with her expressions of joy at reunion with the baby. Fairbairn now draws the necessity of distinguishing between the situation in the later oral phase when biting occurs alongside sucking. From the first phase, the sucking experience makes a template for all future relationships with loved figures and of social relationships in general. This first relationship he holds to be pre-ambivalent since the child comes to feel the lack of his mother's love to be due to his having emptied and destroyed her. The reason her love is withheld is that his love is bad. This is a much less tolerable situation than that in the later oral stage when hate develops. Here he refers to Klein's view of the depressive position in which the child's love can remain good, because it is his hate that has caused the destruction. Good love can undo the latter by reparation. Following her terminology he suggests for the pre-ambivalent dilemma the term *schizoid position*.

To him it is an essentially tragic situation in which what is meant to be love destroys 'the thing he loves', as Wilde expressed it, a haunting theme for so many poets and writers throughout man's history. This schizoid dilemma adds another reason for the schizoid keeping his love inside himself. It is not only too precious to part with, but it is too dangerous to release. One consequence of that feeling is that the love of others will be equally devastating, so that he must not be loved at all. Indeed, many schizoid characters are carried by this anxiety to the point of inducing others to hate them rather than to love them. Thus the schizoid's condition involves two tragic dilemmas: (1) he must not love, because his love is destructive; and (2) he must avoid being loved by hating others and making them hate him. To these there have to be added two further reasons for substituting hate for love.

First is what Fairbairn calls an immoral motive, because it involves adopting the joys of hating since love is denied him. Second is a moral motive in the policy of it being better to do the inevitable destruction by hate, which is bad, than by love, which is good. He then finishes his paper with a third tragedy for the schizoid person, wherein he may be driven to adopt a reversal of moral values. For this situation he draws upon the Miltonic reference that not only is it a case of 'Evil be thou my Good', but also of 'Good be thou my Evil.'

THEORETICAL IMPLICATIONS OF THE 'SCHIZOID POSITION'
The genetic accounts given for the major schizoid phenomena have carried
widespread conviction and Fairbairn has proved the value of the analytic approach to this group of patients who had been hitherto deemed as generally
not suitable for it. His findings add up to the necessity for analysts to gain
understanding of their patients' problems by approaching these with an open
empathic attitude resting on an inner world that does not constrict their perceptions by either intellectual or emotional rigidities. From what we have
learned of Fairbairn's inner world we can see its reflection in almost every
observation he makes. The early environmental deficiencies he had encountered, to use Winnicott's phrase, had later been added to by a strong sense of
injustice about how his mother had responded to his sexual curiosity in childhood. His own early anxieties and inhibitions in relationships with others let
him respond to his patients' withdrawn and negative attitudes as defensive
expressions of their anxieties over very different longings towards himself in
the transference and in their closer contacts with the figures of their inner
worlds. Melanie Klein's work had shown him how powerful these inner
worlds are and how they can be made conscious when the analyst is sufficiently freed from anxiety to stay with them and not to impose a framework of
interpretation whose lack of fit with what the patient feels puts him back into
the frightening early world in which he was unrecognized and not understood.

Freud had the empathic capacity for permitting his patients to expose
much of what they felt anxious and guilty about, a capacity that became
more comprehensive as his experience enriched it. He had an extremely
toughly integrated ego with which to foster this process, a quality uniquely
strengthened by the self-analysis his patients stimulated in him. The sexual
manifestations in his patients made the libido theory enormously illuminating.
On the one hand, its biological roots plus the notion of energies that had
a reality in the physical world gave a 'real', and so a 'scientific', basis
for the strange new explorations he was making. On the other hand, the
conflicting impulses towards the family figures gave powerful sources for
the anxiety and guilt attached to the sexual instincts. It all had a remarkable
cohesion and explanatory conviction from which to underpin an instrument
of investigation with startlingly new power. Within his own self there were no
splits from relationships with 'bad' parents that were sufficiently pathological
to inhibit the quest into the dangerous areas of the unconscious. Melanie
Klein also had the security in her self to take the analytic approach into the
worlds of young children, in whom the directness with which unconscious
phantasies were expressed evoked in her radical new formulations. She had
the freedom from severe and over-idealized figures in her inner world to

accept the full scope of the young child's remarkably concrete descriptions of his phantasies, especially of destructive hate. Like Freud, she could take for granted an ordinary degree of integration of her self and so view what she saw as the struggle of the child's ego with the great instincts conceived as impersonal drives.

Fairbairn's intellectual powers, whose development had been valued and fostered by his 'good' mother, were linked to his lack of security in the deeper layers of his self and with others and to the undermining influence of the savagely anti-sexual and controlling side of her personality. This later incident is but one example of what he felt had been there previously. Acceptance of her young son was highly conditional from the start. The defensive power of his early intellectual interests in the outer world was such that he effected a notable splitting off from this central self of the original bad-mother experiences. The inner worlds of his patients, reacting with the corresponding sources of anxiety in himself, inexorably took him along 'the line of thought' he referred to in the Introduction to his book as having been there from the early days of his analytic experience. The splits in his patients arose from their experience of the 'bad' mother, starting from the earliest phase and continuing throughout childhood. The difficulties Fairbairn had in integrating his sexuality and masculinity into his ego had little to do with the maturation of the erogenous zones of the libido theory. They had their source in the hostility of his mother installed permanently in his personality. The strength of his intellect, backed by the support of his 'later' mother, even against his father, in the central part of his self was such that he could use the impact of Melanie Klein without a massive retreat from, or denial of, the importance his deep feelings accorded to it. We recognize, however, that his acceptance was only partial. He had shared her view of the importance of oral sadism in the early phases, as was seen in the papers following her seminal contribution in 1935.

The importance of the inner world with its good and bad objects had been assimilated, but some serious disturbance had occurred around this issue of the earliest destructive phantasies. As he put it in his notes, his emotional problem had been converted into a physical one. This allowed him to preserve a great impetus to go forward intellectually on the contribution of the actual relations between the child and its mother and father. His achievement was the radical theoretical one of going, as Ernest Jones said, to the centre of the self to study its development. From this position, in which he felt amply supported by the experiences of his schizoid patients, he had to assert as a general proposition the inadequacy of a theory of instincts operating from innate energies seeking discharge. The conflicts over sexuality with their crippling anxieties and inhibitions could not be accounted for unless the responsibility for the disturbing reactions in the child was shared by the parents and their contribution. In this first paper, he described his clinical data which, despite the condensed presentation, establish the early environmental failures as the major aetiological factors in the splitting of the personality. To see his understanding being shaped by his own unconscious factors does not, of course, invalidate his views. All thinking is influenced in that way, and we judge theories by their goodness of fit with clinical data and their illumination of obscure areas.

To turn to his clinical observations, these are put in a form in which the behaviour of the adult schizoid is described in what may be termed a number of first-level abstractions. Thus he groups most of the manifestations according to patterns of the same form as those in the infant. The oral-libidinal fixation of Freud and Abraham, however, is taken as much wider in its origins than was envisaged in the libido theory. As mentioned, the adjective 'libidinal' described here a quality of affect pertaining to the urge to incorporate not only milk but also to internalize the rest of the experience of the mother and the outer world. The bodily satisfaction from sucking and the assuaging of hunger pangs make a dominant experience against a ground of more general 'stimulus hunger' that is also reaching out for satisfaction. It is also an experience with a firm and well-defined quality.

Fairbairn suggests that, though the incorporation of the experience from all that the mother as a person is giving is distinct from the more sharply defined feelings of sucking the vital supply of milk, it is, nevertheless, as essential as the feeding mother for the development of an effective personality. If it is not given, the infant is aware of something that is missing, and he compensates by intensifying the bodily incorporating experience to devour more of his mother than her milk and her breast. With more serious degrees of this lack of the personal input from his mother, there can be a progressively withering effect to a point at which, as Spitz's studies showed (1965), the loss of the urge to live and to grow as a person, as an individual with a joyous autonomous interest in the world, can shrivel the whole vitality of the organism to death.

The extraordinary feature of the development of psychoanalytic theory, and in the study of infant development, is the time it took to expose the fact that a basic force in the infant's psychological development is centred on this need for being treated as a person. Death of the self occurs in spite of hunger and other bodily needs being satisfied. Lesser degrees of the starvation of the self permit of survival but at the price of a future person with serious distortions and failures in the development of his capacities to relate effectively with others. The growth of the self, as we can best term this holistic force that is mediating the organization of the experience, is clearly founded on an extremely powerful and vital psychological process whose importance biologically is no less than that going on in the body. The two fields are obviously interconnected in the closest way, and yet it is the physical aspects that have been given an importance, virtually a reality, of a different order compared with the recognition of this autonomous force required for survival. Hartmann (1958) saw the need for its recognition, but the way in which his theory of the ego took shape perhaps helps us to understand this striking theoretical situation. For though he saw the necessity of recognizing an independent part of the personality, his ego was conceived as impersonal functions deriving their 'reality' from the biological energies of the libido and aggression, while the self was constituted from representations from ego activity. Fairbairn's self was such that he could not accept impulses as something which could be looked at as coming from outside the self. Too many of his 'impulses' had met with a painful and bewildering rejection. The oral fixations did not represent the failures of satisfactions at the breast as such, but were the result of a deprivation in the overall constellation of 'mothering'. The subjective experience of a powerful need to relate to the person the infant feels 'should be there' would have sources very different from a libidinal energy.

While the self has to be in satisfying relations with the mother as a whole person, Fairbairn is explicit about its autonomous differentiation from its objects. He was still aware of the reverberations from the controversy between the Viennese analysts around Anna Freud and the London group allied with Mrs Klein which was fuelled by different beliefs about when an infant could differentiate an object from its self. He found no difficulty in conceiving the infant as an autonomous organization which could sense from the start the difference between a real breast and a hallucinated one. This issue seemed to have arisen from assuming that the perception of an object as external would only be possible when it could have a fully developed content that only sub-sequent maturation could bring, instead of an activity which like every aspect of organismic growth had its embryonic precursors. His position is indeed identical with that of the later researchers in infant development. He sees the infant growing psychologically only within the environment of the mother's love, which treats him as a person and so engenders within his self the feeling of becoming one. Another source of difficulty in conceptualizing the infant's autonomous development was the current psychoanalytic conception of affects. This was largely inspired by Freud's early views which regarded the emotions as charges of energy derived from the underlying instincts. As such, they were often taken to have an independent status as stimuli for action. In the view of most British philosophers and psychologists, the emotions were the sensed specific quality that accompanied activity aroused by the innate propensities of the instincts. Every emotion thus had a quality of uniqueness from the situation in which action had been evoked. It was what was embodied in the everyday language when people said 'I don't know why, but I *feel x* is right (or wrong).'

This conception of the affects, not specified by Fairbairn, must have facilitated his intellectual work since it gives a metapsychological basis for the phenomena of splitting into clusters of similar affective tone. Furthermore, the experiences of relations with good objects could have structural biological underpinning not from energies, but from patterns in some form of fields of force which could merge or repel each other according to their compatibility. Subjectively, such interactions would be experienced with pleasure, a positive cohesive affect, in contrast with pain and its negative fields. Splitting, in other words, can be seen at the earliest phases as deriving from the properties of the central nervous system, as an innate rejection of what brought pain and thus had to be avoided. It follows, too, that the process of repression originates from emotional incompatibilities arising in later more sophisticated experience.

Fairbairn's pre-ambivalent splitting would seem to be of the earliest variety. It rests on the dichotomy between what is felt to be 'good' in contrast with 'bad', like the infant's spitting out or pushing away as he put it. Here we can get an impression that the bad, having been emotionally categorized in this way, can be pushed into the background. The rejection, however, is not carried out as an unemotional turning away but has, because of the frustration, 'an aggressive quality to it'. The 'badness' of the mother has little or nothing to do with an innate instinct of destruction but is there because of what she has not provided. The contrast here between his view and Mrs Klein's is sharp. For her the badness of the primal part object is a consequence of the intensity of the innate sadism or death instinct projected into it. The role of oral sadism had made a great impact on Fairbairn, as was seen in his short paper describing the reactions of three patients to the King's death. In this paper on the schizoid factors, the patients are disturbed by their negative reactions but these are conceived as originating from the feeling of having caused mother's lack of response or her disappearance. There is no hint of the innate ruthless aggression that characterizes Klein's oral sadism. Indeed it is quite remarkable that the words sadism or sadistic do not occur in this paper, and we may wonder if his symptom was creating a reaction formation.

Klein, in her paper on 'Schizoid mechanisms' (1946), while valuing his descriptions of developmental schizoid phenomena, considers that Fairbairn's rejection of Freud's primary instincts leads to a failure to understand the role which aggression and hatred play from the beginning of life. As a result of this approach, he does not give enough weight to the importance of early anxiety and conflict and their dynamic effects on development.

Apart from their different theoretical approaches, there can be no question that the aggressive reaction and the sadistic attacks had been recognized earlier in his patients – the young man in the present paper (1940, p. 13) whose dream is reported to illustrate the regressive depersonalization of the relationship with his mother was the same patient who 'had projected a considerable charge of oral sadism' upon his mother in the earlier paper – but the conspicuous absence here of the very word raises questions. His emphasis is certainly on the theme of what happens to the ego when the mother fails to convey to the infant that he is loved for himself. While he has drawn attention to a whole range of aetiological factors in the making of his case, we cannot but feel that the picture is more complex. Whether or not we believe in the death instinct as a primary motive in development, there can be little doubt that Mrs Klein established the role of violently aggressive reactions in the infant. Fairbairn acknowledges such feelings as having the features Klein describes when he refers to the development of hate once biting of the nipple starts. This hate, however, is for him a new and later development compared with an innate sadism. Yet we have to allow that, even before the infant acquires biting, the violence of his rejective behaviour can be of great intensity, as we can infer from the negative rejective reactions that are manifest, for example with its screams and its frantic pushing-away behaviour. Whether his conflict over his own urinary sadism was repressing too much is the question that comes to mind.

Publication of this paper had to be laid aside because of all the wartime restrictions. (At this time the Battle of Britain had recently preoccupied everyone, and the disruptions in London through the air raids were becoming serious.) His family arrangements were complicated. There was the travelling to Carstairs hospital three days per week and a good deal of travel to pick up his boys from school at weekends. His wife and he lived for some months in their home and then decided to move to Gifford, a village about twenty miles from Edinburgh. Small and pretty, it had an old-world charm and a sense of being a part of a stable society over the centuries. (John Witherspoon, the only theologian to sign the American Declaration of Independence, was born in the manse here in 1722.) At first in temporary homes, they acquired early in 1942 a lease of an attractive villa into which they settled a few weeks later and in which they lived for the next seven years.

With all these many demands upon him, especially since his wife was not in robust health following her meningitis, Fairbairn maintained both his clinical work and his writing. During the week he stayed in Edinburgh, where he had five or six analytic patients as well as his hospital work. He was also able in this way to keep in close contact with his widowed mother, now well up in her eighties. The drive to continue the theoretical task he had begun with his first paper was sustained at a high pitch throughout 1941, and his commitment was manifest to his colleagues in the hospital. He had described his goal as the recasting and reorientation of the libido theory, together with a modification of various classical concepts, and his next step was to suggest how the splitting of the ego originated. He completed this second paper by the end of 1941, and soon afterwards he read an abridged version to the Scottish branch of the British Psychological Society. Again the reception was appreciative and encouraging with discerning comments from some of the analysts who were now stationed in Edinburgh as part of a new unit set up by the Army to improve the methods of selecting officers. His title clearly expressed a major challenge yet his attitude, as seen externally, was never in any way an arrogant one. He felt his clinical findings left no option if psychoanalytic theory was to advance; there simply had to be 'A revised psychopathology of the psychoses and psychoneuroses'.

'A REVISED PSYCHOPATHOLOGY OF THE PSYCHOSES AND PSYCHONEUROSES'

In the accepted account of the development of the ego, he considers carefully the part played by the libido theory as formulated by Freud and later expanded by Abraham. The main consideration that permeates his arguments is again his conviction that the seeking of libidinal pleasure is an inadequate basis on which to found any biological theory of development. He had already asserted that the organism and its self can only be developed through the constant interaction with its environment; they cannot be considered apart. The paramount importance of the object-relationship had never been adequately assimilated, and it was largely by thinking of the organism in isolation that its development could be conceptualized in terms of urges towards libidinal pleasure. For him, it only made biological sense to view pleasure as a reward for finding the object. The concept of erotogenic zones with the object as the means of providing libidinal pleasure was to put the cart before the horse. He points out that in Freud's original version of the libido theory, the object reference was implied in the terms for its three stages, namely, auto-erotic, narcissistic, and alloerotic. In Abraham's scheme, however, the object disappears to be replaced by each phase being related to the libidinal aim. The oral and genital phases have biological objects in the breast and the sexual organs, and for Fairbairn only a biological object could justify each stage. Faeces are only a symbolic object. Furthermore, he believed that his findings demonstrate that the common classification of the psychopathological conditions cannot be linked to the different phases of libidinal development. Paranoid, obsessional, hysterical and phobic states on deep analysis all prove to be techniques of defending the self against the effects of conflicts originating in the early oral or incorporative sucking phase, or in the later oral biting phase. With inappropriate experience these phases are productive of two states, the schizoid, in which the autonomy and integrity of the self are endangered, and the depressive state, in which the functioning of the self is threatened with the loss of crucial object

relationships. For Fairbairn, these states are in a different category from
the other psychoneurotic conditions, for they represent ultimate disasters
to the self, and in order to avoid them the other conditions act as defensive
techniques. Moreover, because these conditions have this defensive function,
they are extremely resistant to change in analysis, and it is their tenacity that
gives them an appearance of having a biological origin similar to the two
disasters. Their status as protective reactions is also to be seen in the fact
that they are common precursors to the emergence of the more serious states.

Having abandoned libidinal phases, Fairbairn sees development of the
self as based on its relationship needs in successive stages. He has taken
here the biological perspective of considering the essential characteristics of
the adult self to which development is oriented. Thus, although not making
these explicit, he clearly sees 'the objects' required by the adult for effective
living as whole persons with their own unique identity. He takes mature adult
sexuality, for instance, as a component within a relationship which is to be
sustained for other reasons than sexual gratification. That the evolutionary
development of mankind is an important theme in the background of his
thinking is clear in the paper he had written a few years previously about
the survival of the family. With human beings, the individual is destined by
nature to be a social person. He has to acquire the capacity to live in mature
dependence with others, that is, with the full acknowledgement of their
'otherness' while sharing survival tasks that can only be done in collaborative
relationships. Fairbairn is imbued with this conception of what is innate in
humans for their development as persons being realizable only within the
setting of the family group. (This point was stressed by Yankelovich and
Barrett (1970, p. 388) when they quoted the anthropologist Malinowski: 'Sex
in its widest meaning is rather a sociological and cultural force than a mere
bodily relation of two individuals.' Fairbairn met Malinowski when he gave a
lecture in Edinburgh about 1932 entitled 'The sexual life of savages'.)

From this viewpoint, he describes the development of relationships as
stages within a process which started with the infant being predominantly
preoccupied with incorporating or sucking with regard to nutrition, and
psychologically 'taking in' from the mother, while completely dependent upon
her for the satisfaction of these innate personal needs. On reaching maturity,
this whole pattern has to change to one in which giving to others will be more
to the fore than taking. The core characteristic of this developmental process
is the incorporation of 'objects', that is, the assimilation of imagos of other
selves from which the individual's own self is to be fashioned together with
a perpetuation of imagos representing the objects with which an internal
relationship is maintained. The first stages include the two oral phases,
sucking followed by biting. The final one is not incorporative, since its aim
is in keeping with mature genital sexuality. The stage of transition between

them involves Abraham's two anal phases and the phallic or early genital one.

In most of Fairbairn's references, internalization and incorporation are virtually synonymous terms. He takes the standpoint of the infant's subjectivity in contrast to the more behaviouristic one commonly adopted in the psychology of cognitive development. In the latter, what is stressed are the constant perceptual and imaginal processes whereby the outer world is represented internally. There is here the adoption of the common analytic stance in which perceptual selection is of what is given significance or meaning by developing *Gestalten* in the self, and subjectively this is an act of incorporation, that is, one that is actively desired. The attribution to the personal self of the role of agent even in these early stages is very much in line with his stress on the 'personal level' of human functioning. With him this is no 'soft' humanistic thinking, but a deliberate emphasis of what he believed to be scientifically accurate, namely, that mental processes at a holistic or personal level are mediated by structures at this personal level. Indeed, it was not much more than a year previously that he had been asserting his criticism of academic psychology for being unscientific by ignoring most of what went on subjectively in the person. Over forty years later the infant researchers are moving increasingly into the importance of the subjective and inter-subjective factors of central importance in early development. In following his accounts this factor has to be kept in mind.

Internalized 'objects' are primarily imagos of persons, even though in the earliest stages the perceptual content may be embryonic. They are not neutrally or mechanically recorded representations, but are actively 'incorporated' into the inner world so that they can satisfy needs, or because they are attached to preoccupying concerns or threats. They are thus predominantly imagos of the significant family figures. The term unfortunately preserves the connotations of what discharges instinctual tensions instead of conveying the essential quality of being personal and inter-personal. Part objects are also internalized but often as 'deteriorated' or degraded substitutes for the whole person. When he writes of the internalized object as being a libidinal one, however, it seems he is using this term in a wider sense than the classical one, because he is usually referring to the need for the object that has a more complex origin than this term would usually indicate. At the risk of moving into the *élan vital* notion, there is the fact that the needs of the self stem from the wide range of forces that bond the living organism to the environment, and especially to the mother from whom birth has separated him: but it operates as a whole.

In his first paper Fairbairn describes the earliest internalized object as pre-ambivalent. With the later oral phase, frustration experiences lead to the splitting of the external object into an accepted one that is loved and a rejected one that is hated, both of which are internalized. Subsequent development is inevitably much concerned with the rejection of the bad object from inside the mind. Paranoia and obsessional neurosis, instead of deriving from the two anal phases, are to be understood as states patterned on excretory rejections. Hysteria is usually taken as rejection of the genitals because of oedipal guilt. On Fairbairn's proposed scheme of development, the oedipal situation does not originate in the triangular rivalries, but from the incestuous wish stirring up the earlier rejection of the demand for love, with one parent being treated as the accepting, and the other as the rejecting, object. Correspondingly, the hysteric's rejection of the genitals stems from an identification of them with the breast as the original part object in infantile dependence. Unlike the paranoid and the obsessional, the hysteric does not try to externalize the rejected object. It then forms the content of the characteristic dissociation. A further differentiating feature in the hysteric is that the attitude of giving love is retained in an idealizing love, that is, love with genital organs, and what they mean, is repressed.

The conflict in each of these conditions is thus between the developmental urge towards mature dependence upon the object and the clinging to infantile dependence. It is this clinging to the objects of the primal stage because of the failure of feeling loved when the self began to experience and to assert its autonomy that constitutes the central difficulty in schizoid individuals. Without the experience of being loved, the self cannot trust external figures, and since it cannot tolerate the anxiety of being without attachment to some figure it is compelled to hold on to what it has, despite a degree of badness. Hysterics retain the yearning for a breast as also do male homosexuals who, having failed with mother, hope to find it in the form of father's penis.

What happens in the transition phase is next discussed in more detail because of its importance in the development of the psychopathological patterns of defence. Though these may be laid down in the early phases, they do not become established firmly unless the parental patterns are continued during the post-infancy years.

A critical issue is how the nature of infantile dependence is conceived. Fairbairn assumes that it essentially rests on identification with the mother and anxieties associated with the process of becoming free from her. In referring to this identification, he does not use the word 'merged', although he does describe the maturation towards adulthood as becoming differentiated from this primary identification. I do not find it a satisfactory term, because it conveys a loss of the autonomy of the self in fashioning its own 'shape'. There is an assumption that the intense closeness or clinging the infant needs with the mother in this period somehow removes its psychological boundary and submerges the autonomous strivings of the infant. I believe, as Stern holds (1985), that it is more accurate to conceive of the developing self, not as absorbing a copy of the mother's self, but as requiring during this period of initial emergence of his self, with the feeling of being a person, a more or less constant input of the subjective states of the mother, and her empathic sensitivity to reflect, and more especially to encourage, the development of his own growing intentionality and selfhood within his own boundaries.

In recent years I have had experience with several individuals whose analysis many years previously had not changed a powerful feeling of never having achieved a confidence in their sense of autonomy. I believe there is here one of those issues so manifest that it has not been given adequate theoretical consideration for itself. To the external observer, the required closeness is what is noted and the notion of undifferentiation is an assumption about what is happening. No symbiotic relationship, however, takes away the thrust of the organism to realize its own nature; the acorn can only become an oak-tree. The growth in security and confidence in the self, however, rests on the extent to which the two independent subjectivities respond adaptively to each other. Given the right experiences, the infant moves with his own maturational thrust towards separation in his own time from this instinctively required closeness. When the developmental needs are not met, that is, when the self remains 'hungry' for the emotional experiences that will enable it to separate gradually, it remains fixated to the mother. Fairbairn describes the transitional stage by the two processes of identification and incorporation. He comments that apparently when the mother does not succeed in fostering the autonomous feeling, incorporation can proceed somewhat like a forced feeding, with the individual incorporating a mother who has incorporated him. This strange anomaly, he believes, may well prove the key to many metaphysical puzzles. For his own inner world, it may well reflect the deeper structures in his own self.

The conflicts of the transitional stage are thus focused on the growing away from this vitally necessary period of attachment to the mother, as Bowlby (1980) has stressed. The developmental urge, with its need for the mother's input to be incorporated, can give rise to fears of isolation, of emptiness and of the terror of having no figure at all, alternating with a compulsive clinging to the mother with the fear of being imprisoned or engulfed by her. In this latter connection, satisfactory development relies on the impetus in the infant being matched by the mother's understanding. Forcing her own image upon her child of what he should be can be as catastrophic as deprivation. The phobic state Fairbairn sees as derived from this conflict between being imprisoned or having no reliable self-feeling, as when enough good contact has been missing.

From this conceptualization in terms of the quality of the relationships in the inner world, he makes a neat table of the topographical positions of the accepted and rejected internal objects that give rise to the four main psychopathological conditions. Which technique is employed, and the extent to which it is used, depends on the nature of the objects incorporated in the phase of infantile dependence and the relationships established between them and the central self or ego. With the latter qualification he is allowing for the internal objects being influenced in their relative dominance by subsequent experience. As was being dramatically illustrated by many of the 'war neuroses' patients, traumatic changes in the outer world could upset the whole balance that the individual had reached in his particular environment. As a diagrammatic summary of the psychopathology of the four common psychoneuroses, the scheme has a useful fit with the foundation patterns of each.

From this exposition of their status as defences against the two states arising from the basic dangers to the development of the self and its ego, he proceeds to complete his theoretical understanding of what happens in these. Starting from the total dependence of the infant for his physical and psychological development, Fairbairn notes that there is only his mother, so that he has no choice but to accept her if he is to survive. This dependence, moreover, means that the infant proceeds from the uterine state and its absolute degree of identification with the mother who is presumably completely undifferentiated. The progressive differentiation goes hand in hand with the decrease in identification. The state of primary identification Fairbairn takes to be identical with primary narcissism, though this seems a gratuitous linking to classical theory with which his line of thought is incompatible. Secondary narcissism is the identification with an internalized object. In the early oral phase, emotional identification is merged with oral incorporation, which he considers to be a libidinal urge. Here he emphasizes as of the greatest importance that, while the object may be rejected or refused, the incorporative urge is not aggressive in aim. The affective state is pre-ambivalent and ambivalence does not arise. The conflict that can emerge is between loving equated with sucking, because the sucking has occurred with sensed expressions of the mother's love, or sucking which has become mechanical or depersonalized, that is, bad.

Because of the very limited resources of the infant at this stage, the outcome is much more critical than at any later one. There is the obvious dilemma that incorporation can lead to the loss of the breast, which at this stage is the affective focus; but with the good feed, the incorporative need dies down, and by the time it comes to life again the breast is once again full and loving. A failure in adequate good experiences has the most devastating effect for it means the infant's love is bad; the libido is no longer freely directed to the breast, which reduces the infant to a devastating impotence. The infant's whole existence is compromised because he loses the wish to express himself. The characteristic affect is thus one of futility, the feeling which later on can chill the analyst when the schizoid patient, overwhelmed by his despair, asks the question, 'What is the point?' When Fairbairn adds to these schizoid phenomena the intense self-consciousness, the sense of looking on at oneself, then for him the splitting of the ego becomes more fundamental than the impotence, because the withdrawal from others intensifies all these effects. The dependence of the self upon its relationships is beyond doubt. In acute schizoid states, the withdrawal of libido from consciousness can proceed until the individual is in the last phase of dementia praecox. Emotional tension can then be relieved and the danger of explosive outbursts lessened, but the underlying anxiety is frequently associated with the fear of madness and disaster. The individual approaching such a state feels he no longer exists. This is the ultimate disaster that is dreaded and the state to be defended against at all costs.

The depressive individual remains capable of relationships with external objects because he does not feel his love is bad. Nevertheless, he has to guard those objects, because his early experience has not fostered the development of a separate bad object which he can freely hate. This freedom requires the acceptance of his hate by the mother, who showed she did no permanent damage by her survival and the continuation of her love. His primal experience has left him able to make good relationships with external persons and with enough of this reassurance he can live quite successfully. With the loss of his libidinal relationships, his hate is turned upon his internalized object, leading to depression. Fairbairn here adds that because the depressive relationship with his internal object has retained the identification characteristic of infantile dependence, which is suffused with the bodily feeling, then loss of bodily parts or functions can readily lead to a depressive attack or to involutional melancholia. The internal object cannot then be restored.

Both of these psychologically crucial phases only reveal their full potential when the unsatisfactory aspects of the early relationships are continued in later childhood, and because they are frequently the result of the mother's personal difficulties, usually deprivations in her own childhood, the early patterns tend to be maintained. When the later experience provides more empathic understanding, then, if not undone, the pathological legacy of early lacks can be compensated in some degree. Subsequent histories also show that according to the circumstances of later life, the individual may have difficulties deriving from both schizoid and depressive factors. In relation to the existence of the two sources of psychopathology, he does not claim that they represent any more than phenomenological significance, and he does not ignore the possibility of hereditary factors contributing to difficulties at either phase. He notes in this connection the work of Kretschmer (1926), which was a prominent psychiatric topic in the earlier period of Fairbairn's career. Kretschmer postulated two basic psychological types, one predisposed to schizophrenia and the other to manic-depressive psychosis originating from constitutional factors.

The most striking feature about this second paper is the intellectual conviction with which Fairbairn builds his outline scheme for the understanding, and hence also for the treatment, of the psychological disorders. This conviction is clearly not itself an intellectualization of a defensive position. It is more like a manifesto for the full acknowledgement of the proper theoretical status of the psychological in psychoanalysis. Instinctual energies are quite incapable of being the philosophical assumptions on which Freud's work stands – and apart from the basic principles, no one was more respectful or more fully understanding of it. It was a uniquely creative feat to give Freud's edifice new foundations without detracting in any way from its importance. Fairbairn's views in some measure were anticipated by Suttie in his book *The Origins of Love and Hate* (1935). This book was known to him, and he thought it important. For Fairbairn, however, Suttie's arguments were apparently couched too much as a generalized protest without the carefully assembled clinical data and structural theory required – a view that was shared by Ernest Jones and Edward Glover, who did not dismiss it lightly. Harry Stack Sullivan's work, so close to his, was practically unknown in the UK at this time.

With the possibilities of publication slightly improved, he sent this paper to Jones, who accepted it for *The International Journal of Psycho-Analysis* and it appeared there in 1941.

THE 'WAR NEUROSES'

The experience Fairbairn had with the 'war neuroses' was a rich one. He was not involved in treating these patients but in making appraisals of their state when leaving the hospital. Treatment was discussed a great deal with him, though mainly in an informal way. When the hospital closed at the end of 1941 he continued to make appraisals of those discharged from the Services and who were being considered for possible pensions by the Ministry of Pensions. This was a complex situation, as his concern and interest in the patients' conditions had to be very carefully assessed when it came to attributing their incapacities to the effects of war service. He nevertheless managed to get a great deal of early history from these men as well as an account of their traumatic experiences.

From his experience he wrote two papers, one specifically about the origin and treatment of these conditions, while the other developed into a more general discussion of bad objects, their repression and the failure of repression. The first one was entitled 'The war neuroses'.

'The war neuroses – their nature and significance' was read to the Scottish branch of the British Psychological Society in December 1942. The psychiatrists and psychoanalysts who had been in Edinburgh for the first part of the year had now moved with their unit to London, and so the audience was smaller and less informed psychoanalytically. It was published in an abridged form about two months later in the *British Medical Journal* (1943), the journal covering the whole range of medical practice (Fairbairn had always wished to keep psychoanalytic work before the medical profession and the topic was of interest to a variety of groups at this time). The full version of his paper is the one included in his book.

Commenting on the enormous range of incidents that could act traumatically, he concluded that the chief common factor in these individuals was the trauma of being separated from their families and the figures there who fulfilled their infantile dependent needs. This factor was exposed in the universal prominence in these conditions of the compulsiveness of the desire to return home. Its origin was, as he had described in his 'Revised psychopathology', the persistence of the primitive identification with the mother because of the unsatisfactory early experience with her. Since the persistence of this identification had such a damaging effect on the capacity to form relationships, especially within the groups so essential in facing a common danger, the questions of the neuroses and of group morale have to be considered together. Indeed, the incidence of the neuroses in war is a criterion of morale and their treatment had, therefore, to be approached from this standpoint. One issue he was confronted with was the claim that the individual had upon the State when he had suffered from a war neurosis. Fairbairn pointed out that, while social rehabilitation was a matter for national concern, the question whether a pension should be awarded specifically as a *war* pension, in view of the considerations he had advanced, should be considered afresh.

When this paper appeared in his book almost ten years later, an anonymous reviewer in the *Listener*, the highly regarded publication of the British Broadcasting Corporation, made the rather pejorative comment that, since Fairbairn believed such pensions to have little justification from a national point of view, he ought not to be working for the Ministry of Pensions. Fairbairn was extremely angry at what he felt was a serious slur on his professional integrity and proceeded to institute legal action. I had never seen him incensed in this way and agreed to support him in court. The incident certainly emphasized how much his professional self was at the centre of his being. However, I got to know that the reviewer was not, as Fairbairn and I, too, suspected, Edward Glover. This seemed a surprising thought in view of his friendship with Glover, but he knew by this time of Glover's strange attack on the psychiatrists engaged in the War Office Selection Boards, several of whom were analysts well known to him, after he had paid an apparently friendly and appreciative visit to their unit. In fact the review was written by Geoffrey Gorer, the social anthropologist. He had obviously not assimilated Fairbairn's full statements on the issue and, not being a medical practitioner, did not appreciate the seriousness of his slur. (He also did not like Fairbairn's views on object-relations.) I felt the best thing was to get this situation settled without any legal proceedings, especially as Gorer was a friend of mine. I therefore talked to the literary editor of the *Listener*, who was very understanding of Fairbairn's concern. A full apology from Gorer was subsequently published in the *Listener*, and the matter was dropped.

REPRESSION OF BAD OBJECTS

The second paper arose from further theoretical considerations of the nature of the 'war neuroses' and especially of those in which severely traumatic experiences had occurred. Its title 'The repression and the return of bad objects', defines its scope and it appeared in the *British Journal of Medical Psychology* in 1943.

He distinguishes two main groups in the 'war neuroses'. The first included those states in individuals who could not maintain their integration when removed from the environment which had given support to the infantile-dependent factors in their personalities. The second group comprised those who had had severely traumatic events suddenly forced upon them. Losing the attachment to their good objects, the first group found themselves living, for example in the Army, in a highly persecutory world. The second group had suddenly been precipitated into situations in which they had to contend with extreme danger from a frightening world. The effects of these situations in which bad objects were released upon the individual, whether gradually or suddenly, had an immediate appeal as clearly related to what was happening to the relationships in their inner worlds. His understanding of these conditions had also the importance of contributing to an urgent national problem.

With his attention mainly directed to the instincts, Freud had focused on the repression of impulses. When he turned to the agency of repression, the ego, he had to postulate the super-ego as an internalized object with which the ego is identified. It is a good object for the ego whether it is obeyed or not. Internalized bad objects had been made prominent in Melanie Klein's work. Fairbairn's clinical findings all pointed to the prominence of bad objects as being repressed, one of those obvious phenomena which are often the most difficult to discover. He was struck, for example, by the reluctance of child victims of sexual assault to talk about their traumatic experiences. The common explanation at that time, namely that this repression was due to unconscious gratification, never seemed satisfactory to him. Fairbairn now saw the experience as reviving a relationship with a bad object. He also noted that victims were ashamed, a reaction which he attributed to the identification of the child with its early objects, bad or good. This observation he then linked with the way in which he had found delinquent children extremely reluctant to admit that their parents were bad, even when they were physically violent, drunk, and so on. In contrast, these children would readily regard themselves as bad, a defensive attitude apparently to make their parents good and to internalize them as such, a much more tolerable situation, because it gave a sense of security and hope. This manoeuvre he had named a 'moral defence'.

How do bad objects come to be internalized with such power over children is the question Fairbairn raises, and his answer is simple. They are not allowed any opportunity to reject them because the parents are too powerful to be resisted. He attributes to the children an attempt to control them by internalizing them, but their power as a rule makes the bad objects into evil spirits that possess them. The critical factor is that, whatever their power, they are internalized because the child cannot do without them. This moral defence belongs to a higher level of development than the original situation. It is the level of the super-ego. At the deeper level, the individual's guilt acts as a resistance since he releases his bad object if he gives it up. Fairbairn concludes that such release is too terrifying to be faced by most patients, and in analysis, the analyst has to become felt as a secure good object who can take away the patient's devils when he projects them into the analyst. His non-persecutory attitudes then show he has transmuted them.

This theme reminds Fairbairn of Freud's paper on 'A seventeenth-century demonological neurosis' (1923b), which has an amusing side for myself. He had been discussing the ideas in this paper with his colleagues in the hospital at Carstairs, and I happened to read Freud's paper that night. I was so struck by its relevance for Fairbairn's thinking that I telephoned him quite late, excusing my intrusion by saying I thought he would find it a good story. Hence his remark that he cannot refrain from directing the attention of the reader in search of a good bedtime story to this fascinating paper! It certainly supported his line of thought. It illustrated the essential goal of libido as the repressed object who, in the story, was the artist's father. Thus it highlighted the fact of the libidinal tie to the unconscious object maintaining the resistance to analysis. This conclusion was directly opposed to Freud's view that the repressed material itself offered no resistance. The evidence here pointed to the refusal of the libido to renounce its object, that is, Fairbairn was accounting for Freud's notion of excessive 'adhesiveness of libido'. Analysis has therefore, according to Fairbairn, to be directed at the repressed relationship with the internalized object. The libidinal strivings should be accepted as object love even when the object is bad, and caution should be exercised in relation to interpreting in terms of aggression. Again the relationship with his own father is called to mind and his anxiety over his hate being taken as his only feelings for him. The essential release of the bad objects within the transference is very different from a spontaneous release in which the main consequence is a paranoid terror of being attacked. It is the latter situation he found in the traumatic neuroses. When there is no therapeutic opportunity to dissolve the tie to the bad objects, the individual compulsively repeats the trauma until the bad objects can again be made unconscious. The ties to such bad objects become as a rule markedly sadistic or masochistic because of their intense frustration, and the persistent anxiety they arouse can be accounted for in Fairbairn's view without recourse to a death instinct as responsible for the compulsion to repeat.

His theme finally leads to the role of the group in treating such casualties from acute stresses. The super-ego has a highly positive supportive role as well as defending against bad objects, and the importance attributed to it by Freud (1921) in *Group Psychology* would suggest that the problem of neurosis on a social scale becomes one of group morale.

Again the vividness and sensitivity of Fairbairn's understanding impress us along with the cogency of his arguments when he starts from the actual data. It is interesting that though they did not have a great deal of time together, Fairbairn did have the opportunity of meeting Bion, who was in Edinburgh at the War Office Selection Boards for the first half of 1942. He was very impressed with Bion's work (see Pines, 1985) especially on the use of leaderless groups. Bion's later work at Northfield Hospital was based on his view that the treatment of neurosis in such situations as the Army at war must rest on the problem becoming a group one. The wide perspectives of these creative thinkers in psychoanalysis are particularly striking.

The special Army unit remained in Edinburgh for eight months, during which time Fairbairn met several of the analysts who were attached to it for short periods prior to moving to the new Selection Boards being set up. John Bowlby and I spent a day with him in Gifford, and John Rickman, Adrian Stephen and Eric Wittkower saw him in Edinburgh. Michael Balint was a visitor to Edinburgh in connection with his British medical qualification and he also spent a day with Fairbairn at Gifford. Many other psychotherapists, psychoanalysts and psychiatrists met him in this period.

A 'FINAL' EXPLANATION OF THE PSYCHONEUROSES

For much of 1943 his working pattern was back to that of the fully committed psychoanalyst. He was seeing daily eight to ten patients intensively, with a few consultations for the Ministry of Pensions in most weeks. The preoccupation clinically with the problems of the schizoid and hysterical conditions was paralleled with a thrust to take his structural theory into the form that he had long thought was necessary for psychoanalysis and, above all, directed to the problems of hysteria. The prominent role of the relationships with internal objects and the phantasies to which these gave rise must be the central concern. His formulations never seemed to come as sudden insights, but from the constant notes he made of the questions his day-to-day work raised.

What he felt to be a more or less 'final' formulation of the explanation of the psychoneuroses was written during much of 1944 and presented, as usual, since it was his only readily available opportunity, to the Scottish branch of the British Psychological Society in early October. The title, 'Endopsychic structure considered in terms of object-relationships', accurately conveys his aim. Psychological conflict at the personal level had to be accounted for in psychological terms, with no resort to speculative physiology, for example, to supply energies. The need to consider the psychic structure whose activity was 'the impulse' he sees in such concepts as 'sublimating' impulses. Patients, especially schizoid personalities, could revel in endless sadistic phantasies with floods of associations, all of which were practically unaffected by interpretations in terms of such impulses as their contents could reflect. Schizoid persons, indeed, seemed to obtain great satisfaction from providing the analyst with a dramatic display in which they are involved solely as observers and recorders. Fairbairn had come to realize that the important dynamics were in the identity of the figures playing the parts, several being split-off parts of the self while others were the persons with whom these sub-selves had or wished to have a relationship. The repression of one part of the self by another had been introduced by Freud in the activity of the super-ego, and it appeared that 'the impulse' being repressed was embodied in another figure acting as part of the self. There was thus a need to postulate a number of sub-egos, or sub-selves.

Looking at the origins of this failure to put the object relationship to the fore, Fairbairn was impressed by the degree to which Freud's structural theory had been stimulated by the phenomena of melancholia, as also were the views of Melanie Klein. He found this influence difficult to reconcile with his own clinical experience, in which the central problem of most psychoneurotic suffering seemed to be schizoid and not depressive. Melancholic depression in fact was not a frequent symptom in those seeking analysis. He refers again to the prevalence of futility and not depression as the characteristic affect in so much disorder. Futility can produce in so many individuals a state of inertia or apathy, physically and mentally, for which 'depression' is an apt word. It is the failure to distinguish this despondent aspect from melancholic depression that has helped to perpetuate the avoidance of the more intolerable schizoid position. This neglect is also greatly increased by the extent to which the common neurotic symptoms cover it.

Fairbairn believes the central importance accorded by Freud to the depressive phenomena of melancholia was largely due to the need to deal with the problem of guilt. His concern about subjecting this issue to critical appraisal leads him to repeat his views that it is not adequate to derive it from the Oedipus situation and the evolution of the super-ego. It has origins much earlier, as Klein advocated, but for Fairbairn, there is the almost passionate urge to reassert the phenomena preceding her depressive position, that is, the phase in which the first expression of the need for the object is made to feel bad because of the failure of the mother in the attitudes with which she gave the breast. As he stated in the paper, 'Schizoid factors in the personality,' the breast may well be the focus of interest, but it is a part object within the *Gestalt* of the whole object, that is, the loving mother. The mother who does not give her love unconditionally at the start lays the foundation for the 'bad' mother being established internally. In this intolerable situation, the infant identifies with this bad, persecutory mother, and in Fairbairn's view thereby adds a component of guilt that is not in keeping with the massive inhibition of libidinal needs that so frequently occurs in hysteria. The latent urges to get this issue properly understood culminates in his plea to go back to where Freud started it all, that is, to hysteria.

The structural consequences of his line of thought that what was repressed were not bad impulses but bad objects, now crystallizes for him in the analysis of a woman who had come originally for the relief of her frigidity. He had remarked in his first paper that he had come to conclude that dreams, instead of being wish-fulfilments, were primarily the enactment of relationships amongst the different parts of the divided self. The figures in the dream were representations of those persons, or parts of persons, with whom the individual was currently concerned.

The analysis of this dream is an outstanding piece of sustained analytic work in its attempt to do justice to all aspects of the suffering and conflicts of the patient and so to provide an appropriately comprehensive theory. She is presented as having a personality or self that is a perpetual cast of characters in conflicts that range in the depth of their contents from the relationships of everyday life to the savage hate in the most primitive frustrating relationships. The manifest dream presented four figures: (1) herself subjected to attack and the alternation of this attacked figure with (2) a man into whom it turns; (3) the actress who is the attacker; and (4) her husband who is a helpless onlooker. To these Fairbairn adds another figure, namely, (5) the dreamer as the observer and recorder. He notes that it was only as the dream developed that the attacked self changed to the man, and he then suggests that, had the dream continued, the attacking figure would have revealed that it was a composite of the dreamer and her mother. There are thus six figures in the dream and he then notes that these can be grouped into three ego structures each of which has an object with which it is in relationship. One is the dreamer's central self, and the others are subsidiary egos cut off from this central self of which they had been parts. One of them is the object of attack from the mother. Because there is little guilt present, Fairbairn regards this attack as not coming from the super-ego, but from a level beneath this, from an attacking ego he describes as an 'internal saboteur'. The structural implications thus led him to abandon any attempt to understand the inner situation in terms of the traditional tripartite theory and to postulate an original ego structure split into: (a) a central ego, the 'I'; (b) a libidinal ego; and (c) an aggressive persecutory ego. He further concluded this pattern was a universal one.

Having delineated the ego structures, he has to consider what is involved in the relationships they make. The central ego of the dreamer is closely related to her husband, who is very important to her. He was very much in her mind on the night of the dream, as he was due to come home on leave from the Services the next day. Her attitude to him is ambivalent, especially in regard to marital relations. Her libidinal attitude to him is a severely repressed one (her presenting symptom was frigidity), and her aggressive feelings towards him are also hidden. The primitive need for him is seen in her getting a sore throat on the night of the dream, an event that had happened on previous occasions. In the dream, however, the libidinal ego alternated with a man closely associated with her husband. Her longing for him is thus present, but deeply repressed from contact with her central self. Her aggressive feelings likewise are kept away from her central self and embodied in the 'internal saboteur' which is primarily attacking her husband, and only secondarily the libidinal self. The libidinal attachment therefore is apparently of the primal identificatory nature, for it to persist against the suffering it causes. Fairbairn refers to her anxiety on awaking from the dream and comments that what he has described as going on within the relationships casts light on Freud's original conception of neurotic anxiety as libido converted into suffering, a concept he had always found difficult to accept. The apparent passivity of the central ego towards her husband thus covers the repressed aggressive feelings absorbed in her internal saboteur which attacks her sexual self as well as its objects. In short, he is illuminating such otherwise obscure statements as 'aggression turning against the self' or 'libido turning into anxiety'. The internal saboteur, or *rejecting* object because of its disruptive effects, must in Fairbairn's view be tied to the self or ego in a relationship of primitive identification.

With his conviction of this basic endopsychic situation as a tripartite one, with the three ego structures constituting it as the standard pattern of development, a comparison with Freud's description of the psychic apparatus must be made. There is a general correspondence between the two conceptions but important differences exist. Freud's ego derives its activity from the instinctual impulses which fuelled it with their energy. From these energies are constituted the drives to discharge tensions, with consequent pleasure, and the ego organizes experience with reality into which it is driven. Fairbairn's central self is the sentient organizer of the organism's inherent needs to be interacting with the environment. It thus is in a permanently dynamic state, activated at times by specific instinctual stimuli from within and other stimuli from without and endowed with the means of encoding experience to foster optimal adaptation of the whole. As the main organizer, it cannot be other than a unity from the start.

Fairbairn does not put his basic conception into those more modern terms, but his whole outlook, in keeping with modern biology, views all organismic development as a process of differentiation from the encounters with the appropriate environment. (In papers written shortly after this one he declares this influence.) It is from the organization of early experience that the central ego separates these clusters of painful experience around specific figures as incompatible with the emotional tone of the central self. It is clear that he is conceiving the whole self as the organizing agent from the start. The two sub-selves can be seen as consequences of unsatisfied needs. First, as parts of the total open system of the self in action they are also selves, although now they are sub-selves embodying restricted aims. The frustrated need for the optimal contact sought with the mother constitutes one part of the self which attempts to find satisfaction with the aid of the capacity to create appropriate internal imagos. Relationships with such figures will be readily conceived as fashioned by the rapidly developing symbolic action in phantasy and play when need arises. In parallel with this relationship, there is established another in which experience evolves an image of the negative response from the mother to the self for having such needs. These sub-selves being part of the self in action have aims that are incompatible with those of the central self which is seeking to make the best adaptation to the mother as she is. They, therefore, have to be segregated by the central self from its adaptive organization. Thus what is split off are dynamic systems embracing a part of the self with the related object. These are not 'anthropomorphic concepts', as has been said of Fairbairn's scheme (see Greenberg and Mitchell, 1983, p. 167), because each is the essential 'anthropos' in integrated goal-directed behaviour, but in conflict with another human being. There is no physical substrate conceived of as a more 'real' reality and to which Fairbairn is attributing human qualities. Indeed, it is in the essential spirit of Fairbairn's thinking that most theory seeks, wrongly in his view, to dehumanize the description and conceptualization of human action at the personal or holistic level.

In addition to the relationships of each sub-self with the central self, the two sub-selves have a reciprocal and powerfully dynamic relationship with each other. As an identification with the mother who rejects part of the libidinal self the internal saboteur is inevitably and permanently at war with the unacceptable libidinal needs. In addition to its hostility to the forbidden object, it also attacks the part of the self that seeks to get a relationship with it. What we note here is a change in the nature of the internalized objects for these are 'anthropomorphized' into dynamic imagos of people with human attitudes. The object of the libidinal ego is now 'exciting', in that it has the potential for giving satisfaction. The former 'bad' object is now actively rejecting as well as being rejected. In describing the dynamics, it is surprising to find Fairbairn, in spite of all his mission to eliminate the entities of 'libido' and 'aggression', retaining the language of 'the disposal of volumes of both aggression and libido'. This may be attributable in part to the wish to take his internal psychoanalytic audience along with him and not to be put off by too radical a change in their familiar concepts by losing their habitual language. On the other hand, I strongly suspect that in a vivid identification with this patient, his own deeper relationships were stirred up to the point where his hate of the bad objects in its urinary-sadistic form was intruding into the activity of his central self in its integrative activity. His hydraulic metaphors had a profoundly literal meaning.

We also note that whereas he was careful in his previous papers to view primitive rejection as getting rid of, without aiming to destroy, the object, here the patient's infantile rejection by his internal saboteur is 'vindictive' in a savagely destructive way. He reasserts, however, his view of aggression as reactive to frustration. Moreover, with the infant's situation in our culture entailing frequent separation from the mother, there is ample occasion for aggressive feelings to create sustained ambivalence.

While emphasizing the strength of the dynamics within the subsidiary egos, he says relatively little about the central self. Obviously the passivity here in regard to libidinal and aggressive feelings is relative to strength in the central ego. In the first instance, the patient has to use considerable power to repress both of the sub-selves and their objects sufficiently successfully to be a very effective person as a wife coping with her own difficulties and apparently with somewhat unsatisfactory conduct in her husband. The central self with its constant and expanding relations with the outer world enlarges its dynamics greatly with the satisfactions from all its achievements and the very real sense of being a developing achieving person. Fairbairn is not considering these aspects at this stage, presumably because he can take a lot for granted about this part of the self. We see more clearly now that for him the central self, the adaptive section of the self in which learning and planning take place, is synonymous with the ego in ordinary use. The sub-selves, being denied free interaction with the outer world, tend to remain fixed in their aims and scope, though not losing any of their dynamics – and indeed ever ready to exploit external opportunities in keeping with their aims.

His sense of achievement in formulating his scheme for the basic situation is perhaps expressed in the diagram he constructs to illustrate it. It is closely modelled on the one Freud used for the tripartite theory. He thus demonstrates that while he is challenging radically their philosophical assumptions, Freud's discoveries about the organization of the mind retain for him their original brilliance. The super-ego is a striking omission in it because of its primitive form being now in the internal saboteur, but as he had indicated in his previous paper he believes Freud's super-ego formed as the moral defence at a later period.

The origin of the basic endopsychic situation is manifestly in the early splitting of the self that he has maintained as being an inevitable universal occurrence. In particular, he is convinced that the schizoid position is the most appropriate basis for the understanding of hysteria, as his patient shows. The earliest frustrations make for the infant an ambivalent object of his mother. Fairbairn suggests that it is to cope with this intractable reality situation that the infant internalizes this 'bad' mother; he cannot see why a satisfying and available mother would need to be internalized. He uses here the term 'unsatisfying', because 'good' and 'bad' objects are commonly confused with 'desired' or 'undesired', and the frustrating object remains highly desired. It is then that the internal object is split into two parts, one that is 'needed' or 'exciting', and another that is rejecting; and each takes with it the parts of the ego attached to it when both are split off. Fairbairn in this paper seems to have in mind a slightly later stage of development than in the first paper, because he now speaks throughout of hate of the frustrating object, whereas in the 'Schizoid factors' paper the earliest rejection consisted in getting rid of the bad object – spitting it out, so to speak. What is striking about the earliest relationship in his view is the singularly devastating experience it is for the infant to express his need for the object and find nothing that fulfils it. For the slightly older child, the experience is one of humiliation and shame. At the earliest stage, as he has stressed, the experience is one of threatened disintegration. The schizoid dilemma is much more serious than the depressive one, because it establishes a permanent inhibition in regard to making personal relationships.

It is the rejection of the subsidiary self systems by the central ego that constitutes repression. The attachment to the repressed objects is clung to because they represent the original ambivalent attitude. The direct repression from the central ego is reinforced with regard to the libidinal object by the unconscious hostility of the internal saboteur. Libidinal components are thus more strongly repressed than aggressive ones. The latter are repressed by topographical redistribution if too strong.

Since Freud made the Oedipus complex the chief aetiological factor in the neuroses, Fairbairn examines where it fits into his scheme. For him, its place is occupied by the schizoid factor in the emergence from infantile dependence. Since Freud's original statement, the importance of pre-oedipal factors has been increasingly recognized, a finding that prompted Melanie Klein to postulate the start of the oedipal conflict in the infantile phantasies. Fairbairn spells out how he sees his basic endopsychic situation determining events. He had in the first paper stated that in the light of the development of the earliest conflicting relationships around the mother, the split in the ego from the ambivalence entailed a fresh look at what the child faces when the Oedipus situation arrives. The encounter with the father evokes the same difficulties of ambivalence with the same consequence of splitting him into a good and bad figure. The internalized bad father is likewise split into an exciting object of libidinal desire and a rejecting, internal saboteur. He takes the relationship with the father to be almost exclusively emotional, because the father has no breasts. Nevertheless, the unsatisfied component in the relationship with the mother leads the child to want the father's penis as a breast at first, a desire that is increased as infantile sexual phantasies appear. The ambivalence over the parents' genitals, Fairbairn regards as revealing itself in the phantasies over the primal scene, and by this time jealousies and rivalries are greatly affected by the quality of the relationships with the parents. Apart from the extent to which biological factors determine the issue, the psychosexual attitude of the individual is made up from a complex layering and fusion by successive objects. Good and bad genital figures of both parents are internalized, with various aspects from both being embodied in the exciting and rejecting objects. The frequency of inverted and mixed oedipal outcomes are thus accounted for by the variations in the internalized objects. Moreover, the salient influence of the original ambivalence to the mother emerges, according to Fairbairn, in the deep analysis of every oedipal situation, as also does the longing for the breast in all hysterics, male or female. The child thus constitutes the Oedipus situation for himself. The genesis of anxiety, as he described earlier, he believes is akin to Freud's early conception of the conversion of undischarged libido, because this tension evokes an intense threat from the internal saboteur.

After describing how he conceives the oedipal situation, Fairbairn has virtually completed the outline of his task. There is a close analogy between his views and Freud's. Freud's whole thought was concerned with object-relationships but he adhered to the concept of the libido as pleasure-seeking, that is without direction, whereas Fairbairn maintains it has an innately pro-grammed direction to seek specific objects, and pleasure is the affirmation of finding them. A more fundamental difference is his rejection of the concept of energy with aims. There is a looseness of language here that is out of keeping with his general thesis. He clearly is implying libido to be not an energy but an experienced quality of the innately structured activity of the organism that mediates the need for objects. As mentioned, he later drops the substantive and states libido to be a function of the ego. Fairbairn allows for Freud's views being dominated by the scientific philosophies of his time, in which energy was separated from structure. If for no other reason, a psychoanalysis which retained such basic principles would be totally out of line with modern science, and especially modern biology, and so a psychology founded upon dynamic structures created from experience would appear to be more likely to progress when on a better scientific basis. In support of this view, Fairbairn remarks that amongst the advantages that it would bring would be to provide a satisfactory explanation for group phenomena along with a much greater range of aetiological possibilities. Freud's theory reduced the main endopsychic drama to the conflict between the libidinal ego and the super-ego in its anti-libidinal capacity, that is, a dualistic one. Fairbairn's theory enables all kinds of psychopathological and characterological phenomena to be described by the complex relationships amongst a variety of structures and permits of justice being done to the understanding of symptoms as deriving from the personality as a whole.

The therapeutic task can be conceived primarily as reducing the original split in the ego by restoring to the central ego what was split off into the sub-egos, and also as to bring the internal objects into it along with their associated parts of the self. These topographic changes are difficult to achieve. The basic endopsychic situation, however, can be changed much more readily in its economic aspect by reducing the attachments of sub-egos to their objects and the aggression of the central ego and the internal saboteur towards their objects. The basic endopsychic situation is characteristic for hysterical states, and so it is a schizoid phenomenon.

Freud's only dynamic structure is the super-ego. Fairbairn has not conceived his internal objects to be dynamic structures but only as objects of such structures. They must, however, as structures be dynamic in some measure. He has adopted this course to avoid complicating his description and also to avoid diverting attention from the primary importance of the ego structures associated with them and which bring the internal objects into being. These objects can appear in dreams as highly dynamic, though it is often difficult to distinguish whether their activity belongs to them or to the associated sub-self.

The completion of the 'Endopsychic structure' paper marked the finish of his main task, and during the next several years his writing was confined to shorter papers in which he gives general statements of his views. As usual, there was also a regular output of occasional addresses to professional groups plus reviews of books which appealed to him.

When he came to publish his papers in book form in 1952, he prepared a careful synopsis of the development of his theoretical views, which was included in the book. In the course of this summary he recognized some contradictions between the views expressed in the 'Revised psychopathology' paper and this last one, and he therefore wrote an addendum in which he sought to resolve them.

The original internalized objects were the 'accepted and rejected' ones from which he moved to those termed 'exciting and rejecting'. He points out these adjectives refer to qualities of the objects, whereas the first descriptions refer to attitudes in the ego. The major contradiction, however, arises in the accepted object being a 'good' one, whereas the later terms refer to objects both of which come from a split in the 'bad' one. He suggests that the originally internalized object should be taken as the pre-ambivalent one that is both satisfying and unsatisfying. The unsplit ego then copes with it by splitting off both exciting and excessively frustrating aspects into separate objects. From these parts, the libidinal ego and internal saboteur along with their objects are created, while that part of the object not included in them becomes the accepted object of the central ego as a desexualized and idealized object. This is the form into which the child wants to convert his parents and so makes an ego ideal or nucleus for the super-ego. If the 'accepted' object in the scheme of the defensive techniques is taken to go with the central ego, then the 'rejected objects' can cover both the exciting and frustrating objects, since they are both parts of the 'bad' or 'rejected' object. In the scheme for the transitional phase, therefore, the 'rejected object' should now be replaced by 'rejected objects', with both objects treated in the various defensive techniques in the same way as the single one.

6 Consolidation and recognition

WITH THE END of the war, the Psycho-Analytical Society resumed its normal activities. Fairbairn, however, did not visit London often. When he did he met Glover, Jones and some of the senior analysts. Glover with his family spent a weekend twice with him in Gifford and there were occasional visits to Scotland by other analysts. In 1946 he read to the Society a statement of his basic principles with the title 'Object-relationships and dynamic structure'.

His introduction is unusually interesting in the light of what we know of his inner world. He states that his line of thought was stimulated after reflecting upon the protesting cry of a patient that the analyst was always talking about him wanting various desires satisfied when what he really wanted was a father. Fairbairn himself seems to have felt strongly that his own father, with his Calvinistic attitudes and his urination difficulty, was inadequate as a masculine model, not so much in the direct physical sense as in the man who had some of the dynamic quality invested in living and in the affairs of the world and contributing significantly to them, and especially the man who was stronger than mother. It was his father who took him regularly to Church and with whom therefore the figures of God and Christ were closely connected. After his father's death, however, Fairbairn joined the Anglican Church, in which his mother had been brought up. This step may have represented a deeper repression of his father that he was undoing in his symptom, now that his wife had become linked to the bad object. There is the theme of the missing father here and also in his interest in the painter described by Freud in his paper on demoniacal possession. He goes on to say of the recognition in practice by analysts of the importance of object-relationships, that the theoretical implications of this situation are left aside by them. He describes his various reasons for adopting a new standpoint with some aspects which he had not previously stressed, for example, the still prevalent atomism in science, involving building up the whole from components, rather than the modern biological conceptions of development as differentiation within an organism that is a functioning whole from the start. This latter view was rooted in his philosophical and psychological training and made more vivid by the many discussions of these biological developments along with those of the new *Gestalt* psychology in which he had participated during his years in the University Psychology Department. I recall at this point his keen interest in the embryological work of Coghill (1929), who showed that, in the development of co-ordinated movements in the newt, it was the movement of the limb as a whole that was governed by an innate pattern which appeared before any learning from the co-ordination of simpler movements.

In keeping with his paramount hostility to the concept of instincts sending independent energies into the ego, he underlines repeatedly that they operate modes of response only through the total self-system from the start. They are thus inconceivable without reality being involved. Possibly to emphasize his adherence to psychoanalytic principles he states that, although he thought Freud's basic theory should be changed, he held firmly to his clinical method. The reception of his paper was in no way negative, though somewhat subdued. It was, however, the first time many members had encountered his views, and challenges to basic assumptions need much further study.

Overlapping with the work on this paper for the Psycho-Analytical Society, he prepared a Memorandum to the Scottish Advisory Council on 'The treatment and rehabilitation of sexual offenders' at their request. This, like his other papers on social issues, shows careful thought with a highly realistic appraisal of the contribution of psychoanalytic experience. Its points are as valuable today as when they were written. He differentiates treatment for the individual in normal circumstances from the aim to rehabilitate. In the former, the individual seeks help for the relief of personal distress, whereas in the latter group the aim is to obtain a change in relationship with the community. The problem is similar to dealing with the 'war neuroses'. Fairbairn cannot share the view common amongst psychiatrists that perversions are 'symptoms', that is, like unfortunate excrescences attached to an otherwise normal person. They are the consequence of a personality that has become perverse in its basic structure. Neuroses are similar, but as Freud pointed out, there is a fundamental difference in that neurotic difficulties are defences against perverse tendencies, whereas in the pervert the pathological tendencies are given a dominant place in his personality. In the conventional psychiatric terminology, the pervert is thus a psychopath. As with the neurotic soldier, the problem becomes one of rehabilitation, of securing a return to, or the adoption of, the requirements of the group. But the pervert is merely seeking a reinstatement to the group in order to get back whatever advantages he has lost; he does not as a rule wish to be cured. The sexual offenders are thus not usually amenable to treatment. Imprisonment, however, is not helpful, because he is placed in a very abnormal group. What appears to be required is the creation of special communities or groups, and Fairbairn draws attention to the work of some Army pyschiatrists that would appear to be well worth experimental trials. (He refers here, without naming it, to Bion's work.) He further specifies group psychotherapy as a possibly useful resource, because it focuses on the individual's attitudes to others and the attitudes one tends to evoke in others.

The practical value of his suggestions can be readily appreciated, and methods of this kind have become widely used during the last few decades. At deeper levels, it is doubtful if the distinction between treatment and rehabilitation remains valid, for the basic aim of normal development is to become an effective group member, and groups have paradoxically to foster a sense of personal autonomy in each individual within the matrix of group membership.

Two months before these last two papers were presented, Fairbairn's mother died, at the age of ninety-two. This loss did not interfere with his intellectual self, yet he was more affected than he showed. The early bad experiences had engendered a continuing strong attachment to his mother, and he saw her almost daily in the years of the war. His widow thought that he was somewhat depressed for a considerable time afterwards. One result, perhaps not unconnected, was that he was incapacitated with quite severe influenza in each of the years from 1945 to 1948.

These last two papers nevertheless show that his working self was preserving the commitments to his guiding aims. The domestic setting was as it had been since the move to the country. There were, sadly, increasing difficulties due to his wife's becoming progressively addicted to alcohol amd almost detached from him. The result was that Fairbairn had to undertake much of the parental care in arrangements for the children. Soon after the war he had obtained a secretary who replaced the earlier residential one, in that she had a sympathetic appreciation of his analytic work as well as being a helpful support generally. While not residing with him and his wife, she was later an increasingly frequent visitor to Gifford. She gradually became the 'good woman' whose caring attitude he recognized as one he deeply needed, and several years later they were married.

AN OBJECT-RELATIONS THEORY OF THE PERSONALITY
It was two years before his next paper was read, on this occasion at the International Congress of Psychology in 1948 at Edinburgh. This short account of his 'Steps in the development of an object-relations theory of the personality' is again a model of brevity and clarity. It brings out the disciplined

quality of his thinking with the list of the steps he has taken and the reasons for them. Since he wrote a fuller statement in his next paper, little needs to be noted about its contents.

The year after this short paper was a busy one with domestic and family matters. The lease of his house ended and there was a move to another one in Gifford. His elder son finished school and left home to do his military service as still required. In the summer he spent about a month in London seeing friends and attending a residential conference near London. This was a meeting between senior staffs of the Tavistock Institute and Kurt Lewin's Institute of Group Dynamics that had been founded in Ann Arbor, Michigan. From the Tavistock there were several members whom he had met in Edinburgh, for example, Wilfred Bion, Eric Trist, A. T. M. Wilson and H. V. Dicks, and who had invited him as a guest because of what they knew of his ideas. He enjoyed this event, in which he contributed to the discussions, and although he was keenly interested in the subject, it did not stimulate him to write more about groups.

A short review written in this year has an interesting personal reference. The review was of the book by Marion Milner, *On Not Being Able to Paint*, which appeared in the *British Journal of Medical Psychology* (1949). Her previous books had attracted considerable interest because of the highly personal way she wrote about problems she had encountered in her inner world. By the time she wrote this book, she had become an experienced analyst. She had become interested in why, despite acquiring the technical competence, her efforts always petered out because of uncertainties about what she was trying to achieve. She responded to this situation by letting her hand and eye have free rein, whereupon her pictures were much more aesthetically creative and satisfying than when she worked by all the rules. She discovered that the painter's concern was with 'being a separate body in a world of other bodies which occupy different bits of space'. In other words, she encountered the problems of her self in relation to others by allowing a process of spontaneous emergence. Fairbairn writes that her remarks struck a special note of conviction in him, because when setting out to write he neither knew where it would lead nor did any conscious planning. He was most impressed by the way her problems are discussed entirely in terms of object-relationships, especially since she confirmed some of his conclusions about artists' work in his two papers on the psychology of art.

Perhaps the most significant event in this year was the start of Guntrip's analysis in the autumn. (It was through H. V. Dicks, who was the Professor of Psychiatry at Leeds University at this time, that Guntrip had been introduced to Fairbairn's writings.) After the war Fairbairn's clinical load increased until he was seeing about ten analytic patients daily. The urinary symptom was unchanged, and he was making brief notes on some of his dreams, so that the effort to understand it was maintained but sadly without any change in its restrictive effects. In 1951, he gave what was virtually an annual paper to the Scottish branch of the Psychological Society on Vigeland's sculptures, of which there had been a recent exhibition. His main writing during this year, however, was the substantial review he made of his papers on the object-relations theory. This paper was published when it appeared in his book the following year.

'A synopsis of the development of the author's views regarding the structure of the personality' is an excellent account written in his characteristically condensed and precise style. He describes at greater length the arguments given in the paper on 'The repression and the return of bad objects'. The 'moral defence' is distinguished from repression, and the transference neuroses are held to be largely determined by the working through of the return of repressed bad objects. The resistance from the attachment to the latter is emphasized, not only because it is a different view from Freud's, but mainly because the individual cannot give up objects without the threat of disintegration. The return of bad objects is therefore given as a more acceptable explanation of the repetition compulsion.

His theory of the basic endopsychic situation naturally receives most attention. Because impulses cannot be divorced from structures or parts of the ego, he replaces impulse psychology by a new psychology based on dynamic structures, a step which makes the id and ego redundant. It is also this step that makes the concept of the splitting of the ego necessary to give the structures that can repress other structures. The inconsistencies in the concept of the Oedipus situation are brought by the need to postulate the super-ego, conceived by Freud on the basis of the studies of melancholia, as internalized in a pre-genital oral phase, plus the later development from the 'moral defence'. Beneath this level are the persecutory attacks of primitive bad objects. The conception of internal objects developed by Melanie Klein constitutes a major development in theory, although in Fairbairn's view her retention of instinctual impulse and libidinal stages prevent its full significance from being realized. No new ideas are introduced, and the great value of this paper is its completeness as a synopsis of all his ideas that led up to his theory of the basic endopsychic situation, including the modification he added to that paper to overcome the contradictions between the original 'accepted' and 'rejected' objects.

Early in the following year, 1952, he gave a paper to the University Psychological Society on 'Theoretical and experimental aspects of psychoanalysis'. He puts forward the claim that the psychoanalytical technique itself constitutes a valid experimental method, and more effectively so when using the newer concepts of relations with internal objects and their projection in the transference on to the analyst. The interactions between the analyst and patient can then be dealt with entirely in terms of 'here and now' phenomena, thus removing a main basis of criticism of the method from a scientific point of view, namely, that historical material was untestable by itself. The real significance of transference, in other words, is that its manifestations belong to the actual activity of inner reality in the present.

This paper is strikingly similar to one written by Henry Ezriel and published just prior to his own in the *British Journal of Medical Psychology*. He acknowledges Ezriel's work, which obviously provided him with the stimulus for what was an address to academic psychologists and their students, and the paper as a whole seemed to show an unusually close adoption of Ezriel's views, with little added by himself.

In September 1952 his wife died relatively suddenly. There are no recorded comments by him on his reactions though these must have been profound. Despite the fact that he had separated from her emotionally, she was a very important figure for him. As with his father's death, there must have been superficial relief, but there was also a deep attachment. She was the first woman he loved, and they had been married for twenty-six years. He referred to his shock in a letter to Guntrip.

The degree to which his working self was insulated against the deeper reactions to his wife's progressive hostility over close on twenty years is remarkable. He kept up his writing despite the inevitably increased time he had to devote to domestic affairs in keeping the home going and to his parental responsibilities. His younger son was a student in Edinburgh University and so in and out of the home a good deal. In the following spring his daughter was married, and in July he attended the International Psycho-Analytic Conference in London. During the year he wrote two articles for publication. The first was a review and the second a major clinical paper. The review was on Ernst Kris's *Psychoanalytic Explorations in Art*.

When this impressive book appeared in 1953, Fairbairn was an obvious choice for me to ask to review it for the *British Journal of Medical Psychology*. He readily agreed, as the subject was of special appeal, and he wrote, as always, an extremely thoughtful commentary on it. Kris's scholarship and intellectual calibre struck him forcibly and, although expressing some disappointment at the absence of any formulation of a psychology of art, Fairbairn admired greatly the way Kris set out the lines along which this could eventually be developed. Since my concern, however, is with statements of special relevance to his own make-up I shall restrict myself to these. He notes the importance attached by Kris to the capacity of the artist 'to detach certain ego functions from conflict and thus establish autonomy in certain activities' – a comment with unusual relevance just after his wife's death. In response to Kris's use of sublimation, Fairbairn points out the difficulties in this concept, which he had remarked upon in his papers. Similarly with

Kris's use of the distinction between primary and secondary processes as basic to his researches. In spite of the brilliant manner in which Kris does this, Fairbairn believes that he would have achieved greater insight had he adopted a revision of these concepts in terms of an object-relations theory. Fairbairn apologizes for intruding comments about his own views on the role of dynamic structure in the psychology of art on the grounds that it was the best way he could respond appreciatively.

In the autumn of 1953, he wrote what was to be his last clinical paper, 'Observations on the nature of hysterical states'. An abbreviated version was read in London to the Medical Section of the British Psychological Society in October, and the full paper appeared in its *British Journal of Medical Psychology* in the following year. It was thus too late for inclusion in his book.

'OBSERVATIONS ON THE NATURE OF HYSTERICAL STATES'

Fairbairn's thesis for his MD degree had been devoted to the distinction between Freud's concept of repression and Pierre Janet's one of dissociation, and the subject of hysteria took him back to its central position when modern psychopathology was founded. In regard to hysteria he points out that in these patients the resistance is not so much to the psychotherapeutic process as a resistance to the psychotherapist himself.

Although repression became the accepted view, he sees the eclipse of dissociation as a loss, because it implies a splitting in the personality, and when repression is retained it has to relate to what occurs between parts of the personality and not between the personality and impulses. Indeed, for him, repression and splitting of the ego are two aspects of the same fundamental process. A somewhat misleading statement is that attempts to interpret the personality in terms of post-Darwinian biological concepts such as instincts are inadequate, though he himself invokes modern biology to support his concepts of development. Again, however, it is the reification of instincts which he deplores. When he summarizes his general views, he gives the first defence of the ego in dealing with an unsatisfying personal relationship as mental internalization or introjection. In a long footnote, he clarifies two points arising from his previous formulation. First, with regard to the Kleinians' stress on the internalization of good objects, he draws attention to the change in his opinion, whereby he sees the first internalized object as neither 'good' nor 'bad' but unsatisfying, and since such experience is inevitable there is a universal motive for introjecting the maternal object. His second point takes this first introjection as *a defence*, by which he implies that this process is not merely a representation of instinctual incorporation of the mother's milk, nor the general process described as 'memory'. As a defence, it is the expression of a significant meaning, that is, it is a purely psychological process. He believes that the difficulty for Kleinians in appreciating his views stems from the problems of how good relationships are perpetuated within the psyche and of how the personality is moulded by such experience. He thinks the key to these problems is to be found in the relationship of the central ego to the ideal object, a subject needing extensive consideration. I believe that here he has in mind the large question of an adequate metapsychology of the self as well as rounding off his structural theory. However, he does not elaborate further on the central self other than to amend the terminology in his developmental scheme in order to bring each of the split parts of the self into a relationship with an internal object. The persistence of old terms is odd, for example, in 'structures cathecting objects', but the new terms do make for greater consistency and clarity in the dynamics.

In a summary statement of his scheme of the endopsychic situation, the central ego 'cathects' the ideal object, and the two split-off and repressed structures each cathect a repressed internal object. The former ego ideal is replaced by 'ideal object' to bring it into the general line of his thought, and the internal saboteur correspondingly becomes the *anti-libidinal ego*. As a dynamic structure it maintains an aggressive persecutory attack on the anti-libidinal object and thus adds its 'induced repression' to the repression by the central ego. Compared with the super-ego, the anti-libidinal ego is directly repressed by the central ego which parallels Freud's regarding the super-ego as repressed in part. In Fairbairn's scheme, the anti-libidinal ego, the rejecting object and the ideal object all join in Freud's super-ego, thus illuminating the intensity of the hysteric's repression of sexuality.

When he illustrates the basic endopsychic situation, he describes a dream of a woman in which a child is in a passage with a door at either end. In front of one door is a figure of her father with a stick in front of his penis, while at the other, another figure, again her father, holds a whip about to punish her. She stands in a state of excitement between them, seeing through the window at the same time, couples of men and women who scorn her in her predicament. The actual relationship with her father had been one of sexual provocation along with rejection. Substitute a fierce-looking woman for one of the men, and this is very much the inner world of Fairbairn – shut out of the primal scene. A male patient is also described who felt his mother holding down his erect penis and crushing his testicles at the same time. This patient was an only boy with several sisters, whose fussy, possessive mother forbade any manifestation of sexuality and on one occasion slapped him for showing his penis to her. This situation was aggravated by a remote inaccessible father who failed to rescue him from his mother and to encourage the development of adult male independence. In a third patient, a woman, he illustrates the phantasy of a sexless marriage to a husband who indulged her in every conceivable way and with children appearing with no obvious origins. She is thus showing a somewhat extreme ideal object, freed from any element of sexuality – a relationship that hysterical patients try to realize with the analyst until the split parts of the self are threatened by the intrusion of the repressed objects in the transference.

In dreams from other patients, the pattern of circumstances in the family is again brought out as the origin of the basic inner situation. He supports his case for the crucial role of the early relationships of simultaneously exciting and rejecting attitudes in the parents as the causal factors in psychopathological development of the personality. Moreover, the later psychosexual symptoms are also manifestly related to the frustrations in the early oral stage. He comments, however, that while the hysteric's sexuality is at bottom extremely oral, his or her basic orality becomes extremely genital. Although stated in a footnote, Fairbairn emphasizes that while he is describing essentially *personal* problems in hysterics, these are staged in specific fields, especially the genital one. This question of the close link between genital sexuality and more general aspects of the person comes up in the case of the patient Jack. In one of his dreams he was holding down a leopard lying on the floor while he slipped out of the room. The patient recognized the leopard as a fierce sadistic part of himself, and he related the holding down to his passivity in early childhood following his displacement from his mother's care by the birth of a younger brother. Fairbairn notes that he had to draw the patient's notice to what he was ignoring, namely, the leopard representing his penis that must be kept down. It is a matter of some interest that many years later Guntrip told me that he was Jack, a fact very much connected with the incident he described later of seeing his dead brother on his mother's lap and which haunted him without resolution for many years.

There is for me a much more central aspect which I believe has been largely avoided in psychoanalytic thought, namely, the powerful urge of the self to possess its autonomy. The patient's first association for the leopard is that it represented a vital, energetic side of his personality. Fairbairn regards this as the 'libidinal ego', which was certainly there. However, this ignores the specific needs of the central ego for the recognition of its autonomy in all its activities, and Guntrip's account of the early relationship with his mother gives ample evidence of her constant attempt to be as she appeared in another dream, that is, the female keeper with whom he entered a lion's cage and who then cowed the lion as it was about to spring.

Having postulated the origins of hysterical manifestations as the primal splits in the self, instead of being in the Oedipus situation, he then gives his previous interpretation of the latter from the triangular situation of the basic endopsychic situation.

In the final section he discusses some aspects of the characteristic hysterical process of conversion which have a very close connection with his own symptom. This defence is only employed when repression cannot be maintained and transference phenomena threaten the patient with acting out the repressed situation. Fairbairn believes that the defence is a reaction to outer situations that reactivate the repressed inner situation. It is frequently precipitated by a bodily condition associated with the anxieties of the inner one, and the conversion is an avoidance of these by the substitution of a bodily state for a personal problem. When not localized, the conversion frequently appears as attacks of pain in various bodily parts, thereby expressing the attacks of the inner aggression on the inner object. Two of his patients had attacks of sinusitis as a conversion symptom dramatizing the state of imprisonment by a controlling mother. When he observed a concurrent anal and urinary retentiveness he conceived the possibility of these symptoms providing an explanation for the phenomena of erogenous zones, a suggestion supported by the fact that personal conflicts between the child and its parents frequently relate to behaviour involving those zones. He describes one woman patient who became very angry with him in the sessions, because he had seen her at the theatre the previous evening. She then denied the anger with him but wanted to smash things in the room. Upon pointing out that this represented an attack upon him, she denied being angry at all and merely felt certain kinaesthetic sensations – a conversion *in statu nascendi.*

A male patient is then described who illustrated a conversion being confined to phantasy. This case is of particular interest because of its close fit with his own inner situation. In phantasy the patient was constantly arguing with his mother about his right to possess and use his penis as he wished. He felt his mother was adamant in her rejection, and he could not use it without her permission. To escape from her clutches was impossible for him because of the guilt about his hatred of her for keeping him castrated. If he were angry with her she would injure his penis or have it cut off. Castration was a lesser evil than getting his head cut off. He thus localized the clash with his mother in his penis, and when he felt the analyst was encouraging him to express his angry feelings he wanted to break off the session. Further case material brought out the artificial circumscription to the areas referred to in their erotogenic states, and Fairbairn points out it is the functional activities, not the restriction to anatomical considerations, that give them their prominent role. Thus 'oral', should be replaced by 'alimentary', 'anal' by 'defecatory', and 'urethral' by 'urinary'. With regard to the erotogenic status of the mouth, he quotes a male patient whose whole personal problem receded at one point in his analysis when he became preoccupied by his infant daughter who was most distressed and was failing to put on weight. The patient wanted to give the baby a richer mixture, which was encouraged by Fairbairn, and she put on weight. Her distress remained, however, with a great deal of crying and sucking at her blanket. Fairbairn thereupon suggested that since the problem was in the mothering, the parents should take professional advice. This was given by one of his colleagues, who found the baby was being completely rejected. (I am indebted for further insight into this to Dr Jessie Sym, who undertook to help the mother, with considerable improvement developing in her relationship with her child. Dr Sym informed me that Fairbairn was quite anxious about the situation his patient was in because while asleep, his patient's wife had caused their first baby's death by suffocation through lying upon her.)

The 'oral' need was thus a conversion of the unsatisfying relationship with her mother. A further example is given from the male patient already mentioned as having a castrating mother. He had been circumcised and the loss of his foreskin felt as if he had been deprived of the only thing that gave him pleasure, that is, playing with his foreskin which had become a substitute for his mother. In short, the vicissitude of childhood relations can readily produce the conversion of the defecatory and urinary system into isolated erotogenic zones. Fairbairn thus refutes the theory of an originally inherent auto-erotic orientation with object-seeking developing later.

The audience to whom he read this paper included many analytical psychotherapists and so was a much wider one than that at the Psycho-Analytical Institute. It was well received, though some analytic eyebrows were raised at his giving the patient advice. There was a general reaction, however, of realizing that something important had been presented.

By the early 1950s, Fairbairn began to enjoy a much more congenial academic and professional atmosphere in Scotland. In Edinburgh the Davidson Clinic under Dr Winifred Rushforth had brought together a number of Jungian analysts, and in its Glasgow centre there were, as mentioned earlier, a few analytical psychotherapists including K. M. Abenheimer and R. W. Pickford, who was a senior member of the staff in the Psychology Department of the University. W. M. Millar, who had had analysis with Fairbairn, had become Professor of Psychiatry in Aberdeen. He established a notably psychodynamic climate in his group, as did T. F. Rodger, who become the first Professor of Psychiatry in Glasgow. MacNiven was still superintendent of the chief psychiatric hospital there, and he had become a close friend of Fairbairn, while Rodger had also been well known to him from the pre-war years. Rodger soon recruited to his staff T. Freeman, who had completed his training as a psychoanalyst in London while he worked in the Tavistock Clinic. Freeman was an enthusiastic researcher in schizophrenia, and there was an active group of young psychiatrists who became involved in this field, one of whom was R. D. Laing. There were also two other young psychoanalysts in the Lansdowne Clinic, a unit devoted to out-patient psychotherapy. It was closely linked with MacNiven's hospital and

Rodger's department, so that a relatively large group of professionals existed, all of whom were psychodynamically oriented. There was also J. L. Halliday, a consultant physician whose publications showed a sophisticated understanding of psychosomatic conditions and attracted considerable attention. In short, compared with the pre-war years there was a remarkably different atmosphere sustained by these groups whose members, if not analysts by training, were actively interested in the whole field of analytical psychotherapy.

For this enlarged group of interested professionals, Fairbairn was naturally a figure whose importance had been indicated by the esteem in which he was held by a large proportion of the senior academics. He was receiving substantial recognition in psychoanalytic fringe areas following the publication of his book in 1952 and Guntrip's articles, which appeared both in the professional journals and as semi-popular accounts of the nature of psychotherapy that attracted a wide readership.

Following the paper on hysteria he seemed to be satisfied with his picture of the endopsychic situation, and he responded to opportunities at scientific and professional meetings, or when some book expressed views that interested him, by pointing out the importance of appropriate structural theory in general as well as his own contribution. Guntrip (1961) has recorded the reactions to Fairbairn's book in reviews by analysts, and all I need to mention here is that by and large they greatly disappointed Fairbairn. He was surprised both by the manifest lack of grasp of theoretical issues by analysts and, more striking, the lack of interest, along with the apparent unwillingness to examine basic assumptions. The reviews were in fact notable for this, and I could only assume that these reactions were prompted by deeper resistances to the implications of what Fairbairn implied rather than being solely the superficial initial responses of rejection of unfamiliar concepts and accusations of substituting quite 'unnecessary' new terms. As Guntrip pointed out, the new terms were not fanciful creations to attract attention but were carefully chosen to relate to new concepts. The resistance seemed to me to be a remarkable demonstration of the extent to which the intellectual tools of analysts become welded into their personality. This fusion is general enough in all scientific work, but it seemed a particularly strong one for those investigating the disturbing areas of the unconscious mind. The security of the familiar is especially tenacious when new views threaten the personality and not only at the intellectual level. Winnicott's dismissive remark, 'if only Fairbairn didn't knock Freud . . .', was particular striking. Greenberg and Mitchell in their perspicacious, objectively critical, and frank study of the development of *Object Relations in Psychoanalytic Theory* (1983) refer to being quite puzzled by it, because Winnicott's whole work was in such complete support of Fairbairn's line of thought. (This matter will be referred to later – see page 174.)

There was relatively little notice taken of Fairbairn's work in the British Psycho-Analytical Society following the appearance of his book. Melanie Klein was not enthusiastic about it, though valuing his observations, while Anna Freud gave no indication that she had noticed it, and they each exerted a powerful inhibiting brake on any of their associates wasting time on unorthodox theory. Miss Freud's exclusive investment in the classical principles of her father, theoretical and practical, also had its inhibiting effect in the USA because of her status amongst the European analysts who had moved there. Klein was for many years kept as taboo there by a much more active campaign. Fairbairn scarcely merited 'a campaign'; he was merely ignored. His non-participation in the International Psycho-Analytic events had, of course, contributed to this position. Amongst the 'independents' there was no great enthusiasm stimulated by the prominent figures such as Balint and Winnicott, and any influence he gained in these early years after his book appeared came from those analysts and senior psychotherapists in the Tavistock Clinic. Again, I do not wish to give any impression that there was any concerted or shared negative judgement. I felt it was more a case of the general attitude of withdrawing from the hard intellectual work required in appraising basic principles; in psychoanalysis this work has powerful emotional resonances. Doubtless, too, the work had evoked deep personal factors.

ABENHEIMER'S CRITICISM AND FAIRBAIRN'S REPLY

In contrast with the reviews, there was a major criticism from Glasgow. Karl Abenheimer, who had been trained in Europe as a Jungian analyst, had an intellectual background of German philosophy and psychology in which the existentialists and phenomenologists featured prominently. Within the group of psychotherapists in Scotland he was highly respected for his modest, friendly attitude, along with his scholarly dedication. Fairbairn's themes had greatly interested him from the time he heard his papers at the Psychological Society meetings and as they appeared in the journals and then in his book. Abenheimer (1955) wrote what he termed 'a severe criticism' of Fairbairn's factual and theoretical viewpoints, although recognizing Fairbairn's contributions as important.

In a somewhat reproving tone he states that with his psychology of 'complexes' Jung had anticipated by twenty-five years what Fairbairn tries to do with his concept of dynamic structures. He finds much about the internalization of objects valuable, though as a complete description of the inner world it is untenable. He considers the primal acts of splitting postulated by Fairbairn to be conjectures, because we have no exact observations from this early period. Also, the inner world, as Jung and his school have shown, is incomparably richer than Fairbairn indicates. He then reveals the very different standpoint he brings from his own training. For him, to speak of an internal and external world in the infant mind is meaningless, because all objects belong in large measure to the internal world, and it is only with development that the objective object is differentiated. Special acts of incorporation are therefore unnecessary to explain objects. Ego elements that arise from primary identification with objects often conflict with one another, and the theoretical problem is how unification comes about. Internal objects are frequently created, not from external ones but from imagined ones. Of particular importance because of their pathological effects on the child is a category of introjects that are themselves not external but internal in the psyche of the mother or father, for example, the internal male imago of the mother, or her animus, which is often more influential than the external father. Because it is not a reality, this kind of introject can be particularly disturbing.

On the role of libidinal stages, Abenheimer believes these play an important part in infantile dependence because of the phantasies that originate from them. For Freud, they gave rise to a variety of aims and objects, whereas Fairbairn, by focusing solely on the whole object, loses such aims. Fairbairn's abstract terminology, based on his holistic point of view, leads him to regard the various sexual urges only as techniques for securing the relationship with the other and not as final aims. Abenheimer considers Freud's findings are valid, although it was this conflict which split Freud and Jung, and he is on Fairbairn's side in this issue. In furthering the move to independence, Fairbairn ignores the tendencies from libidinal stages, tendencies (about which he had written in a previous paper) such as those relating to acquiring material and maternal power from anal symbols and male paternal power from phallic symbols. He thus reckons with three pairs of primitive ego-object complexes, namely: infantile dependence and the good breast/mother; independence through possession of the phallus; and maternal power from possession of the belly/mother opposed to the breast/mother. Each of these pairs is ambivalent, and therapy has to aim at their assimilation into the ego. Abenheimer considers that this scheme agrees with Fairbairn's in so far as it is based on whole psychological situations. In contrast with it, his three stages of ego development indicate the way in which these complexes are dealt with.

Fairbairn's contention that repression relates to dynamic structures is according to Abenheimer a fundamental insight. He takes issue with him, however, in saying that repression is mediated by aggression, because he believes many different emotions instigate it. Also, he cannot understand the use of the substantive, in view of Fairbairn's disowning of the concept of instincts with aims. Aggression should not be used unless it is clearly defined who is being aggressive and what the aim is. The last of Abenheimer's factual criticisms concerns the scheme for the transitional techniques. He believes these cannot be based on the object relations alone but must bring in such facts affecting the state of the development of the ego as he described in these three complexes.

When he turns to the theoretical papers, he finds them excessively abstract, a consequence, Abenheimer believes, of Fairbairn's belief that analytical psychology is a natural science in which the individual experience can be reduced to general laws and a general scientific theory. The human sciences are interpretative studies with concepts of dynamic psychology that seek to unify and integrate the field of motivation, whereas the natural-scientific standpoint isolates aspects that are causally relevant to the formulation of general laws. Only muddle arises when these two logically different operations are identified. Fairbairn's starting-point with the whole self is that of the *Geisteswissenschaften*, that is, the interpretative human studies as opposed to the natural-sciences, and so his far-reaching abstractions cannot be justified. Thus in using the term 'objects', which comes, as general abstract terms do, under the influence of the 'natural-science' outlook, it comes to mean everything. In using 'good' or 'bad', 'exciting' or 'rejecting', the qualitative and evaluative differences to which they relate are all left to the reader. 'Taking' and 'giving' are again such generalizations that they make them relatively meaningless terms which in fact hide the most important contents of Fairbairn's teaching and his most striking deviation from the orthodox Freudian ideas, namely, to counteract the atomistic approach. By treating these qualitative statements as factual ones he perpetuates the type of science he wants to disown. The four techniques are Fairbairn's nearest approximation to natural laws, which then appear too good to be true. For example: (1) the paranoid person is still full of inner attackers after all his externalizations; (2) the obsessional tries to control external as well as internal evil by internal magic yet has the greatest resistance to true introversion; (3) the hysteric tries to identify with the external accepted persons and to remain unaware of the internal rejected structure; (4) the phobic represses all rejected structures and so feels nice but powerless. He panics in face of external powers or when alone with no support from external powers. In short, the scheme works because each term is used in a variety of meanings. With his subject-matter, Fairbairn is much closer to the humanistic studies than to the orthodox Freudian teaching. The gap this makes between theory and practice is a glaring one which he wants to narrow with his views on practice. For Abenheimer the subjective contents we observe are naïve interpretations, mainly in terms of motivation and in no sense representative of reality. The further back we go in development, the less do psychological contents correspond to any 'scientific' reality. The research methods of dynamic psychology cannot eliminate the subjective and so the experiment plays no role in them. The muddle with regard to the concepts and subject-matter of dynamic psychology can only be cleared up by recognizing that the infantile and the disordered personalities apperceive the self in animistic and mythological terms. Dynamic psychology is therefore the study of the mythology in and through which we live.

The Jungian/phenomenological viewpoint of Abenheimer is not in itself my concern. For one thing, the changes in theoretical biology and in the conceptions of the nature of science have made much of it (and of classical Freudian theory) out of date and Fairbairn was much nearer the modern standpoint than was Abenheimer. His essay, however, was the first serious effort to analyse and appraise views Fairbairn was advancing, and, perhaps because of its Jungian standpoint, many of his points relate to crucial questions. My purpose in quoting from it so fully is twofold. First, I wished to show that the intellectual world around Fairbairn was more varied in its representatives and also in many ways more challenging than that of the orthodox psychoanalytic groups. In his Scottish situation, the different viewpoints were being exchanged in a friendly open-minded manner without the inhibiting atmosphere that psychoanalytical institutes tended to impose upon really free discussion. My second purpose is to show the quality of Fairbairn's thinking in response to challenges at different levels and on very different grounds. In the course of defending his position he makes some very useful statements about it.

Fairbairn replied at length with an essay 'Observations in defence of the object-relations theory of the personality'. Commenting on Abenheimer's Jungian standpoint, he says in his customary somewhat formal style – though on this occasion I picture him with the twinkle in his eyes he would often adopt when many others would be more sarcastic – that Abenheimer contends that (a) in so far as his conclusions conflict with Jung then they are erroneous and (b) he should have adopted Jung's views from the start in his struggle towards their light. He himself has always deprecated 'Freud versus Jung' controversies, because truth should take precedence over scholastic arguments. When he first became interested in psychopathology he had no controversial axe to grind and chose Freud because his view seemed to him more illuminating and convincing. The three general criticisms Abenheimer makes can be summarized as: (a) in so far as his approach conforms to scientific criteria, his conclusions are wrong in many respects; (b) his approach is not really scientific but pseudo-scientific; (c) he is misguided in attempting to adopt a scientific approach since the inherent nature of 'the psychopathological disciplines' is not scientific in the natural-science sense. He feels he is thus faced with a formidable proposition for his defence.

As a preliminary, he points out that his general theory is essentially a theory of dynamic structure, but he regards the *developed* psyche as a multiplicity of structures of two classes, ego structures and internal objects. The latter are conceived as introjected and structured as representations of emotionally significant aspects of persons upon whom the subject depended in early life. The internal object is an endopsychic structure, other than an ego structure, with which an ego structure has a relationship comparable to a relationship with a person in external reality. As regards 'libido', the real libidinal aim is the establishment of satisfactory relationships with objects; the object thus constitutes the true libidinal aim. Sexual aims are essentially personal, but all personal aims are not necessarily sexual.

The statement of Abenheimer that his dynamic structures are exactly what Jung has described as complexes is for Fairbairn astonishingly wide of the mark. He then quoted from Jung's writings to show that he endows the term with so many meanings that it has nothing in common with his concept of dynamic structures, even though there is at times an approximation to the latter. Fairbairn showed in his MD thesis that he had studied Jung carefully. When Abenheimer says his conception of the origin of the inner world is unsupported by clinical data, Fairbairn refers to his essay on 'Endopsychic structure . . .', in which the psychical structures are directly derived from the clinical material, and all of his theoretical concepts are based upon his daily experience with human beings. On the more detailed criticisms he finds extraordinary the one attributing mere conjecture to processes happening before exact observation is possible, because inductive inferences of this type are widely prevalent in other sciences. He rightly dismisses the claim that his findings contradict those of Jung and his school, but he takes up the criticism that his assumptions contradict each other. Thus by saying that the idea that psychological life starts with a primary identification of ego and objects is inconsistent with internal objects originating from specific processes of introjection or incorporation, Abenheimer does not understand that he has described identification as a *specific affective* process which is essentially *active* rather than cognitive.

Abenheimer also confuses psychological issues with philosophical and epistemological issues when he says, 'all ego needs are experienced in the image of the corresponding object'. It is his confusion of internal objects with images that leads him to say special acts of incorporation or introjection need not be assumed. The internal representatives of objects undergo considerable changes according to the individual's needs and emotions. So far from being mere images, the internal objects are specific structures established during the most formative period of life from ego activity serving specific purposes in the economy of the psyche. What Fairbairn described at length in his papers was the necessity to postulate special acts of incorporation to explain internal objects in order to make external reality more tolerable.

Fairbairn cannot agree with Abenheimer's view, an obviously atomistic one, of the ego with its unintegrated elements often in conflict. His postulate of the ego as an integrated structure from the outset is in conformity with contemporary biology. With regard to the criticism that he ignores the importance of anal and phallic tendencies, Fairbairn rejects this, because the exploitation of techniques does not arise, in his view, from a temporary salience of these phases but from challenges to active emancipation from dependence in excretory and sexual activities. He points out, too, that there is always an element of hate underlying all the emotions of fear, disgust, shame, and so on, cited by Abenheimer as a factor in repression other than aggression. Fairbairn agrees that the use of aggression as a noun is inconsistent with his rejection of the hypostatization of 'libido' and 'aggression', but abstract nouns are a part of all rational thought just as the terms used by Abenheimer are. He notes that regarding the accusation of the omission of manic or hypomanic denial, he actually quotes this as a *specific defence* called into play by the state itself rather than by the underlying conflicts. Again, the presence of persecution in the paranoid does not constitute a paranoid attitude.

Fairbairn cannot easily discuss theoretical criticisms in a short space. He states that he regards analytical psychology as a scientific discipline and not as a 'natural science', though in research investigations it is not necessary to use methods appropriate to the physical sciences. Also, although he may have resorted to abstract concepts in creating his theoretical framework, he considers it better than having no framework; that to him constitutes the chief weakness of Jung's writings. To the charge that the word 'object' is too impersonal, Fairbairn responds with the great range of objects which appear in the vicissitudes of emotional life. His classification of objects is his attempt to take into account the qualitative infantile judgements, for example, as 'good' or 'bad'. He does not believe that this is a valid reason for rejecting these terms as indicating a subjective factor that makes theories into pseudo-science. Fairbairn thinks Abenheimer has not understood that his formulation of the four techniques rests on processes of internalization that are unconscious, nor that the accepted and rejected objects are essentially internal objects, that is, they remain as internal whether they are *treated* as internal or external. At the same time he expresses his appreciation of the clinical comments Abenheimer makes upon these techniques.

Replying to Abenheimer's statement that dynamic psychology is concerned with the content of mental acts, Fairbairn thought that would account for his difficulty in giving validity to his views, which are conceived in terms of dynamic *structures*. For him, science is nothing more than an intellectual tool which does not provide in any sense a picture of reality. Instead, it gives a construct which offers a coherent account of the phenomena of the universe through general laws established by inductive inference under conditions of maximum objectivity in the observer. The only real value recognized by science is an explanatory one, and this applies to general medicine. Adopting scientifically tested knowledge does not make a good doctor nor a good psychotherapist. Scientific truth is not an ultimate value, though he attaches the greatest importance to it. What patients seek from the psychotherapist corresponds to the religious quest, for they want to find salvation from the past, from the bondage to their bad internal objects, from the burden of guilt and from spiritual death. In this process he believes the transference situation within the relationship with the analyst is of crucial importance.

The style in which he presents his defence represents his thinking at its best. He felt Abenheimer had taken his papers seriously and had paid him a handsome tribute in his lengthy critiques. Today, many would regard a fair amount of what Abenheimer says as perhaps not meriting the effort which Fairbairn took in his reply. There was then much debate and unclarity about the issue of the status of psychodynamic knowledge and its theories. Indeed they are still alive, although the developments since then have answered several of the questions. The precision with which Fairbairn takes up Abenheimer's points and the straightforward way in which he deals with his evaluation of his points, dismissing sharply what he considers irrelevant yet without being contemptuous, and the extent to which his thinking is rooted in his clinical data, are all exemplary. His own personal answers to complex questions of what is scientific suggest that he had clarified these for himself in the past and after a great deal of careful thought.

THE SCHREBER CASE

His next essay was stimulated by the appearance in 1955 of an English translation of Schreber's *Memoirs of My Nervous Illness* by Dr Ida Macalpine and her son Dr Richard Hunter. Freud's original explanation of Schreber's illness rested on his concept of a conflict between homosexual and hetero-sexual libido, when the frustration of one tendency gave rise to the salience of the other, that is, the choice of illness was explained without any reference to object-relations. Such factors must be assumed to account for the oscillation. Macalpine and Hunter adopt a negative attitude to psychoanalytic theory, because of its inadequate foundations in the phenomena of the artificial situation of the transference. They offer an explanation of Schreber's illness in terms of procreation phantasies, of which there is evidence in his descriptions and a plausible precipitating factor in the childless nature of his marriage. Fairbairn rejects Freud's views as based on impersonal factors. This essay, however, has been rendered almost irrelevant in the light of Niederland's researches (1963) into the way Schreber was treated by his father. Had he had that knowledge, Fairbairn would really have enjoyed making use of the father's actual behaviour in his relationship with his son.

The final section of his essay arouses specific interest in regard to Fairbairn's own unconscious phantasies about the primal scene. He notes with surprise that neither the authors nor Freud take into account the primal scene, especially because of its close association with procreation phantasies and with phantasies of the parents as persecutors. The importance of this theme was very much on his mind around this time, as I knew from conversations. He now makes the bold assertion that the anxiety over reviving the primal scene is the source of the greatest resistance in analysis, a resistance that can assume quite fantastic proportions. Fairbairn considered that it was so terrifying a theme for Schreber that he was driven to create his delusional belief of parentless or spontaneous generation of pregnancy; in all his phantasies of cultivating voluptuousness he never mentions any sexual intercourse. Fairbairn also quotes the intense anxieties of one of his male patients, evoked in childhood by his mother's hostility to his having a penis. The patient had a profound doubt about his sexual role, and it was accordingly not surprising that he had difficulty over urinating in public lavatories. There can be no doubt about the impact this theme was progressively making on Fairbairn.

The intellectual quality and the feeling of satisfaction in these last two essays is reminiscent of that of the artist achieving his aim. There is also conveyed a parallel feeling of enjoying life generally. Throughout most of the 1950s, he did have a much more social life. His friendship with Mrs Mackintosh, his secretary, had now been well established, and they intended to be married. As she had not obtained her divorce this could not be done, and it was a few years before it became possible. They saw a good deal of each other outside their working relationship, and he was also drawn into various social events by his younger son, who was now studying in Edinburgh University and was prominent in the student life.

Since moving his home to the country, he had become a keen gardener, a hobby which continued to give him a great deal of pleasure for the rest of his life. In this year, 1956, he was rather proud of winning a first prize for some of his flowers at the local flower show. His widow recalled how entertaining Fairbairn was in these years, laughing a good deal and a lively interesting person to be with all the time. However, the long hours he spent at work in the evenings showed his continuing dedication, and she found him maintaining in all his writing his usual punctiliousness about every word.

In this year also he gave the opening lecture at the annual Summer School of the Davidson Clinic in Edinburgh. Dr Winifred Rushforth, its moving spirit, was a woman with tremendous enthusiasm and drive in her efforts to make psychotherapeutic help available. She had a group around her in whom there were some Jungian analysts and analytical psychotherapists and a number of others whom she 'trained' despite their lack of the usual mental-health experience. She was an able 'dynamic' person, but one whose enthusiasm outran discrimination, so that she did not always draw boundaries in regard to 'movements' and methods that were of dubious status intellectually and professionally. Although not involved in any of its activities, Fairbairn valued its work in spite of the lack of the usual professional and academic requirements in all trained staff and in regard to the scientific principles of their work. He also admired the unique way the Clinic flourished in the unsympathetic climate of opinion towards psychotherapy created by the academic world, especially the medical and psychiatric communities, and maintained facilities for psychological help for extremely low fees.

He chose as his subject for the occasion a strictly psychoanalytic one which had a specific relevance to the centenary year of Freud's birth. As always for such occasions, his address was carefully prepared for publication, and it appeared in the *British Journal of Medical Psychology* the following year entitled

'FREUD: THE PSYCHO-ANALYTICAL METHOD
AND MENTAL HEALTH'

His starting-point is another excellent summary of Freud's theory and the stages in its development, from which he goes on to the need to bring in the personal relationships of the child in the structuring of the personality. Drawing upon the recently published book by Glover, *The Technique of Psycho-Analysis* (1955), he describes the strict principles of the psychoanalytic method as laid down by Freud, to which Glover stresses the need for close adherence. Fairbairn, however, goes back to the publication by Glover in 1928 of a study on the technique of psychoanalysis adopted by twenty-four practising analysts. He found that, in practice, analysts holding to their classical principles varied in their methods in every imaginable way. From his independent position this finding was probably more appreciated than by those subjected to the pressures of orthodoxy. He remarked that Glover's study suggested the personality of the analyst may in the last resort prove to be at least one of the decisive therapeutic factors.

Turning to Freud's outlook on the problems of mental health, he cites his stoical philosophy and his pessimism as resting mainly on his concepts of the nature of the id. Fairbairn's own conception of conflicts arising from the relations with inner objects offers a more hopeful prospect, though he is mindful of unrealistic optimism, for experience shows the intractability of the forces of resistance. Some findings of psychoanalysis, however, should gain recognition in the interests of prevention, for example the importance of the early relationships. His last precept is noteworthy, namely, that the child should be safeguarded against 'any risk of his being a witness of sexual intimacies between his parents'.

In each of the last few years he had had at least one debilitating attack of influenza, and in November he had a suspected urethral infection. He had to be examined in hospital, but no specific treatment was given.

The year 1957 was one of much domestic activity and hence with little time for writing. The separation of his home in Gifford from his consulting room in Edinburgh had been increasingly felt as imposing strain on his health. He therefore took the opportunity early in the year of buying a beautiful Georgian villa situated in the small historic village of Duddingston which was within the city boundaries of Edinburgh and preserved from urban encroachment. Here he could do such work as he wished in a country setting with a fine old garden and yet within easy reach of the centre of the town. Not long after this decision, his daughter had a second daughter, so that he now had two grandchildren. Following that event, his younger son qualified in law, while his elder one finished his degree at Oxford. His family were thus established as he moved into his new home. The move was hardly completed when he had to take to bed with an acute urethral infection. Before the end of the year, however, he was seeing six to seven patients on most days.

Early in the next year he met Dr T. A. Watters, an analyst from New Orleans who was visiting a psychiatrist friend in Edinburgh. Fairbairn's work was now becoming known in the United States, though because of his private symptom he did not accept invitations to visit. Another visitor was Don Jackson who knew of his work from his period in Chestnut Lodge through Frieda Fromm-Reichmann. She appreciated the relevance of Fairbairn's ideas for Jackson's own work with the family relationships of schizophrenics.

'ON THE NATURE AND AIMS OF PSYCHO-ANALYTICAL TREATMENT'

During the early months of this year he wrote what was to be his last paper. Szasz had sent Fairbairn a copy of his paper, 'On the theory of psycho-analytic treatment', before it was published in 1957 and he began to write reflections upon it. After a brief summary of his theoretical position, he informs us that his views clearly have the most far-reaching implications for treatment, and it is because of the major issues they present that he has put them to the test with the greatest circumspection. Stimulated by the paper, he now expresses disagreement with some of Szasz's views and formulates some of the changes he considers his own theories suggest.

Szasz, following Kurt Eissler, believes the analysand should possess a relatively mature, strong and unmodified ego, a requirement that Fairbairn points out would at once rule out child analysis. Indeed, if overemphasized, it readily justifies the joke that the most suitable analysands are those who don't need it. On his theoretical grounds, which regard the ego as modified by reality from the start, the splits created in it by early experience become the fundamental factor in the development of the psychopathology, for which the patient is seeking help. On this latter point Fairbairn queries Szasz's view of analysis as not a form of treatment conceived in the medical model but a form of scientific education. This he believes to be misleading, because the dynamic of the request made to the analyst in the first instance – the motive that starts the whole analytic endeavour – is the patient's wish to be relieved in some measure from his 'suffering'. It may be that scientific education is the means of removing the suffering, but that is not the patient's motive. Since medical treatments are frequently not related to what the patient complains about, it may be thought that this is not an issue to which attention needs to be drawn. This, however, raises a fundamental issue for Fairbairn. Education is not one of the ways in which the individual formulates his request in terms the culture of our society accepts. Neither is it an attitude engendered by the deep motives, religious and otherwise, of 'doing good' or 'giving help to the needy', which might be attributed to Fairbairn's early adoption of religious values. He believes a caring attitude is basic to the whole process of analysis; it is a requirement dictated not by sentiment but by the scientific facts of infant development. The patient's original experience was of not being 'loved' for himself, and it is the need for such an attitude that he will inevitably sense. Apart from the facts of development, Fairbairn again harks back to his paper in defence of his object-relations theory, where he enlarged on this question and in which he quoted Glover's findings that showed that the success of analysis rested on the relationship with the therapist. It is this personal relationship that provides both a means of correcting the pathological effect stemming from his inner relationships and an actual relationship with a reliable and beneficent parental figure. This latter experience was denied to the patient in his childhood. He adds that a psychology conceived predominantly in terms of impulse tends to discount the importance of this factor, and he believes this is reinforced by the growing extent to which the work of senior analysts is devoted to trainees, a situation which also fosters rigid adherence to the classical method. He admits his chief interest having been in promoting a more adequate theory, and there can be no question that here as in all situations concerned with effecting change there is nothing so practical as a good theory. Questions of analytic technique must start from the understanding the analyst brings to the situation. Purism leads to apotheosis of the method, with the common circular position of failure with the patient being taken as due to his unsuitability for analysis.

Fairbairn had adopted the position with patients who were not making satisfactory progress of asking if the technique of analysis was defective and what the analyst was trying to do and how what he was doing worked. As for its aim, he considers 'analysis' to be a misnomer, because the analyst is trying to promote a maximum synthesis of the structures into which the original self has been split. This aim involves the further aims of reducing the infantile dependence still persisting and the hatred of the object responsible for this splitting. In this endeavour the greatest source of resistance is the maintenance of the individual's inner world as a closed system. It is the fixation to inner objects that gives rise to the transference, for under its influence the analyst is responded to as though he has become an inner object. Fairbairn notes, apropos of this process, that in neurosis outer reality is treated as if it were inner reality, whereas the converse occurs in psychosis. For a change to occur, the real relationship with the analyst has to replace that with the internal object. This process is what is so familiar in Klein's terminology of introjection and projection. The primitive relationships are present, for Klein, largely with part objects, whereas, in the examples he gives, this process occurs more frequently between whole persons. It is because the whole person is, in his view, the original source of the deprivation in the satisfaction sought that he emphasizes the necessity for the patient to feel that the analyst is an understanding, accepting person, that is, a good object.

The nub of resistance to changing the closed system is often expressed in the patient's remark when experiencing his frustrated rage with it, that 'there is nothing to be done about it'. Illustrating this dilemma, Fairbairn quotes the 'frozen dramas' described by two male patients. One felt if he became good, even by castrating himself, his father despised him, and his mother always put him in the wrong no matter what he did; so he remained permanently in this state of enraged impotence. His mother possessed and imprisoned him. He needed her and couldn't possibly release his rage until he had got away from the gaol. The other patient dreamt of raising his hand to strike his mother who had reproved him for exposing himself to a maid. He then found his hand mysteriously arrested in mid-air, and he became convinced he was in the grip of a fatal heart attack. This incident of inhibited sadism towards his mother and hypochondriacal anxiety about his heart became established as a static situation.

In the origin of this inner situation becoming completely fixed or static, he again comes back to the readiness with which primal-scene phantasies create it. A third male, for example, described waking up in his parents' bedroom to find them having intercourse, whereupon he felt 'pushed out' by his father. This scene remained a static one for him, like a tableau. If his parents came together there would be an explosion and disintegration. Sexuality and intercourse are of the utmost danger, and the whole atmosphere of sexuality inside him is one of terrific aggression and anger. Fairbairn does not regard the static scene as necessarily to preserve the internal object from destruction. On the contrary, its function can be to perpetuate the destruction. One female patient had a phobia of meeting accidents on the road. The body she dreaded seeing was that of her father. This fear, however, was a defence against the murder of her father which was in turn a defence against an incestuous rape. The patient on one occasion saw an accident ahead of her. She was immediately panic-stricken and dashed up a side-street to avoid it but at the same time was clasping the accident to her as she ran. Fairbairn interprets this reaction to the traumatic event as attempting to deal with it by incorporating it into the closed system of inner reality. The obstinate attempt to keep aggression and libido localized as a closed system in the inner world is for Fairbairn the phenomenon Freud described as 'the death instinct'.

In treatment the patient is seeking relief from this inner closed system. He attempts, nevertheless, to coerce the analyst into it through transference, and it is the determination on the part of the analyst to reach the closed system within the therapeutic relationship by developing a quality in the latter which induces the patient to open it to outer reality. However neutral a role he may assign to himself therapeutically, he must intervene by his interpretations. The actual relationship between patient and analyst is the decisive factor, and the suitability for treatment can only be assessed on the extent to which the inner closed system is entrenched.

This paper had a mixed reception. Discussion brought out the difficulties of defining what Fairbairn meant by the analyst making a good personal relationship. He had described in the paper that his main modification to the treatment situation was to do away with the couch and to sit so that the patient could see him if he chose to look. Fairbairn had come to believe that the couch isolated the patient in the way a crying child is left alone or is isolated in his cot during the primal scene. Apart from that change he had not altered the way in which he made his interpretations. There was an impression gained that he was changing the method to present himself as a good object, and Mrs Klein was heard to remark that he was no longer doing analysis, or words to that effect. He was certainly ready to be more 'human' if he thought the occasion merited, for example when he gave advice to the patient Richard about the nutrition of his child. (See his 1953 paper, 'Observations on the nature of hysterical states'.) It was perhaps the way in which his interpretations were framed in whole-person terms with not enough of the constant references to projection and introjection that irked. Mrs Klein was of the opinion from his earlier papers that he did not give enough weight to the infant's destructive hate.

The importance of the analyst being a good parental figure is a statement lending itself to very varied interpretations, some of which are inimical to the amelioration of the core difficulties in the patient. The concern of the psychoanalyst must always be with the pathological conflicts that are brought out in the relationship between him and the analysand. The image of the rigid, sphinx-like analyst who operates not as a person but as a book of rules is more a myth than a reality. Yet it is extraordinary how reticent analysts are about admitting in what ways they might depart from this model. The enormous advantage – it might well be a necessity – of refraining from action outside the task of improving understanding is that any other course, as the least of its effects, confuses the situation. Much more serious, it can intensify demands for gratification or raise the resistances, especially to the uncovering of the crucial destructive feelings, so that the analysis becomes blocked. At the risk of over-simplifying the situation, it seems to me Fairbairn's comments to the patient Richard could have explored why an urgent reality problem had come up at this point and the problems of his own infancy that might be covered over. Such apparent ignoring of the reality problem can be put to the analysand without it being felt as the attack the analysand might be expecting from his own hate. In short, the essential way of being a good figure is by showing the scope of the analyst's empathic understanding. Giving 'advice', if that was thought urgent, is best kept out of the immediate analytic work. In all his references to the therapeutic component, it is not enough to say that the essential feature is for the analyst to be a real good person over time. What makes him the real person the patient needs is the patient's experience of him as the parent who can understand his feelings, his frustrations and hate, and stay alive and concerned for him after being the object of all of these feelings. Only his interpretations can demonstrate that empathy in the analytic situation, in which verbal interchange is what is eventually helpful. There are at least two selves to be addressed by the analyst, namely, the analysand's adult self and his infantile one.

THE LAST YEARS

In the second half of 1958, Fairbairn's ill health kept him off work for about six months. Mrs Mackintosh, his secretary, obtained her divorce later in the year, and the following April she and Fairbairn were married. Though better, his general health remained variable with occasional febrile states or influenza. Fortunately he was well enough by the autumn to meet some of the psychoanalysts from London who visited Edinburgh to make preparations for the International Psycho-Analytical Congress in 1961. He was also able to attend a dinner in London in November to honour his seventieth birthday. This was an informal occasion arranged by his many psychoanalyst friends, which he and his wife greatly appreciated.

Another spell of influenza stopped his clinical work in the early months of 1960. He was able to enjoy his garden in time for the summer season, and it was a particular pleasure for me that he took the chair when I gave the opening address at the Summer School run by the Davidson Clinic, as he had done some years previously. In September, he welcomed a visit from Dr Karl Menninger. It was characteristic of him that he travelled to London shortly afterwards to attend Mrs Klein's funeral at Golders Green. He had a very great respect for her work, and he had that strong sense of expressing such feelings that made paying his tribute on these occasions very important to him. (This was in rather marked contrast to the absence of her daughter from the service, although she was then in London.)

By 1961 there was a noticeable deterioration in his health with signs of arteriosclerosis. He was seeing three or four patients on most days but was completely off for two spells. It was a sad circumstance that the International Psycho-Analytical Congress, which was held for the first time in Edinburgh in that year, saw him unable to participate other than by inviting a number of visitors to his home.

The recognition of his work by the international psychoanalytic establishment was still understandably limited, since he had never presented papers or made himself personally known in the international scene. This was because his symptom interfered with his being away from home and prevented him from accepting many invitations to visit various centres. He still kept in touch with the literature, though with mixed feelings, for in his view the practice of analysis was becoming increasingly like a technology of interpretation, with diminishing attention to what was happening at the personal level.

Following his marriage, he and his wife maintained a fairly active social life with friends and neighbours for the next few years. With his younger son's marriage in 1962, all three children were now established in their own homes. When I visited him (two or three times in each of these years) he seemed much older, yet he was always eager to discuss what was going on in the psychoanalytic world, and he was still seeing three or four of his old patients on most days.

It was very gratifying to him that Guntrip, through his articles over the previous few years, and now by his book, *Personality Structure and Human Interaction* (1961), had made his theories widely known. Many younger analysts and analytical psychotherapists, especially from the USA, were making contact with him and this pleased him. In 1963 there appeared a monograph on *Freud and Fairbairn: Two Theories of Ego Psychology* by Charles T. Sullivan. This was a carefully considered appreciation of his work, the first from the USA, and he was accordingly delighted with it. In the same year, the *British Journal of Medical Psychology* devoted a special number to honour his contribution. During the last years of his life there was thus, if not from the centre of the psychoanalytic establishment, a gratifying response to his achievements.

The absence of articles in what were to be his last few years reflected his diminished energy, though not any loss of interest in psychoanalytic theory. This was constantly stimulated by his continuing to see a few of his patients daily and by an active correspondence with Guntrip. In frequent letters the latter raised issues concerning theoretical statements in his own papers as well as continuing to check on some of Fairbairn's.

'SYNOPSIS OF AN OBJECT-RELATIONS THEORY OF THE PERSONALITY'

In 1963 he wrote a very brief 'Synopsis of an object-relations theory of the personality' in which he lists its main points. The first states that 'Libido is a function of the ego and so is fundamentally object-seeking'. The use of the substantive is somewhat surprising as also is the retention of the old term cathexis in later parts. 'The earliest form of anxiety is separation anxiety' is also a change in emphasis with respect to the frustrating features in the early relationships. He also stresses again that introjection is a distinct process not to be regarded as just the product of a phantasy of oral incorporation. He was again in bed for a spell in the early part of 1964 but was soon enjoying a fair amount of socializing with friends. In most weeks he saw two of his old patients daily. Although I was not aware of it on the occasions on which I saw him, he began in these last years to take much more alcohol than he had ever done. This was very much out of character, and I wondered if the prospect of death was evoking a primitive identification with his first wife.

In the summer of 1964 Winnicott gave the address to the Summer School of the Davidson Clinic, in Edinburgh, and Fairbairn and he met a few times at the Clinic and when he had lunch in Fairbairn's home. He had to take to bed again in November, and this time he had to remain there in a progressively weaker state eventually leading to his being transferred to a nursing home. I visited him on the 29th of December, by which time he was very weak. There were some members of his family present, and we chatted quite ordinarily about various things. Although he looked tired, the familiar twinkle could still come into his eyes. Two days later he died. His relationship with the Church was preserved to the end, with the funeral service held in St Mary's Cathedral, after which he was buried beside his first wife in a cemetery not far from their home. I add some excerpts from remarks I made as a personal note at a meeting of the British Psycho-Analytical Society in January 1965.

At a memorial service in St Mary's Cathedral in Edinburgh it was said by the rector, who as a boy had been well known to Dr Fairbairn, that he was always impressed by three qualities: his kindness, his courtesy, and his humility. These certainly were very prominent in his make-up as I knew him and they were aspects of what gave him his very human interest in, and concern for, all with whom he came in contact. I remember three years ago talking to Dr T. A. Watters from New Orleans, who had come to work in London with Dr Balint, when it suddenly emerged to my surprise that he was not only interested in Fairbairn's views but that he seemed to know him quite well personally. He then told me of how his experience of Fairbairn had shown him very vividly what 'good object relations' meant. He had been visiting Edinburgh to see a friend who had arranged for him to meet Fairbairn. Dr Watters unfortunately turned ill and could not keep the appointment. He said that he was then quite overwhelmed for Fairbairn came in and out of his hotel for the next few days making sure he was getting all the medical and other care he needed. To me, of course, this was no surprise. I do not think I have ever known anyone who took what one might say was such a responsible attitude to others. I always felt, no matter whom he was dealing with, they were always deeply respected as individuals.

It would be quite wrong if any impression were to be given at this point of Fairbairn as taking the human scene with a kind of puritanical sense of duty. Quite the contrary. This concern for, and care of, others, for the dignity of the individual, were deeply spontaneous in him, and he combined them with a marked feeling of enjoyment and a good sense of humour. He was a delightful host. It was typical of him, I thought, to make the following remark when I visited him on his death-bed. His wife had said about one of his sons that he had plenty of time ahead of him for some work – and at once the old twinkle came into his tired eyes as he smiled to me and said 'He has plenty of time – not like me!'. . .

Obviously I cannot devote space in a short note of this personal kind to his psychoanalytic work. He was certainly not the kind of man who would like to be thought of as having founded a school. Nothing could be more foreign to him. He was devoted to, and cared for, psychoanalysis with much the same responsible feeling as he had for people. Although his own ideas represented a different way of conceptualizing certain basic phenomena in human relationships, he always thought of them with modesty and as belonging to psychoanalysis; and he hoped they would be useful to the development of psychoanalysis. When he was made a member of the British Psycho-Analytical Society many years ago, I knew from the way he mentioned it that he felt deeply rewarded. I am sure it gave him great support in his isolation. Years before the war he would sometimes say after he returned from a visit to London to attend a meeting of the Society that he wished he worked in London to be with the other analysts there. And after the war, he remained eager to know what was going on, both in the affairs of the Society and in what was happening in the world at large to psychoanalysis and psychoanalysts.

As I got to know more of Freud's early struggles I often thought of how Fairbairn had lived through closely similar experiences. It was a great satisfaction to him too, and knowing his early struggles it was a particular pleasure to me that he got quite a measure of interest in his work in his lifetime. He was particularly appreciative of the large number from the British Society who came to the party in London that was organized to celebrate his seventieth birthday. He received many invitations to go to the United States of America in recent years, and perhaps it was because of the conservatism I mentioned, plus the constraints of his symptom, that he did not care to go. He certainly became progressively absorbed in his home and garden in later years. Ronald Fairbairn was a full man – a rich personality, a man of great integrity, and, in the best sense, of great dignity. He valued the worth of every human individual and he would fight for, and go into the wilderness for, his convictions. This trait was to be seen not only in his work but in other matters; thus a few years ago he took a prominent part in resisting the demolition of the old houses in George Square in Edinburgh for the University buildings.

Perhaps I could best end this note by saying that, while I shall always feel especially privileged and grateful for having had him as my colleague, teacher, and friend for so many years, he was a man of whose character and work all psychoanalysts can be proud.

7 Fairbairn's achievement

WHEN I ask myself what the significance is of Fairbairn's contribution to psychoanalysis, my answer will strike most analysts as making grandiose claims. I believe, nevertheless, it is entirely accurate to say that he was the first to propose in a systematic manner the Copernican change of founding the psychoanalytic theory of human personality on the experiences within social relationships instead of on the discharge of instinctual tensions originating solely within the individual. In short, he replaced the closed-system standpoint of nineteenth-century science with the open-system concepts that were evolved by the middle of the present century to account for the development of living organisms, in which the contribution of the environment has to be considered at all times.

His viewpoint is receiving increasingly sympathetic and careful appraisal. Here I wish to stress that his specific theories about the structuring of the personality will certainly be amended, but such advances will be made by the adoption of his basic assumptions.

In judging the importance of his work, it is appropriate to comment first on his challenge to the fundamental assumptions upon which Freud's classical theories were based and which he retained until his death. Having asserted the vicissitudes in the personal relationships between the infant, his mother, and his family, as the primary consideration for the development of the personality instead of the instincts, there was, of course, no question of the instinctive endowment being ignored. The issue was how the interaction of the innate factors and the environment was conceived. Fairbairn was highly critical of the way in which instinctive energies were reified, one could almost say deified, in early psychoanalytic theory. Guntrip, following on this lead, has been interpreted as dispensing with 'the instincts', and at times he can give this impression. Like Fairbairn, however, he was in no way a naïve thinker.

What they both felt strongly about, and it was this aspect of Fairbairn's writings that attracted Guntrip in the first instance, was that the concept of 'drives', the motivating forces originating in the instincts, was being used to create a quite inadequate picture of human nature.

The danger they reacted to was the insidious dehumanization of man with no adequate account of his nature at the personal level. With Guntrip's background as a clergyman it was easy to 'explain away' his arguments, though these were put forcefully. (It was not so widely known that Fairbairn had started out to become a clergyman and had retained an active membership of the Church, otherwise he, too, might had an even less serious reception.)

The accepted theory of the instincts had, therefore, to be questioned as an appropriate foundation for the understanding of the conflicts underlying the presenting problems. Though that was naturally of the first importance, there were also dangers from its influence on social and cultural values. The pleasure accompanying the satisfactions of instinctive needs did not lose its importance; it was essential in selecting and maintaining relatedness. When pleasure-seeking became the foremost motive, however, this was the result of a deterioration in the essential relationships, a failure in the attainment of the capacity for rich and mutual relations with others in which the individuality of the other provides a deeper satisfaction than the use of him or her to provide gratification. The unfortunate consequences of adopting Freud's instinct theory as making gratification the aim could be seen when the writings of social philosophers like Herbert Marcuse (1953) and Norman O. Brown (1929) were taken to justify sexual indulgence as something with little or no restraint – for 'kicks', as the saying went. Fairbairn was not concerned with moral values here. The biological importance of his views stemmed from his conviction that the family is the crucial agency in the development of healthy, creative individuals. For it to fulfil this function, sexuality is an essential component in the maintenance of the optimal relationship between the parents and between them and their children.

Both Fairbairn and Guntrip were trained in philosophy. In their book, *Ego and Instinct* (1970), the social scientist/philosopher Daniel Yankelovich and the philosopher William Barrett gave a highly pertinent critique of psychoanalytic theory. While neither was a practising analyst, both were well informed and deeply convinced of the importance of psychoanalysis for the human sciences in general. Their concern was to further its acceptance and development by getting its basic assumptions right, for in their view no science can progress unless this is done, and they thought those of psychoanalysis were wrong. Despite a great deal of discussion with a group of distinguished analysts in Boston in the USA, they make no reference to Fairbairn, presumably because his book was not made known to them. (Elizabeth Zetzel, a leading figure of the psychoanalytical establishment in the Boston area, may have contributed to this neglect. In an article on 'Recent British approaches to problems of early mental development' (1955) she treated Fairbairn's views as an ingenious intellectual exercise, without seeing the fundamental challenge that his powerful clinical data had forced upon him.) I have always felt this was a great pity, because these thinkers reached conclusions closely similar to his and so might have added to the impact of all of them. They propose as a fundamentally required step the replacement of the 'id' by one of 'developmentals'. These are the dynamic structures that are formed when instinctive activity interacts with critical experience at specific stages in the life cycle. Their concepts derive from a wide consideration of human development, social, cultural and biological, and their arguments add up to conclusions which cannot be ignored, the more so when placed alongside those reached by Fairbairn twenty-five years earlier. Nevertheless, their line of thought has had little effect upon psychoanalysis. The response to their book reassured me that the reluctant recognition of Fairbairn's views could not be justified by the commonly expressed superficial reasons.

The issue that they and the 'object-relations' theorists had introduced has been a preoccupying one amongst analysts for the last fifty years. In an admirably critical and comprehensive account of its history, Greenberg and Mitchell (1983) have described this dialectic as showing the progressive encroachments of the object-relationships viewpoint into the drive theory. These challenges have been met by a succession of accommodations made by tenacious analytic thinkers which bring out the increasing strain of defending an untenable position. In their constructive critique of the psychoanalytic view of human nature, Yankelovich and Barrett describe a similar process with which they draw a parallel in the development of astronomy, with the constant addition of epicycles to the traditional scheme of the solar system.

As an evaluation of Fairbairn's views, I believe that of Greenberg and Mitchell is quite unusual in its scope and penetrative accuracy. They note that the abstractness of his language can mislead the reader into thinking that, in his stress on libido as object-seeking rather than pleasure-seeking, these are somewhat Talmudic and arcane distinctions. What Fairbairn is suggesting, according to them, is really a fundamentally different view of human motivation, meaning and values. The orientation of the infant to others is there from the very beginning because the infant has adaptive genic roots for his biological survival. Moreover, this urge to seek and maintain interaction with others is characteristic of adults at all stages of life.

Development begins in the total dependence of the infant, at which stage a security is normally established that lays the foundation for the later transformations towards the normal personality. Fairbairn's views of the transitional stage between this infantile dependency and maturity are not spelled out, and this is a weak feature of his developmental theory, though this lack is easily remedied from the wealth of data on childhood and adolescence. He does stress, however, that the earliest structuring from the experience in relationships forms a basic pattern which shapes the future patterns of relationships.

Clearly Fairbairn has left much that needs to be expanded, and what he ended with points to tasks for a more complete theory of the self as fashioned from relationships. His primary text, so to speak, is that the individual from the very start has to be loved for himself by the unconditional loving care of (at first) the mother. This loving care has then to be continued by the father as well, and adapted within the family to the specific behavioural stages brought about by maturation and the cultural environment. In all development and in maturity, persons have to be in satisfying relationships for their own survival together with that of their groups.

Assumptions about the infant not having any ego or self at the start contributed to the long period in which the self was scarcely mentioned. Freud's 'Ich' had the significance of the personal self until, as Bettelheim (1983) suggested, the absorption in instinct theory led to it being replaced by the impersonal 'ego'. When Hartmann found it necessary to postulate an autonomous ego, he described the self as the separate structure that was cathected in narcissism. He did not elaborate the concept of the self, however, because of his inability to free himself from the traditional drive energies, even though he realized these were making a theoretical impasse.

If we take Fairbairn's basic statement we have clearly got to conceptualize a potential structure, operating as a whole, that only becomes functional, in the effective way for which it is designed, through certain experience with the mother, the father and the wider society. It 'seeks' to become the organizing agent of a conscious 'person' who remains aware of the continuity of his past with his present and of the future as immanent, and with a unique sense of himself as having an identity in relationship with other persons.

As mentioned earlier, Fairbairn accepted that 'self' is a more appropriate term in most of his considerations, since it refers to the whole from which sub-selves are split off. The ego is useful for the central self, that is, the dominant part of the self that incorporates the main purposes and goals of the individual in his relationships with the outer world and with which consciousness is usually associated.

Along with his humanistic and philosophical background, the understanding of the personality for Fairbairn had to be firmly based upon its evolution, that is, its biological roots. A modern image of man must illumine his essential properties, and for this I find Chein's definition invaluable. I have already referred to this but it will bear repetition. 'The essential psychological human quality is, thus, one of commitment to a developing and continuing set of unending, interacting, interdependent, and mutually modifying long-range enterprises' (Chein, 1972, p. 289). When we start with a modern biological outlook, we depart from Freud, for whom the science available allowed only the Newtonian base with its emphasis on the second law of thermodynamics. Chein concludes that man's motivation is a unique development. As a living organism, man is removed from the closed systems characterized by entropy, and this focus has to be replaced by a commitment to accomplish something – even if only the survival of his family in the environment.

As an open system, the living organism is 'negentropic', a feature maintained by its perpetual incorporation of energy. All organisms are created from other organisms. (For a modern perspective on evolution I am indebted to Jantsch (1980) and Jantsch and Waddington (1976).) They are wholes which cannot be made from the aggregation of parts. Their constant exchanges with the environment mean that constant transformations are proceeding, despite which they maintain their own characteristic form by a process of self-regulation. What is essential in these continuous self-renewals and self-expressions are the self-bounding processes rather than the changing structures. While evolution has led to many subsystems in the organism which maintain an equilibrium or steady state, this 'homoeostasis' does not obtain for the organism as a whole. At this level, equilibrium means death, because of the ending of the never-ceasing interaction with the environment in which processes of self-transformation and self-maintenance constitute life. As Sir Julian Huxley said, our perspective for man must be *sub specie evolutionis* rather than *sub specie aeternitatis*.

In the lower levels of the evolutionary scale the form of the animal along with its behavioural repertoire is directly determined by the genic inheritance. Thus, given that the dinosaurs lay their eggs in places that provide the appropriate environment, and with some early protection against external dangers, the embryo can emerge and fend for itself. An 'organizing principle' within the fertilized egg provides for successful maturation under these conditions. Life can be lived in an action mode with learning restricted to the limited skills required to feed, to fight and to mate. Evolutionary development does not greatly require increased adaptive capacities as long as the environment provides what is needed. Their huge physical bulk could evolve along with a relatively small brain being adequate for perceptual-motor learning and the co-ordination of all the bodily parts by the organizing principle its nervous system carried. Clearly this organizing principle is of the greatest importance, since it embodies the management of the life process as a whole. In the lower animals we can conceive of it carrying out this function on the basis of an affective field which controls the fitting together of sentient experiences from bodily and environmental changes according as the overall state is within the range of what feels 'right' or not 'painful'. Innate patterns for finding the objects required for survival can be transmitted by the genic inheritance, as they are in the human infant in 'desiring' and seeking the breast. In an unchanging environment little need for complex information storage arises. Any threat to its autonomy is a threat to life and so is reacted to ferociously and the individual and the species group survive.

When man is reached, an extremely complex behavioural equipment has been evolved. In brief, he has become a social person who survives not only by adaptation to, but largely by the creation of, his environment. Social animals survive by the evolution of innate mechanisms to keep them together, thereby gaining protection against predators and facilitating the rearing of the young. The common mode of achieving this grouping is by innate mechanisms creating attachment to dominant members. With the enormously increased psychological resources and creative capabilities required to cope with life in human communities, there has been an evolutionary development in which these are maximized by each individual acquiring a high level of autonomous creativity. The innate equipment for each has to provide for such development and the relatively huge cortex in man's brain emerges to meet it. As well as the behavioural systems providing for basic actions, there is now a great range of behavioural properties required for community living, especially for the amount of activity that has to be shared if optimal creativity is to be achieved. Relationships are mediated by holistic features in each human being, the essential character of which we describe as 'becoming a person'. The individual becomes aware of having a self and, moreover, a self which can transcend itself in order to observe and appraise its inner processes and its position in the world. When this subjectivity can be shared an enormous facilitation occurs for co-operative action in joint plans and purposes. *Homo sapiens* has emerged with all his unique characteristics. Added to the innate equipment that provides for the specific behaviour survival requires, there is now much behaviour that has innate components sufficiently influential to ensure its emergence, although not such as to restrict too narrowly the fit with the environment. The adaptive behaviour is then given a final pattern by training within the family and its society. Thus, what has been evolved in the genic inheritance is not the complete structural basis for the required behaviour, but a 'potential' for it, as in the acquisition of language.

The notion of inherited potential was thought by many biologists until recent years to be a somewhat vitalistic notion. Critical evidence came from the Cambridge ethologist W. H. Thorpe in the 1950s when he and his colleagues showed that while the basic song units in chaffinches were inherited, the young birds could not perform the adult song unless they heard this from the adults. The possession of the song as shared by all members of the species is critical for survival. Learning from experience provided by the parents or adults had thus entered the process of evolution. With the mammals, prolonged parental care has become a necessity for dependent young.

In man this care becomes loving care, and powerful love feelings have evolved as the great means of creating and maintaining the most vital human relationships, those in the family and in the group. (In connection with this outline see also Artiss, 1985.)

Yankelovich and Barrett quote from Cantril's study of functional uniformities in widely different cultures which suggest a list of innate potentials in the individual for behaviour at the human or personal level. The potential has to be realized within a specific culture, and in this way great variation exists in specific characteristics such as in languages. Language plays an essential part in many other acquisitions in which a rich range of communication amongst adults and between parents and children is required, while its symbolic function underpins creativity and the extremely flexible use in the development of tools and shared skills. Other innate potentials seem to be the attaining of food and shelter, getting security in a territorial and emotional sense, a need for ordering the data from environment, the need to seek new experiences, for procreation and safeguarding the future, the capacity to make choices, to experience a sense of the individual's own value to himself and others, and the need for a system of values and beliefs to which he can be committed and even sacrifice himself.

All these potentials, when realized, have to be fitted together and in an overall way that is managed by an autonomous self. As Angyal (1965) put it, it is paradoxical that this autonomy can only be attained within the heteronomy of being raised in, and belonging to, the community. In short, optimizing creativity in the individual can be achieved with a simultaneous bonding of the self to the group. This list is not quoted to be a comprehensive one of essential capacities, but to bring out how the highly complex task facing the individual in his development towards being a mature member of the community can be seen from an evolutionary standpoint. These attainments are all expressions of what we mean by becoming a person, that is, of having a mature self. Without these innate potentials and their development within the group to which persons will belong, or enough of them in sufficient measure, and without the integration or cohesive functioning that only a whole can offer, the individual cannot become a person.

Several specific capacities have been listed, but the critical feature has been left, namely, how the 'person' is formed as an essential unity. To put these capacities together in various ways does not add up to being a person. Indeed, to learn to fulfil most of them, the individual has to be a person in the first instance, for it is the sense of autonomous agency that determines the learning. Moreover, much learning, for example language, needs a shared subjectivity between mother and child. (See Stern, 1985.) An intensely dynamic potential power in the self is thus what motivates the sustained purposiveness of the individual to contribute to the well-being of himself and the group.

The answer to how the whole is formed can be given as the simple one that it is there from the start, a view adopted by Lichtenstein (1977). All organisms are wholes, and they create other wholes for survival. Fairbairn long felt critical of the atomism of so much analytic theorizing. He himself found no difficulty in assuming the existence of 'wholes'. That the infant gives the strong impression of being a whole 'person' from a very early stage is certainly vouchsafed by all parents and most infant–mother research workers. Kohut (1971) quotes the way adults react instinctively to babies as persons and treat them as such, usually with expressions to indicate their pleasure in responding to this quality, as strong evidence in favour of a whole self being actively present. It is not difficult to conceive of this potential being present in the innate endowment and giving rise to the 'expectation' to be treated in this way; and this does not only occur at the infant stage. The person at all stages of the life cycle resents not meeting this response from others, with intensities of feeling covering the whole range of aggression.

To return to Fairbairn, it is very much this trend of thought that can be seen in his conception of a unified self that is an autonomous potential, at first, and which is then suffused with a sense of of being a person in proportion as the mother's loving care is assimilated. It can also be inferred that frustrations that interfere with this autonomous development are reacted to as with the animal fighting for its life, for the self is the living centre of the individual.

Since being a person, that is, having a self that is autonomous yet preserving its autonomy or identity by means of its matrix of relationships, is the essential resource for effective enjoyable and satisfying living, the nature and development of the self is the paramount issue for general psychology as well as psychoanalysis. For the latter, the immediate concern is the role of the self in psychopathology. Fairbairn attributes all psychopathology to the splitting of the self in early experience, and Melanie Klein also adopted this position.

Winnicott's therapeutic studies, together with the observation of mothers and babies in his paediatric work, fully supported Fairbairn's assertion of the primacy of personal relationships for the development of the self. He spelled out the mother's empathic responsiveness as establishing a positive attitude to others and to the outer world. This attitude characterized the child's 'true self' in contrast with the conforming self that emerged to maintain the relationship with mother on her terms if not allowed enough scope to express his own. Bowlby (1980) has amply confirmed by his careful research studies the psychological necessities in the mother–child relationship. His theory of attachment stresses, so far, the conditions for the essential development of the self rather than the nature of the processes of the latter. He fully recognizes the complex developments involved in that process, a research area now receiving the attention of psychoanalytically trained workers. (See Stern, 1985.)

Clinical data suggest that, while the mother's initial influence establishes security or otherwise in the sense of being a person, the interaction with the father seems to be essential in the realization of the full autonomous potential. Winnicott (1971) referred to 'male and female elements' needing to be combined, and Fairbairn mentioned the need for a father. It would thus seem that while Fairbairn came to view the Oedipus situation in its relationship with infantile sexuality as a social situation and not a fundamental one for development as Freud had portrayed, there is another dimension to the importance of the relationship with the father in the maturation of the self. Indeed, Fairbairn's symptom can be seen as an attempt to bring back to life the father he had destroyed in phantasy, a need greatly increased when the imago of the castrating mother was revived by his wife's negative attitude to his work.

While it was the formation of splits in the self that formed the start of Fairbairn's line of thought, the defensive reactions against this situation suggest that the original self has retained a holistic dynamic within which these incompatible demands are dealt with, either by repression or by finding some substitute mode of satisfying the need. The structuring of these internal relations is much more complex than is apparent at first sight. Some of the internal objects have a relatively separate structure which is recognized as such, for example Freud's super-ego. The variety of objects and their topology seems to be quite large. Thus, Fairbairn regards dreaming not as wish-fulfilment but as the spontaneous 'imaginative' playing out of relations amongst them. The person, in short, emerges as a cast of characters, each related to a specific kind of object. These systems of self–object relationships have constant dynamic effects on each other and are also in perceptual contact with the other world, so that when it presents a situation that fits what an inner split self is seeking, then the latter can become activated to the point of taking overall control of the self. We see here the mode of action in compulsive relationships when the activation is intense.

These subsystems, like the self as a whole, do not require to borrow energy from separate 'drives'. They operate in the quite different way that systems under cybernetic control do. The strength of the drive exhibited is governed by what is switched on by inner releasing mechanisms. The power of the whole self to manage behaviour with optimal adaptiveness is thus the resultant of the integrity of the whole self against the pressure from sub-selves, and these two sets of forces vary according to the past history of the person and the nature of the external enviornment to which behaviour is being directed. The outer world is frequently the main releaser of action, but more important are the internal goals and imagos embodied within the self, again with varying 'distances' from the central self. All of these carry a dynamic of internal origin into the world to mould it, even with considerable coercion, to attain its goals.

With a sub-self becoming dominant, it is difficult to specify where the 'autonomy' of the self is then located. Even under strong compulsions, there is usually an awareness of the situation of being 'possessed', as though the observing self remains intact though powerless to exert enough control over it.

The compelling power of subsystems is not confined to instinctive action from sexual or aggressive arousal. Though less dramatic, it seemed that Fairbairn's ideal self could separate itself from these pressures and retain its own motivation in the sustaining of his creative work. Freud met this problem when he discussed the ego ideal and when he puts civilization into an adversarial relationship with the autonomy of the self. His position is a complex one. On the one hand, he felt the individual has to accept tiresome constraints, yet he observed that with the development of the ideals shared by the group, the individual acquires an identity for his self that he defends against any threat. Furthermore, he does this with a ferocity that has to be conceived as coming from an elemental force, one he linked with his postulation of the death instinct. In short, if we adopt a theory of aggression as a reaction to danger, then threats to the autonomy of the self readily suggest the origin of hate; and its relative permanence follows from structured internal threats.

A comprehensive theory of the self will have to fill in the areas that are largely left out of consideration by Fairbairn. The whole of Fairbairn's transitional phase can be seen as occupied with the final structuring of the self under the influence of the realization of the various potential aspects, such as those listed by Yankelovich and Barrett. In this development, Erikson's contributions (Erikson, 1959) at once seem to fill in the gap, with the epigenetic phases presumably deriving from the maturation of developmental potentials in the experiences which each culture seeks to provide at the appropriate period. Fairbairn gave a theory of the basic structuring that arises from the experiences in the earliest stages of mismatch between the child's needs and the parental responses. The schizoid split has a far-reaching influence because of the early highly formative stage in which it operates. Subsequent stages, for example the phallic–masculine-gender complex, can be more restricted in the disturbance they engender when the schizoid position has been free of deprivation. This freedom from inner constraints is especially important when the investment of the self becomes so much focused in the deep satisfaction of using special talents, for example in the acquisition of knowledge and evolving specific goals for the self. The split-off internalized objects can have a great range in the degree to which they deform development, and here we note whole areas in which much more research is needed. When mention was made of Fairbairn's relationship with his father, it seemed as though his father, at least as a sexual figure, had remained very much separated within his self, though very much present despite his repression.

When we take an evolutionary perspective for the development of the self as a fundamental characteristic structure, then the understanding of the dynamic of the ego ideal becomes much more plausible than that offered by classical theory. Thus in his Introduction to Chasseguet-Smirgel's study of *The Ego Ideal* (1985), Lasch adopts her account, with all the richness of her observations of its development. Her basic assumptions, however, are strikingly rooted in a closed-system perspective from which all the commitments of man are seen to stem from his fear of death and a longing to re-establish a sense of primal unity with the natural order of things. Evolution, in contrast, can be seen as providing man with powerful innate potentials enabling him to strive purposefully, and not as a passive victim of chance and necessity, to alter this natural order. The prospect of death, moreover, is surely altered when it is seen as a planned necessity for the 'progress' of life that evolution appears to embody. The Socratic injunction to examine one's life can thus focus on what has been given to life by the individual.

Jantsch, in his view of the role of evolution, brings in the relevance of myths in man's awareness of his condition. For him, the striving after the 'steady state' of an imagined perfection is reflected in the myth of Sisyphus. The evolutionary perspective on the other hand sees him as Prometheus. From our consideration of the self the vultures would then perhaps represent the deep hate over the frustrations of his autonomy – or the death instinct for Melanie Klein. It seemed to me that Fairbairn was always far more profoundly motivated by the 'developmentals' in Cantril's list than by a longing to return to the 'perfection' of the intra-uterine state. If evolution has a thrust in it 'to evoke', it is not too fanciful to imagine that man, or a proportion of men, get something of it within their nature. Hitherto his religions may have been one of its main expressions. Now he has to find ways in which selves in their groups do not need to eat each other, as the lower forms of life did, for survival. The development in social animals of the submissive action when a fight for domination has ended, exemplifies evolutionary possibilities.

Fairbairn's emphasis on relationships started in his suffering from bad ones. His potential for an ideal self seized on Christianity as a means of realizing it. He then discovered, as Freud did, that only more knowledge of the self would in the long run sustain him towards his goals.

In the formation of commitments, the internal object may occupy a very different position in that it may be suffused in its influence by an assimilation into the central ego. We get a strong impression that Freud was internalized in this way following upon the similar internalization of Christ. The situation is then extremely complex when what was the bad mother becomes the adopted model after a change in her attitude from castration to active encouragement of a masculine autonomy. I am reminded here of Freud when puzzled to account for an instinctual demand being 'tamed' when brought into the ego. His solution was to seek help from 'the Witch Metapsychology' and I wonder if it was his 'bad mother' who unconsciously prompted this suggestion (Freud, 1937, p. 225). Fairbairn recognized the therapeutic problem here because of the deeper hate being overlain by so much gratitude that was felt later for the support of the realization of his masculine ideals. When he referred at various points to the intense resistance aroused by the therapeutic process, this seems to centre on the fear for self-structures that have become so important. In these later internalizations, there is also the problem of the relation between the parents being internalized, as when he felt in later adolescence he was in a secret collusion with his mother against his father. This enactment of the interparental conflicts within the self, with parts identified with each parent, is extremely common, highly destructive and highly resistant to exposure because of the threat to the integration of the self.

In this rather personal version of where I believe Fairbairn would have continued his journey, a particular area is outlined, because I believe that the whole tenor of his work was steadily moving to the conceptualizing of the self. It was, after all, where he started, as Ernest Jones commented. Guntrip, his close student, moved openly in this direction, and Fairbairn was not in any way out of sympathy. Klein's contribution can also be seen as heading in this direction, though I believe with Fairbairn that her theoretical progress was hampered by her adherence to the drive theory, especially in relation to aggression. But when a powerful ideal has been formed, with its inherently committed urges to sustained action, then the anchorage in the outer world keeps the interference of conflicting inner relations to a minimum. Fairbairn was struck by this feature, which Kris (1953) described in the artist, whose chaotic life in many areas was nevertheless not allowed to interfere with the creation of his object.

What is the significance of this approach for treatment? The main implication is what Melanie Klein and her group have expounded so clearly, that is, the need to focus on the inter-subjective process which underlines the transference phenomena. Fairbairn made a minor change to permit the analysand to see him if desired. I doubt whether this is of much importance. The psychoanalyst wants to get to the deepest layers of conflict, and for this purpose the classical method and setting have most to commend them. It is the perspective which the analyst brings to what is presented to him that is of the greatest importance. A consequence of being in practice for a very long time is that one sees several analysands who felt dissatisfied with what they had achieved in previous analysis, often many years earlier. I have been greatly impressed in these cases by the importance of exposing the internal object-relationships that get concealed within the central self and some of its activities. A particular constellation I have met is one in which a highly successful individual has become threatened with the sabotage of his success by, for instance, taking risks with actions that would bring public humiliation, and indeed succeeding at times. Dealing with these problems as related to impulses out of control had not produced appreciable change. What did prove effective in several cases was the exposure of the sadistic attack on the central self, identified with the mother, as a vengeful retaliation for early hostility from the mother to the masculine/sexual self identified with a despised father. A great deal of work in almost all of these cases had to go into the reparation of a deeply repressed destroyed mother who was later idealized. Correspondingly, the father had to be brought back into a state that corresponded with his good aspects. The best results seemed to follow when the self was felt to have brought both parents back internally into a good relationship. The great resistance was prominently related to a fear of going mad over the disintegration of the self or of committing suicide as a way out of the primitive hate for the mother's rejection of the autonomy of the self in becoming 'its true self'.

One feature of working at the primitive levels of the development of the self is the impact on the analyst. What happened to Fairbairn has been described, and sadly with no help he could not work through this situation. For myself, I certainly experienced a good deal of unconscious turmoil from the recognition of much of the analysands' secret selves in myself. This point brings me to Winnicott's accusing Fairbairn of 'knocking Freud'.

Greenberg and Mitchell are quite puzzled by this savage attack. The personalizing of this remark around Freud has to be noted, for what Fairbairn was challenging was not Freud, but his libido theory. Towards the person Freud, along with his work, Fairbairn's admiration and respect were reverential. Greenberg and Mitchell note most carefully that in contrast, Winnicott 'adopts' a version of Freud's theories that is quite at odds with what Freud postulated. In his intellectual work, Fairbairn is responsive all the time to Freud's views and his recasting of some of his assumptions is in no sense a destructive act directed at Freud. Freud was therefore an intellectual father who had been so profoundly admired that Fairbairn 'metabolized' him into his own self. His ideal object became his ego ideal, that is, a less concretely personalized structuring. This seems to be quite a distinct process from internalization of an idol and which persists largely in this form. Winnicott was well known as having a pronounced maternal character and he expressed a disappointment in the relationship with his father, whose busy life had prevented the close contact Winnicott would have liked. In *Playing and Reality* (1971, pp. 72 ff.) he describes a session with a middle-aged man in which he said to this patient: 'I am listening to a girl talking about penis envy.' This remark had a pronounced effect on the patient, but it also set up a deep personal experience that Winnicott needed to live through in the next few months to arrive at the understanding he reached about male and female. It felt to me that the incident had really disturbed Winnicott's envy and hate of his father, feelings in a secret self which he projected into Fairbairn in his attack. Greenberg and Mitchell clearly recognized his attack as quite irrational, in view of the closely related nature of his contribution with Fairbairn's.

In this connection, I have suspected that Kohut had a similar experience in the early stages of his work. There is no question of the value of Kohut's contributions in expanding the concept of the self with his rich descriptions, and I am very much in agreement with his eventual position of coming out boldly against the retention of the drive theory. What disturbed me is his lack of specific recognition of the work of others, a characteristic that Greenberg and Mitchell comment upon. His work has become adopted in a flood of enthusiasm in which the contribution of others is completely lost. Thus in a recent review of his work by Cooper (1988), Kohut is credited with discovering the capacity for transference and its actual prominence in narcissistic patients, and other authors have noted *his* concepts of Tragic versus Guilty Man, the perversions as products of deteriorated relationships, or of the Oedipus complex as a social derivative and not a basic aetiological issue. All of these ideas are expressed in the very words that Fairbairn used fifty years ago to describe his schizoid patients; he also commented on their omnipotence, though this was often concealed. Fairbairn, in turn, when he claimed the unusual readiness of these patients to form transferences, was drawing on Melanie Klein's description of its manifestations in severely disordered personalities. It has been noted by several analysts that Kohut's preoccupations have been a focus for many years amongst analysts, for example Harry Stack Sullivan, Winnicott and Michael Balint. Due accord should, of course, be given to those who introduce innovating thinking, but I am less concerned with the neglect of Fairbairn's contribution than with the avoidance of issues that can confront analysts with a threat to their work self.

I have a strong impression that Kohut read Fairbairn (I have been informed his work was talked about in the Institute of which Kohut was a member), but I do not imagine he was simply plagiarizing. It seems to me much more likely that his interest was deeply aroused, and he then split it off, because it was for him unconsciously disturbing and concerning lest it obtrude in a way that might invoke criticism from the establishment, to whose views he was for many years inordinately sensitive. What has almost convinced me in my belief is a passage very early on in *The Analysis of the Self* (1971, p. 14). He describes a particular defence against the dangerous regressive potential in the narcissistic personality which results in what is referred to as the *schizoid personality* (Kohut's italics), though he says it is not found in the analysable narcissistic disturbances. Such individuals have learned to distance themselves from others to avoid narcissistic injury. He then continues: '*In opposition to his explanation it might be claimed that the retreat of these persons from human closeness is caused by their inability to love and is noticeable by their conviction that they will be treated unempathically, coldly or with hostility*' (my italics). He claims this is incorrect, because many schizoid patients are capable of meaningful contact with others – a rather jejune remark for someone of Kohut's standing. I do not know of any writer other than Fairbairn who asserted that the schizoid personality had been made specifically afraid to love by the experience of rejection, and Greenberg and Mitchell describe this particular view as one of Fairbairn's most innovative ideas. If Kohut's interest was unconsciously aroused in it as something to be developed, it points to a difficulty in taking and giving that Fairbairn described as prominent in schizoid personalities. Fairbairn further suggested omnipotence and grandiosity as reactions to this form of deep insecurity, and to the covering over by these traits of the deep hatred for the early deprivation.

I do not make these observations lightly or disparagingly. For me their value is to draw attention to reactions in one's own self as one becomes immersed in the earliest phases of its development. Fairbairn's own disturbance, as well as Winnicott's, illustrates this possibility, which may account for some of the resistance to its close study.

Any borrowing, even if repressed, has had a valuable outcome in the way Kohut has developed his ideas in much more detail than Fairbairn did. Perhaps, too, much of what has been reacted to negatively in Kohut's work might well be overcome by the adoption of some of Fairbairn's rigorous and uncompromising statements of the basic assumptions that psychoanalysis must build upon. Fairbairn, I am certain, would have greatly welcomed Kohut's work with generous approval.

I am grateful to Professor Henry Walton for drawing my attention to a passage in *The Dean's December* (1982) where Saul Bellow gives his thoughts about the contemporary human scene in an interchange between the Dean and his wife, who was enraged by her mother's death. The Dean is reflective and says:

It's the position of autonomy and detachment, a kind of sovereignty we're all schooled in. The sovereignty of atoms – that is, of human beings who see themselves as atoms of intelligent separateness. But all that has been said over and over. Like, how schizoid the modern personality is. The atrophy of feelings. The whole bit. There's what's-his-name – Fairbairn. And Jung before him comparing the civilized psyche to a tapeworm. Identical segments, on and on. Crazy and also boring, forever and ever. This goes back to the first axiom of nihilism – the highest values losing their value. (p. 259)

Such acknowledgement from one of our greatest contemporary writers seemed an appropriate finish.

FAIRBAIRN'S MAIN PAPERS

The papers are dated from when they were published. Those published in his book *Psychoanalytic Studies of the Personality* (London: Tavistock, 1952) are indicated by the letters PSOP.

1927   'Notes on the religious phantasies of a female patient', first published in PSOP.   PSOP, pp. 183–96.

1929   'The relationship of dissociation and repression, considered from the point of view of medical psychology', MD thesis, Edinburgh University, unpublished.

1930   'Some points of importance in the psychology of anxiety', *Brit. J. Med. Psychol.* 9: 303–13.

1931   'Features in the analysis of a patient with a physical genital abnormality', first published in PSOP.   PSOP, pp. 197–222.

1934   'The sociological significance of Communism considered in the light of psychoanalysis', *Brit. J. Med. Psychol.* 15, pt 3.
                                            PSOP, pp. 233–46.

1936   'The effect of a king's death upon patients undergoing analysis', *Int. J. Psychol-Anal.* 17, pt 3.   PSOP, pp. 223–9.

1937   'Arms and the man', *Liverpool Q.* 5: 27–34.

1938   'Prolegomena to a psychology of art', *Brit. J. Psychol.* 28: 288–303.
'The ultimate basis of aesthetic experience', *Brit. J. Psychol.* 29: 167–81.

1939   'Is aggression an irreducible factor?', *Brit. J. Psychol.* 18: 163–70.
'Psychology as a proscribed and a prescribed subject', first
published in PSOP.   PSOP pp. 247–55.

1940   'Schizoid factors in the personality', First published in PSOP.
                                                          PSOP, pp. 3–27.

1941   'A revised psychopathology of the psychoses and psychoneuroses',
Int. J. Psycho-Anal. 22: 250–79.
                                                          PSOP, pp. 28–58.

1943   'The repression and the return of bad objects', *Brit. J. Med.
Psychol.* 19: 327–41.   PSOP, pp. 59–81.
'The war neuroses – their nature and significance', *Brit. Med. J.* 10.
                                                          PSOP, pp. 256–87.

1944   'Endopsychic structure considered in terms of object-relationships',
Int. J. Psycho-Anal. 25: 70–73.   PSOP, pp. 82–136.

1946   'The treatment and rehabilitation of sexual offenders', first
published in PSOP.   PSOP, pp. 289–96.
'Object-relationships and dynamic structure', *Int. J. Psycho-Anal.*
27:30–7   PSOP, pp. 137–51.

1949   'Steps in the development of an object-relations theory of the
personality', *Brit. J. Med. Psychol.* 22: 26–31.   PSOP, pp. 152–62.
Critical notice: *On Not Being Able to Paint, Brit. J. Med. Psychol.*
24: 69–72.

1951   'A synopsis of the development of the author's views regarding the
structure of the personality', first published in PSOP.
                                                          PSOP, pp. 162–82.

1952   'Theoretical and experimental aspects of psycho-analysis', *Brit.
J. Med. Psychol.* 25: 122–7.

1953   Critical notice: *Psychoanalytic Explorations in Art, Brit. J. Med.
Psychol.* 26: 164–9.

1954   'Observations on the nature of hysterical states', *Brit. J. Med. Psychol.*
27: 105–25.

1955   'Critical observation on Fairbairn's theory of object relations' (by
K. M. Abenheimer), *Brit. J. Med. Psychol.* 28: 29–41.
'Observations in defence of the object-relations theory of the per-
sonality' (a reply to Abenheimer), *Brit. J. Med. Psychol.* 28: 144–56.

1956   'Considerations arising out of the Schreber case', *Brit. J. Med.
Psychol.* 29: 113–27.

1957   'Freud: the psycho-analytical method and mental health', *Brit. J. Med. Psychol.* 30: 53–62.

1958   'On the nature and aims of psycho-analytical treatment', *Int. J. Psycho-Anal.* 34: 374–83.

1963   'Synopsis of an object-relations theory of the personality', *Int. J. Psycho-Anal.* 44: 224–5.

BIBLIOGRAPHY

The place of publication is London unless otherwise indicated.

Abenheimer, K. M. (1955) 'Critical observations on Fairbairn's theory of object relations', *Br. J. Med. Psychol.* 28: 29–41.

Angyal, A. (1965) *Neurosis and Treatment.* New York: Wiley.

Artiss, K. L. (1985) *Therapeutic Studies.* Rockville, MD: Psychiatric Books.

Balint, M. (1968) *The Basic Fault.* Tavistock.

Bellow, Saul (1982) *The Dean's December.* Penguin.

Bettelheim, B. (1983) *Freud and Man's Soul.* Chatto & Windus.

Bowlby, J. (1980) *Attachment and Loss.* Hogarth.

Brown, Norman O. (1929) *Life against Death.* Middletown, CN: Wesleyan University Press.

Chasseguet-Smirgel, J. (1985) *The Ego Ideal.* Free Association.

Chein, I. (1972) *The Science of Behaviour and the Image of Man.* New York/London: Basic.

Coghill, G.E. (1929) *Anatomy and the Problem of Behaviour.* Cambridge: Cambridge University Press.

Cooper, Arnold M. (1988) 'Review of *How Does Analysis Cure?' J. Amer. Psychoanal. Assn* 36: 175–9.

Drever, J. (1917) *Instinct in Man.* Cambridge: Cambridge University Press.

Erikson, E. (1959) *Identity and the Life Cycle.* New York: International Universities Press.

Ezriel, H. (1951) 'The scientific testing of psycho-analytic findings and theory', *Br. J. Med. Psychol.* 24: 30–34.

Freud, S. (1900) *The Interpretation of Dreams*, in James Strachey, ed. *The Standard Edition of the Complete Psychological Works of Sigmund Freud,* 24 vols. Hogarth, 1953–73. vol.4.

—— (1921) *Group Psychology and the Analysis of the Ego. S.E.* 18, pp. 67–143.

—— (1923a) *The Ego and the Id. S.E.* 19, pp. 1–59.

—— (1923b) 'A seventeenth-century demonological neurosis', *S.E.* 19 pp. 69–104.

—— (1937) 'Analysis terminable and interminable', *S.E.* 23, pp. 209–53.

Glover, E. (1928) *The Technique of Psycho-Analysis.* Supplement No.3 *Int. J. Psycho-Anal.*

—— (1955) *The Technique of Psycho-Analysis.* Baillière, Tindall & Cox.

Greenberg, J. R. and Mitchell, S.A. (1983) *Object Relations in Psychoanalytic Theory.* Cambridge MA: Harvard University Press.

Guntrip, H. (1961) *Personality Structure and Human Interaction.* Hogarth.

Hartmann, H. (1958) *Ego Psychology and the Problem of Adaptation.* Imago.

Jantsch, E. (1980) *The Self-Organizing Universe.* Oxford: Pergamon.

Jantsch, E. and Waddington, C., eds (1976) *Evolution and Consciousness.* Reading, MA: Addison-Wesley.

Jones, E. (1951) 'Preface', in Fairbairn (1951), (see 'Fairbairn's Main Papers', above).

Kernberg, O. (1980) *Internal World and External Reality.* New York: Jason Aronson.

King, P. M. (1983) 'The life and work of Melanie Klein in the British Psycho-Analytical Society', *Int. J. Psycho-Anal.* 64: 281.

Klein, M. (1929) 'Infantile anxiety-situations reflected in a work of art and in the creative impulse', in *Contributions to Psycho-Analysis 1921–1945.* Hogarth, 1950, pp. 227–35.

—— (1934) 'A contribution to the psychogenesis of manic-depressive states', in *Contribution to Psycho-Analysis 1921–1945.* Hogarth, 1950, pp. 282–310.

—— (1946) 'Notes on some schizoid mechanisms', in M. Klein, P. Heimann, S. Isaacs and J. Riviere, eds *Developments in Psycho-Analysis.* Hogarth, 1952, pp. 292–320.

Kohut, H. (1971) *The Analysis of the Self.* New York: International Universities Press.

—— (1984) *How Does Analysis Cure?* Chicago/London: University of Chicago Press.

Kretschmer, E. (1926) *Physique and Character.* New York: Harcourt Brace.

Kris, E. (1953) *Psychoanalytic Explorations in Art.* George Allen & Unwin.

Lichtenstein, H. (1977) *The Dilemma of Human Identity.* New York: Jason Aronson.

McDougall, W. (1923) *An Outline of Psychology.* Methuen.

Marcuse, H. (1953) *Eros and Civilization.* Sphere; Abacus, 1972.

Niederland, W. G. (1963) 'Further data and memorabilia pertaining to the Schreber case', *Int. J. Psycho-Anal.* 44: 201–8.

Pines, M. ed. (1985) *Bion and Group Psychotherapy.* Routledge & Kegan Paul.

Read, H. (1931) *Art and Society.* Heinemann.

Rinsley, D.B. (1979) 'Fairbairn's object-relations theory: a reconsideration in terms of newer knowledge', *Bulletin of the Menninger Clinic* 43:489–514

——(1982) 'Fairbairn's object-relations and classical concepts of dynamics and structure' in *Borderline and Other Self Disorders: A Developmental and Object-Relations Perspective.* New York: Jason Aronson, pp. 251–70.

——(1987) 'A reconsideration of Fairbairn's "original object" and "original ego" in relation to borderline and other self disorders' in J.S. Grotstein, M.F. Solomon and J.A. Lang eds, *The Borderline Patient: Emerging Concepts in Diagnosis, Psychodynamics and Treatment.* vol. 1 Hillsdale, NJ: Analytic Press, pp. 219–31.

——(1988) 'Fairbain's basic endopsychic situation in terms of "classical" and "deficit" metapsychological models', *J. Amer. Acad. Psychoanal.* 16:461–77.

Spitz, R. A. (1965) *The First Five Years*. New York: International Universities Press.

Stern, D. N. (1985) *The Interpersonal World of the Infant*. New York: Basic.

Stokes, A. (1955) 'Form in art', in M. Klein, P. Heimann and R. Money-Kyrle, eds *New Directions in Psycho-Analysis*. Tavistock, pp. 406–20.

Sullivan, C. T. (1963) *Freud and Fairbairn: Two Theories of Ego Psychology*. Doylestown, PA: Doylestown Foundation.

Sullivan, Harry Stack (1959) *The Interpersonal Theory of Psychiatry*. New York: W. W. Norton.

Suttie, I. D. (1935) *The Origins of Love and Hate*, Routledge; Free Association, 1988.

Thorpe, W. H. (1963) *Learning and Instinct in Animals*. Methuen.

Winnicott, D. W. (1971) *Playing and Reality*. Tavistock.

Yankelovich, D. and Barrett, W. (1970) *Ego and Instinct*. New York: Random.

Zetzel, E. (1955) 'Recent British approaches to problems of early mental development', *J. Amer. Psychoanal. Assn* 3.

INDEX

This first edition of
Fairbairn's Journey into the Interior
was finished in May 1989.

It was set in 10/13 Ehrhardt
on a linotron 202 BY Selectmove Ltd.
printed on a Miller TP 41,
on to 80g/m², vol. 18 Bookwove.

The book was commissioned and edited by Robert M. Young,
copy-edited by Peter Phillips,
indexed by Stamley Thorley,
designed by Wendy Millichap,
and produced by Martin Klopstock and Selina O'Grady
for Free Association Books.